Manga in America

ALSO AVAILABLE FROM BLOOMSBURY

The Power of Comics: History, Form, and Culture
By Randy Duncan, Matthew J. Smith and Paul Levitz

Manga and Anime Go to Hollywood
By Northrop Davis

Manga: An Anthology of Global and Cultural Perspectives
Edited by Toni Johnson-Woods

Black Comics: Politics of Race and Representation
Edited by Sheena C. Howard and Ronald L. Jackson II

Manga in America:

Transnational Book Publishing and the Domestication of Japanese Comics

CASEY BRIENZA

Bloomsbury Academic
An imprint of Bloomsbury Publishing Plc

B L O O M S B U R Y
LONDON · OXFORD · NEW YORK · NEW DELHI · SYDNEY

Bloomsbury Academic

An imprint of Bloomsbury Publishing Plc

50 Bedford Square   1385 Broadway
London   New York
WC1B 3DP   NY 10018
UK   USA

www.bloomsbury.com

BLOOMSBURY and the Diana logo are trademarks of Bloomsbury Publishing Plc

First published 2016

British Library Cataloguing-in-Publication Data
A catalogue record for this book is available from the British Library.

ISBN: HB: 978-1-4725-9586-7
PB: 978-1-4725-9587-4
ePDF: 978-1-4725-9589-8
ePub: 978-1-4725-9588-1

Library of Congress Cataloging-in-Publication Data
A catalog record for this book is available from the Library of Congress.

Typeset by Integra Software Services Pvt. Ltd.
Printed and bound in India

*For all of manga's transnational cultural producers
and consumers… past, present, and future*

Contents

Illustrations

Tables

Acknowledgments

It's almost impossible to believe that it's been nearly a decade since I first embarked upon this journey of discovery. But it really has been that long, and needless to say, I owe an enormous debt of gratitude to the many individuals and institutions that have supported this research on manga in America over the years.

First thanks must go to John Thompson, who expressed enthusiasm for my work in its earliest stages, only a few weeks after I'd begun my graduate student career, and eventually agreed to take me on as his PhD supervisee in the Department of Sociology at the University of Cambridge. None of it would have been possible without you.

Sincerest thanks as well to NYU's Department of Media, Culture, and Communication for providing invaluable intellectual foundation for my interests in manga and book publishing, along with an excellent launching pad for future opportunities and endeavors. My MA thesis advisor Aram Sinnreich, along with Rod Benson, Debbie Borisoff, Ben Kafka, Marita Sturken, Mary Taylor, and Aurora Wallace made 2007 and 2008 some of the most important formative years of my academic life. I must also thank Steven Lukes for the best instruction in classical social theory a soon-to-be sociologist could ever have hoped for.

It is true, though, that research can feel like traveling down a very lonely road. What ever would I have done without my fellow Cambridge "survivors" Ozan Aşık, Charlie Barlow, Nick Boston, Rosamund Conroy, Beth Grace, Jonathan Ong, Tomas Undurraga, Peter Walsh, Monica Wirz, Dominic Yeo, and the rest of the PPSIS PhD students to share it?

I am profoundly grateful to Trinity College, Cambridge for their generous financing of my doctoral studies and fieldwork. The offer of an External Research Studentship came with unwritten perks, and the lovely, light-filled room at the top of Blue Boar Court's C staircase proved a blessing beyond measure—there could have been no better place in the world to write up this research. I am also grateful to the Alumnae Association of Mount Holyoke College for supplemental funding and the Department of Sociology at Rutgers University for hosting me as a Visiting Scholar in the 2010–2011 academic year. I'd particularly like to thank Karen Cerulo, Paul McLean, and Ann Mische for their hospitality.

This manuscript was finalized after joining the Centre of Culture and the Creative Industries in the Department of Sociology at City University London. Sincerest thanks to my new departmental colleagues Debbie Dickinson, Cecilia Dinardi, Ana Gaio, Rosalind Gill, Jo Littler, Jenny MBaye, Janet Merkel, Andy Pratt, and Marisol Sandoval for their welcoming support and friendship throughout a period of painful professional uncertainty and transition. Toby Miller and Dave O'Brien, who have since left us to take up posts elsewhere, also have my gratitude. In addition, I have benefited from exchanges with Grietje Baars, Mel Bunce, Rachel Cohen, Chris Flood, Sam Friedman, David Haynes, Malcolm James, Dan Mercea, Ernesto Priego, Lyn Robinson, and Chris Rojek. Above all, however, is the great debt I will forever owe Keith Simpson, who pushed himself past his own reasonable limits during the final weeks and months so that I too might hope to exceed mine. Don't ever surrender to despair, Keith, no matter how things turn out.

David Avital and Mark Richardson of Bloomsbury have been wonderful to me throughout the submission and publishing process, and David M. Buisán's artwork and design for the cover is thrilling. It's an incredible achievement, as well as a faithful visual representation of this book's thesis—I'm sure that there are many manga industry insiders who will see themselves in it! I also really appreciate the detailed comments provided by the anonymous peer reviewers. The final manuscript strives to incorporate their helpful feedback.

Comics scholars in the United Kingdom are easily among the most collegial academic communities in the world. Thank you to Martin Barker, Will Grady, Paul Gravett, Simon Grennan, Ian Hague, Paddy Johnston, Sarah Lightman, Anna Madill, Nina Mickwitz, Chris Murray, Joan Ormond, Julia Round, Roger Sabin, Dan Smith, Nicola Streeten, Tony Venezia, Paul Williams, and Sarah Zaidan for being a home away from home.

Many thanks as well to Daniel Allington, Glynn Anderson, Melissa Aronczyk, Robert Baensch, Anne Barron, Ele Belfiore, Jaqueline Berndt, Gurminder Bhambra, Eve Bottando, Mary Churchill, Clayton Childress, Maureen Donovan, Shai Dromi, Brooke Duffy, Shinsuke Eguchi, Christian Fuchs, Ian Gadd, Katrina Gulliver, Maggie Hames, John Holmwood, Ron Jacobs, Susan Jacobson, Ben Kafka, Jean Khalfa, Mikhail Koulikov, John Laprise, Xinghua Li, Zhan Li, Andrew Lindner, Janet Lorenzen, Neda Maghbouleh, Marianne Martens, Laura Miller, Dhiraj Murthy, Bobby Nayyar, Naoko Nemoto, Gary O'Brien, Fusami Ogi, Gloria Oh, Penn Pantumsinchai, Devon Powers, Jillian Powers, Andrea Press, Matthias Revers, Danielle Rich, Terri Senft, Adrienne Shaw, Bev Skeggs, Sarah Sobieraj, Deirdre Sumpter, Eleanor Townsley, S. Courtney Walton, Junhow Wei, Yoke-Sum Wong, Guobin Yang, Shujiro Yazawa, Elizabeth Young, Nancy Yuen, and Lin Zhang for having shared in this long and circuitous journey. There are surely others whom I've forgotten; even if you are not on this page, rest assured that your names are, each and every one of them, inscribed on my heart.

My family is deserving of an extra-special mention for their years of tolerance of my unorthodox career path. We take a long time to become who we are, and who knows how or where it will finally end?

Last but certainly not least, I wish to extend a gigantic thank you to the seventy American manga industry insiders without whom *Manga in America* would have been but a pipe dream. In order to protect their anonymity, I will not list these people by name here, but that should in no way be taken to minimize the extent of their generous contributions of time and expertise. I am delighted and honored to have had the opportunity to meet and learn from you, and this book, ultimately, is *your* story. Any errors which remain are, of course, my own.

1

Introduction

It had been a productive interview lasting nearly two hours. But as I thanked my informant, an experienced editor at one of the most important manga publishing companies in the United States, once more for his time and stood up to leave, he cleared his throat pointedly and frowned. I paused, half-risen from my chair.

"You're at *Cambridge*, and this is what you're researching?" he asked with a vague gesture meant to take in everything about the situation in which we had found ourselves. "Isn't it too...," he searched at length for a word, "stupid?"

I was momentarily dumbfounded. By that point in my fieldwork, I had conducted well over thirty interviews with his industry colleagues in the United States and Canada, and no one had ever suggested that I might be wasting my time (and, presumably, my university's resources). Yet, here was a person who had dedicated his entire adult working life to manga publishing wondering if it was stupid to try to understand him and his world.

So, I echoed his question back to him. "You work in this industry," I said, stating the obvious. "Do *you* think it's stupid?"

"I don't count," he replied dismissively without missing a beat.

Although we then discussed possible ways in which my research should contribute to the stores of sociological knowledge, this editor, whom I will call Thom (short for Doubting Thomas), simply would not be persuaded that those who actually do the labor of transnational cultural production are important and that this study might be valuable because it is about something that he himself values. He sincerely believed that, in this context, he simply did not matter enough. Furthermore, upon reflection I now realize that many other informants, their initial replies to my email approach skeptical that they possessed any relevant expertise worth sharing, were not merely being obstinate in the face of an inconvenient, pesky researcher making demands upon their already overscheduled lives. Though they may have shared his views, they were too polite (or perhaps too embarrassed) to raise the issue with me as bluntly as this one editor did. Had I allowed my research agenda to be wholly determined by my informants, I would have deemed it unworthy of serious inquiry and abandoned the subject entirely. It is a sobering thought.

It is also, at least on the surface of things, a profoundly puzzling one. According to the research firm ICv2, American manga sales grew 350 percent from $60 million in 2002 to $210 million in 2007, and this so-called "manga boom" effected changes in the publishing landscape that have become spatially inscribed into the floor plans of every mainstream bookstore in the country (Brienza 2009a). Manga, which until the start of the twenty-first century was often mistaken for an exotic fruit in the English-speaking world, had quickly become serious business. Journalists, scholars, and policy wonks all began to write about the importance of manga. To them, the humble comic book seemed to represent a Japanese challenge to the hegemony and cultural imperialism of American popular culture, a global phenomenon in need of interpretation—and perhaps replication.

There are, in short, plenty of people out there on record suggesting that the story of manga in America is an important one needing to be told. And it is one, moreover, that manga industry professionals like Thom had experienced firsthand. As a veteran editor, in fact, he had a direct and instrumental role in manga's overseas commercial success. Why should this not be obvious to him? Why was he so very convinced that his opinions and role in it all did not "count"? What was going on?

The answers to these questions, surprisingly, may be found in how, precisely, these commentators had being telling the manga story and what sort of language they had been using. Sociologist Sharon Kinsella, writing in 2000, likens manga in its original Japanese context to "air" because it has "permeated every crevice of the contemporary environment" (Kinsella 2000, 4). And intriguingly, she is not alone in using atmospheric metaphors either; in his monograph *Recentering Globalization*, Koichi Iwabuchi attributes the success of manga outside of the Asian region to being culturally "odorless" (Iwabuchi 2002, 24). While, in his view, the Japanese origin of many of its cultural objects intended for local consumption hangs about them like invisible but all too perceptible olfactory particles in the air, manga can circulate the globe freely because its national, racial, and ethnic characteristics are undetectable and therefore do not pique the proverbial olfactory sensibilities of non-Asian noses. This odorlessness was not, as it was for goods such as electronics and automobiles specially manufactured for export, a deliberate business strategy. Instead, the reason proffered for the lack of offense is simple: The medium of the cartoon was American before it was Japanese, and its flow is therefore innocuous and easy to reverse.[1]

This discourse on air and odorlessness reflects Japanese common wisdom through the 1990s about the origins, properties, and appeals of its popular culture. For example, famed Japanese cultural philosopher Hiroki Azuma argues that contemporary popular, or as he terms it "otaku," culture in Japan such as manga is the product of "a complex yearning to produce a *pseudo-Japan* once again from American-made material, after the destruction of the 'good old Japan' through the defeat in World War II" (Azuma 2009, 13). The Japanese so fully embraced manga, then, precisely because military defeat had made other older forms of media distasteful. If it is received well in America, that is only because it was already kind of American. This explains why journalist Douglas McGray observed "a strange point of pride, a kind of one-downsmanship, to argue just how little Japan there is in modern Japan" among the Japanese "artists, directors, scientists, designers, and culture mavens" he interviewed in the early 2000s. This, he too goes on to suggest, may be a crucial component in the global spread of what he calls "Japan's Gross National Cool" (McGray 2002, 48).

McGray's article, however, published in *Foreign Policy* in 2002, represented a historic turning point in the way in which the story of manga was represented. Drawing upon political scientist Joseph S. Nye's conception of "soft power" (Nye 1990, 2004), he argues that Japan's popular culture might be actively deployed both to revive the nation's export economy in the postmanufacturing age and to improve its position on the global diplomatic stage.[2] In his view, Japan is "one of a handful of perfect globalization nations," having succeeded "not only in balancing a flexible, absorptive, crowd-pleasing, shared culture with a more private, domestic one but also in taking advantage of that balance to build an increasingly powerful global commercial force" (McGray 2002, 53). For a country which has renounced the coercive "hard power" of military

---

[1] It should be noted that Iwabuchi's views on this subject have developed over time, and he no longer argues that Japanese manga circulate outside of the Asian region so readily simply because they are "odorless" (see Iwabuchi 2004, 2010).

[2] The concept of soft power was first developed in his 1990 book *Bound to Lead: The Changing Nature of American Power* and elucidated upon in detail in the 2004 follow up volume *Soft Power: The Means to Success in World Politics*. Seen as an alternative to the "hard" military power of guns and tanks, soft power, by his definition, "is the ability to get what you want through attraction rather than coercion or payments," and "[i]t arises from the attractiveness of a country's culture, political ideals, or policies" (Nye 2004, x). Nye (2008) readily admits that precisely how this attraction operates and produces tangible dividends for nation-states is not always clear, nor is there always a firm dividing line between relations that attract and those that coerce. Nevertheless, to Japan, which post–World War II constitutionally renounced military power as a path to political influence and seemed to have become an economic has-been after the bursting of the bubble economy in 1989, soft power was—no pun intended—bound to be an attractive prospect.

domination, such an alternative means to influence should be particularly desirable, but unfortunately, it has not thus far had the will or means to tap it. McGray is optimistic about the future, however, finding it "hard to imagine that Japan will be content to remain so much medium and so little message" (McGray 2002, 54). After all, he argues, the rewards could be tremendous: "If Japan sorts out its economic mess and military angst, and if younger Japanese become secure in asserting their own values and traditions, Tokyo can regain the role it briefly assumed at the turn of the 19th century, when it simultaneously sought to engage the West and to become a military and cultural power on its own terms" (McGray 2002, 48).

Gone with the wind, then, went the metaphors of air and of culturally odorless gases that might first have come from America on random currents of global circulation. In their place appeared a militaristic language about "cultural power" and "commercial force," along with the possibility of newfound global influence—and manga, of all things, was among those objects of popular culture to lead the charge. By the middle of the first decade of the 2000s, subsequent commentators throughout the media and the academy, and indeed the nascent manga industry itself, had begun imitating and expanding upon this new style of rhetoric. In their hands, the story of manga in America became one of all-out war. Journalist and critic Roland Kelts was commissioned to write a book subtitled *How Japanese Popular Culture Has Invaded the U.S.* (see Figure 1.1). This book was published by Palgrave Macmillan in 2006. In 2007, *Wired* magazine ran a cover story on how manga has "conquered America" (see Figure 1.2). The magazine also promised to explain, albeit in a slightly smaller font size, "how Japanese comics are reshaping popular culture" in a mere ten pages. Similarly hyperbolic, the largest independent American manga publishing house of the period, called Tokyopop, coined the phrase "Manga Revolution" and used it extensively on published titles and assorted promotional material beginning in 2002. In his scholarly book about American comic books, sociologist Paul Lopes deploys this very same slogan and devotes five pages to "The Manga Revolution" (Lopes 2009, 152), arguing that manga was an "external" force of transformation upon comics publishing in the United States (Lopes 2009, 157). Even Giles Clark and Angus Phillips mention "the irresistible rise of manga" in the latest edition of their publishing textbook, using the intransitive verb "to rise" as if to suggest that the popularization of manga was a phenomenon that had no deliberate actor behind it (Clark and Phillips 2008, 54). This had, in short, become a story of foreign invasion, revolution, and conquest, where resistance is futile, and it was the manga itself doing the invading, revolutionizing, and conquering. Manga was at the forefront of a fight between Japan and the United States for cultural domination; the medium itself had become the agent of social change.

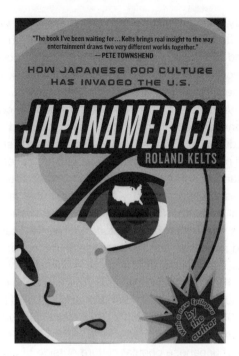

FIGURE 1.1 Japanamerica.

FIGURE 1.2 Wired *(November 2007)*.

Needless to say, this new take on manga was appealing within Japan itself, particularly given its complicated history in the twentieth century with the United States, and the influence of McGray's article on governmental policy since its publication in 2002 has been significant (Valaskivi 2013).Although different government ministries and bureaucrats have quite different views on the potential symbolic and economic value of popular culture, the article, along with the annual Education White Paper published back in 2000 by the Ministry of Education, Culture, Sports, Science and Technology (MEXT), which designated manga as a traditional Japanese art, paved the way for new initiatives. For example, in May 2006 the *Wall Street Journal Asia* reported that "[t]he Japanese Foreign Ministry plans to sell the Japanese 'brand' by marketing national treasures like manga (Japanese comics), animation and music abroad. This new initiative will include an international prize awarded to manga artists and may even certify Japanese animators as 'ambassadors of animation culture,' showcasing their work at embassies worldwide" (quoted in Sugiura 2008, 149). Social scientists again quickly began contributing to the discourse; an anthology edited by Yasushi Watanabe, David L. McConnell, and Joseph S. Nye (2008) titled *Soft Power Superpowers: Cultural and National Assets of Japan and the United States* included chapters on the cultural and economic impact of Japanese popular culture outside of Japan. And in 2009, the nation's 15 trillion yen economic stimulus package included provisions aimed at increasing sales of Japan's popular culture overseas. Prime Minister Taro Aso told reporters that April, "Japanese content, such as anime and video games, and fashion draw attention from consumers around the world. Unfortunately, this soft power is not being linked to business overseas. By linking the popularity of Japan's soft power to business, I want to create a 20–30 trillion yen market by 2020 and create 500,000 new jobs" (quoted in McCurry 2009). While the nationalistic undertones are muted, the debt to McGray's thinking in all of these instances is nonetheless perceptible. As a part of this new initiative to help private businesses more effectively capitalize upon the already popular, the Japanese Ministry of Economy, Trade and Industry established the Creative Industries Promotion Office in June 2010. The stated goal of this new office is to promote the expansion of Japan's cultural industries and export of their products overseas in the hope that this sector will help drive domestic economic growth. The unstated goal is the global projection of cultural power. A press release from the ministry announced that their efforts would be conducted, "[u]nder the single, long-term concept of 'Cool Japan'" (Anon. 2010a).

Of course, it is easy to be skeptical of the efficacy of such reactive, top-down initiatives (Sugiura 2008), and moreover, Japanese commercial interests felt that the government had historically been all talk and no walk in this area. In an August 2010 editorial, for example, the conservative, business-friendly daily newspaper the *Yomiuri Shimbun* called for even more direct state intervention:

> The government seems content for Japan to just be extolled overseas as "cool." However, we think the government has not tried hard enough, or been imaginative enough, in taking advantage of this popularity for the benefit of business expansion.
>
> In June, the trade ministry released its "strategy to promote a culture-oriented industry." This plan to harness "Cool Japan" to revitalize the national economy seemingly reflects an awareness that more must be done to tap this industry.
>
> The strategy calls for an integrated support system—from product development to the signing of overseas sales contracts—for small and midsize companies that lack the expertise and funds needed to develop their business abroad. We hope the ministry's strategy will be steadily implemented. (Anon. 2010b)

However, in the wake of the Fukushima earthquake in March 2011, the now former Prime Minister Aso's passion for popular culture seemed ill-suited to drive international policy in a time of crisis. Yet, manga as one of Japan's most important cultural "exports," "assets," or "brands" has nonetheless become the third and final standard story about manga in America.

To sum up these views, then, manga is airy, odorless, innocuous, and easily transportable; alternatively, it is militaristic, forceful, and powerful enough to project Japan's will even upon the pop cultural and political juggernaut that is the United States. It might also, to take a slightly more modest view, be a newfound global economic asset as a cultural export or brand. Yet, upon what grounds can it be assumed that any of these interpretive options are the best ways of thinking about what has happened in the first place? Certainly, all three modes of talking about manga do, upon close inspection, share one critical error in common: They attribute manga's success to the peculiar and unique properties of the manga medium itself.

Now, while I do not deny the agentive potential of objects (Latour 2005), these accounts, clearly, cannot be the whole story. The manga medium cannot literally circulate around the globe like an odorless gas. It does not, in fact, physically move much at all. While in theory it is possible that a molecule of carbon dioxide exhaled by manga artist Masashi Kishimoto might one day find its way into the body of a person on the other side of the Pacific, a copy of Viz Media's English language edition of *Naruto* shares not one carbon atom in common with any copy of the original Japanese language edition of that same title. Manga is emphatically not riding the jet stream or, for that matter, crossing oceans by any other means—at least in strictly material terms. With the exception of the modest amounts of imported stock to be found in a few specialist Japanese bookstores such as Kinokuniya in San Francisco and New York City, it is not an export in the way that raw or manufactured goods are exports. And it should likewise go without saying that manga is not a sentient being choosing to invade or make war on other countries. It cannot in and of itself conquer America; at best, it is possible that manga is a tool without which a variety of cultural conquest of America would have been impossible. So, something else is happening, something these stories do not capture.

Clearly, all of these metaphorical ways of talking about manga are hardly better than convenient fictions which do next to nothing to illuminate the actual social and cultural transformations taking place. There are people—lots of them, in highly organized groups—responsible for what has occurred. Yet, it is precisely these people who have been written out of the standard stories of manga's success. According to the common wisdom, the innate properties of the manga object itself were the crucial factor, while those individuals behind it have been made invisible, silenced, and superfluous. It is as if the manga is doing it all on its own. No wonder Thom was so certain he does not count. He was, after all, only believing what he was certain to have heard many times, and in doing so he has been grossly deceived about the conditions and consequences of his own lived experience.

Even the published scholarly research has thus far had remarkably little to say about people like Thom. Those scholars who explicitly engage with the concept of the global soft power and "coolness" of Japanese popular culture are primarily working from a cultural studies or cultural anthropological background and therefore focus on describing the attraction generated by signs and commodities—research on fans and fan cultures. The best work from this perspective is penned by Anne Allison (2006b, 277), who observes:

> [F]or American youth, it is not so much Japan itself as a compelling culture, power, or place that is signified (despite the fact that this precisely what the Japanese government tries to capitalize on in all the rhetoric and attention given to Japan's new "soft power" in the globalization of J-pop). Rather "Japan" operates more as a signifier for a particular brand and blend of fantasy-ware: goods that inspire an imaginary space at once foreign and familiar and a subjectivity of continual flux and global mobility, forever moving into and out of new planes/powers/terrains/relations.

The coolness of manga, in short, arises specifically from its quality of "not-the-United-States"-ness but emphatically *not* its quality of "Japaneseness" (Allison 2006b). If correct, this suggests at minimum that the diplomatic war for hearts and minds waged through popular culture is not going to be a particularly successful political project. I would argue that this view ought to be taken seriously; indeed, other studies of anime fans have drawn similar conclusions about consumers' equivocal interests and sympathies toward Japan as a nation-state (e.g., Napier 2007). This story, however, while a very important antidote to *Wired*-style hyperbole, is still about the manga object and its impact. The role of cultural producers remains wholly unaddressed.

The research, which has resulted in the book you are now holding in your hands, aims to cut through this media hype and intellectual fugue to understand what is actually moving, if not the manga object itself, how and why it happens, and what the consequences of that movement truly are. This required mapping out the complex social configuration responsible for this process to understand how it operates. Drawing upon data gathered through participant observation and seventy in-depth, semistructured interviews conducted in and around New York, Toronto, San Francisco, Los Angeles, and Tokyo with industry professionals from September 2010 to October 2011, I have explored the width and breadth of the transnational cultural field which publishes Japanese comic books in English, demonstrating in the process how cultural flow can only be accomplished through an active, labor-intensive, and oft-contested process, which I term "domestication." Only, as it were, by writing Thom and the people like him back into the story can the past, present, and future of manga in America and what it has to contribute to knowledge about the transnational production of culture in the twenty-first century be truly understood.

In this book, I will argue that roiling beneath the obfuscating cover stories of "air," "conquest," and "export" is the rapid transmission and transformation of professional practice from Japan to the United States and back again, driven by cooperative, as well as competing, individual and collective desires and agendas. Straightforward evangelical objectives, to bring manga to the West, to "build bridges" with Japan, led early American manga publishers to wed themselves and their collective corporate destinies to the field of American trade publishing. In doing so, they succeeded in raising the mainstream visibility of manga. But in trying to change the media landscape, they also changed themselves; they became professionalized into the priorities and practices of trade publishing, which emphasize original product development over licensing the product developed by another. An increased interest in e-books and digital delivery of content since 2008 has upped the ante further in favor of original titles, and it is fast reaching a stage where Japanese manga publishers need their American counterparts more than their American counterparts need—or want—them. The movement of this cultural form from East to West ultimately cannot challenge durable relations of inequality because it succeeds only by traveling through those very same hierarchical structures. This leads, in sum, to the paradoxical conclusion that domesticating Japanese manga for the United States actually makes manga everywhere more American.

What is "manga"?

Before proceeding any further, what precisely is meant by manga must be addressed. The word originates from the Japanese compound reading of the two Chinese characters 漫画, meaning "random" or "irresponsible" and "picture," respectively. While the earliest recorded usage of the word dates back to the 1770s, it did not acquire its modern sense until the early part of the 1900s with Japan's exposure to and emulation of Western forms of cartoon art (Shimizu 1991). Today, "manga" may be written in any of the four scripts (hiragana, katakana, kanji, or romaji) of modern Japanese and commonly refers to any sort of comic book or strip, or printed cartoon. The English language loanword "comics," written in katakana as コミックス, is also used in lieu of "manga," particularly in commercial and business contexts (Schodt 1996).

Manga itself is big business. It is estimated that approximately one out of every four books now sold in Japan is a volume of manga (Pink 2007), and this enduring popularity with audiences of all ages and both genders traces its history[3] back to the period immediately following the Second World War. A cheap medium of entertainment sold primarily to children became a site of visual and narrative experimentation by manga artists such as Osamu Tezuka as well as an outlet for antiestablishment social and political commentary in the mid-1900s. The market continued to expand throughout the postwar years, and by the late twentieth century, manga had become thoroughly mainstream, a medium of communication and expression available everywhere and about, potentially, anything (Kinsella 2000).

Despite this diversity, some gross generalizations about content can be made. An astute observer entering the manga section of a Japanese bookstore will notice that all of the books are arranged first by the gender and age of the target audience, then by publisher, then by imprint, and finally alphabetized by author surname and title. Some specialty shops such as Animate and K-Books even put manga for different genders on separate floors. This arrangement represents the ranked priorities of manga publishing in Japan, and the gendering of manga genres is central. While there certainly are, say, horror manga or mystery manga, these genres are not as important as those which explicitly identify the gender and age of the target audience. The latter include *shounen* (for boys), *shoujo* (for girls), *seinen* (for men), *kodomo* (for very young children of both genders), and *josei* or *redisu* (for women). Unsurprisingly, girls are not stigmatized for reading shounen manga—the highest-circulating shounen magazine *Weekly Shonen Jump* has a readership that is about half female (Schodt 1996)—but boys would ordinarily not want to be caught dead

---

[3]For an in-depth treatment of the history of manga in Japan, see Shimizu (1991) or Schodt (1983).

reading shoujo. Some genres, even when implying a unity of content, are implicitly gendered; the most important examples in this vein include boys' love (for women) and moé (for men).

The vast majority of manga published in Japan are, in the strictest sense, what is known as "story manga." Story manga tell a continuous story over a large number of pages, with the shortest, called *yomikiri*, typically around 20–80 pages. Longer titles are serialized in magazines, mostly in monochrome with an occasional full-color page, later to be compiled at semiregular intervals into reprinted volumes with ISBNs called *tankoubon*. While some manga are published in a preplanned number of serials, since the success of Akira Toriyama's *Dragon Ball*, it has become standard for mainstream, large press titles to operate according to a logic similar to television programming—issuing new installments for as long as the series is popular and adjusting themes and plotlines to suit consumer tastes all along the way. The most popular manga can, therefore, be dozens of volumes and tens of thousands of pages long. Eiichiro Oda's *One Piece*, for example, weighs in at sixty-seven volumes and counting as of August 2012.

Although some collections of *yonkoma*, or "four-panel," manga similar to Western newspaper cartoon strips have also been published in English, the word "manga" is typically used by English speakers to refer to exclusively Japanese story manga.[4] Moreover, it connotes certain stereotypes about specific types of narrative and artistic content. These are abundantly evident in the *Oxford English Dictionary*'s current entry for manga: "A Japanese genre of cartoons and comic books, drawn in a meticulously detailed style, usually featuring characters with distinctive large, staring eyes, and typically having a science-fiction or fantasy theme, sometimes including violent or sexually explicit material." Of course, nothing after that first comma of the *OED*'s definition is universally true about manga; characters in manga may be drawn in any number of styles, some of which do not involve large eyes, and many stories are realistic, with no sex or violence at all.

In practice, however, the bestselling titles in the United States nearly always conform to one of more of these aforementioned stereotypical characteristics. Yet the American manga industry itself defines manga rather differently. To wit, on one level, a "manga" is any comic first published in Japan, irrespective of format or genre, but on another level it can be, quite simply, anything a publisher says it is. The industry definition of manga, as I

---

[4]Some English speakers, notably in the United Kingdom, also use the word "manga" to refer to animated cartoons for television, video, or film from Japan. The confusion originates from a marketing campaign in the 1980s by the anime company Manga Entertainment to rebrand what the Japanese call "anime" as "manga," which was deemed easier to pronounce. As this usage is not in common usage in Japanese or accepted in other parts of the English-speaking world, I use "manga" exclusively for printed comics and "anime" for animation throughout this text.

have elsewhere argued (Brienza 2009b; Brienza 2011), has evolved to have less to do with visual style or content, or country of origin, and more about the presentation of the book as a mass-produced commercial object and the intended target audience. In the most extreme cases, manga is simply a comic book of a particular trim size and price point that girls and women would be expected to read. Whether or not it is from Japan is of secondary importance. If this sounds vague, that is because, quite simply, it is, and a rigorous, universally agreed upon definition does not exist among industry professionals themselves. Nevertheless, unless otherwise specified, I default to the nebulous twofold industry definition—comics from Japan plus anything else the industry so chooses to label as such—when I use the word manga throughout this book because the collective and organizational characteristics of this transnational field's continued transformation are articulated, in part, through the symbolic transmutations and boundaries of the word "manga."

Scope of book and outline of chapters

Fundamentally, *Manga in America* is a specialized case study of transnational cultural production situated within the academic discipline of sociology. I would never presume to pretend otherwise. But if Thom was once upon a time taken aback by the keen interest a sociologist-in-training had in his working life, I, in turn, have been equally and endlessly surprised by the wide range of interest this research has garnered outside of sociology and, for that matter, outside of the academy altogether. Students and scholars working in complementary subject areas such as communication, media studies, Japanese studies, publishing studies, American studies, and comics studies (to name just a few) have all sought to engage with it. Manga fans, policymakers, and publishing industry insiders have also expressed interest in the findings and outcomes of my research. So many different groups, with a myriad of different—and often contradictory—needs, motivations, and intellectual and professional commitments, have put themselves forward as potential audiences for this book. Such enthusiasm across such a wide range of stakeholders is, of course, exciting for any author. However, it is also incredibly daunting. How am I supposed to go about writing what is otherwise a conventional scholarly monograph on a topic of such potentially broad appeal?

In the end, I had to give up long ago on trying to be all things for all people. It seemed an insurmountable challenge that would result merely in a surefire recipe for abject failure. Instead, I set myself a slightly less ambitious task: to ensure that there is something here for everybody. In practice, this probably means that nobody will be entirely happy with the scope of the resultant work. Speaking to a wide range of disciplines, for example, means having to provide an extraordinary amount of detail and lengthy reviews of literatures that will be entirely new for some and entirely boring and uncontroversial for others... and precisely what counts as new and what counts as boring depends upon who the reader in question is. As such, I can only apologize in advance for a text that will, inevitably, seem unduly challenging in places and ridiculously simplistic in others. Please remember that what seems elementary to you may well be the most difficult—but rewarding—section for someone else. There are always trade-offs.

In any case, and irrespective of the above, my task for the research at the heart of this book has been to look carefully at the social process I call domestication in the transnational cultural field called the American manga industry, which publishes Japanese manga in English, primarily for the American but also for a global English-speaking market. I investigate how, exactly, this transnational cultural production works and what the consequences of this process are likely to be for its adjacent national fields. As with all cultural goods, the text which has resulted is to some extent a product of the particular time in which it was researched and written. Nevertheless, its thesis, I would maintain, is durable. In subsequent chapters, I will show that manga publishing houses and their networks of production, when closely scrutinized, prove themselves to be both loyal and dysfunctional family units whose success is constituted through and maintained by both cooperation and conflict. To understand what is going on beneath the placid, well-ordered surface, to unearth the many tensions, conditional alliances, and struggles for power and position which foment beneath, I deploy a combination of ethnographic research methods which inform the following chapters.

Chapter 2 reviews the scholarship on the production of culture, focusing in particular upon manga and other categories of trade book publishing. Then, by synthesizing my analysis of Pierre Bourdieu's theory of fields and Gary Gereffi's global value chain framework, I map out the structure of the American manga publishing industry as it will be understood subsequently throughout this text. Finally, I develop a conceptual vocabulary for the labor of the transnational production of culture that is both expansive and precise enough to suit the subject of my research. The word I choose to represent this collective labor and its constituent components is "domestication."

Chapter 3 provides concise overviews of both the larger Japanese and American contexts of book publishing as well as a detailed historical account of manga publishing in the United States. I argue that, although the first manga in English translation was published in the 1980s, American manga publishing did not exist as a formal, professionalized industry until 2005 and that this professionalization has transformed the goals and priorities of those who work in it. This transformation, in turn, has had enormous implications for the movement of manga content from East to West, which will be interrogated in detail in subsequent chapters.

Chapter 4 focuses on the motivations behind the founding of manga publishing companies and the wheeling-and-dealing art of manga licensing. Manga licensing is riven with intense, often heated, disputes over intellectual property and control over the presentation and marketing of the text. The closer the relationship between the Japanese and American publishers, the more interference and regular conflict there are likely to be. However, I show that, particularly in the current adverse economic climate and uncertainties about digital publishing, the American manga industry has, when companies do decide licensing is worth the time at all, increasingly been succeeding in transferring the material risk of publication back onto the Japanese.

Chapter 5 is an in-depth depiction of the publishing industry labor necessary to domesticate manga and the people who do it. I show that this work, which is routinized in theory, is actually far more chaotic in practice, and that there is no universal agreement about how messages within the manga text ought to be conveyed. Perfect communication, in other words, is not the objective. Instead, these underpaid, often precarious laborers derive satisfaction from imposing their will on and inserting parts of themselves into the product. Following the literature on cultural labor, I argue that casualization is not merely a symptom of the contemporary culture industries but rather an integral component to its continued functioning. In other words, a lack of autonomy over one's own professional life increases the desire to assert control over the object being produced.

Chapter 6 examines the various new models with which manga publishers are experimenting, including fan-funded publishing, web aggregation, iPad/iPhone books, and locally produced original global manga titles. The rapid shift toward digital prose books cannot always be superimposed directly onto the manga medium, and the power struggles discussed in Chapters 4 and 5 are being reenacted in this new space. Ultimately, I argue that strategic responses to digitization need not, in themselves, be digital, and a digital future merely intensifies and accelerates the process which makes manga American.

The seventh and final chapter opens with an anecdote from fieldwork which captures the overarching argument this book makes: that the intervention of the publishing industry makes manga progressively less Japanese and more American. I wrap up the book by suggesting that this process of domestication is becoming increasingly manifest through a re-inscription of unequal US-Japan power relations; a decreasing dependence upon licensing and an increasing reliance upon locally produced content; and, finally, the growing influence of the American manga industry upon the production of manga in Japan itself.

2

Theorizing Domestication: Manga and the Transnational Production of Culture

We don't create [manga]; we repurpose it. We are sort of the shepherds of it in our market. We're the shepherd. We put it into the field and take care of it the best we can. (Interview 2010)

A good story can always be articulated in a variety of different media and formats. Two of the oldest, inarguably, are words and pictures; it should come as no surprise, therefore, that sequential art narratives such as comics and manga have no definitive point or place of origin (Mazur and Danner 2014). Academic arguments are stories, too, and most are presented as prose. Indeed, were I to be asked to distill the one developed throughout the text about manga in America down into one sentence—or even a single word—I would have my answer already prepared. But it so happens that this argument could also be made in pictures. One visual image in particular, in fact.

I see a young, casually dressed Caucasian woman hard at work in her home office. Although she is surrounded at all sides by books, posters, toys, and other artifacts of Japanese popular culture, she is probably living in or near one of the urban centers of the United States. She is an American manga publishing industry professional, most likely a freelancer. A page of manga to be edited is open in Adobe InDesign on the desktop computer screen in front of her, while a hardcopy desk reference of the same title is close at hand beside her. This pictorial representation of my argument can, in fact, be seen on the cover of this very book, and, in my view, it exemplifies contemporary patterns of transnational labor and economic organization in the culture industries—deeply implicated and embedded in complex issues of cultural production and consumption; durable gender, ethno-racial, and class inequalities; precariousness; simultaneous isolation from copresent others alongside networked sociality; and the interpenetration of digital and predigital cultures. The only thing missing from the artwork is a feline companion; the woman who lives in my mind's eye adores cats and probably has at least one to keep her company.

In the previous chapter, I have argued that the story of manga in America cannot, as has popularly been the case in the past, be reduced to an exegesis about either the innate or ascribed properties of the manga medium. It is not an odorless gas freely circulating around the globe; it is not, all by itself and of its own accord, invading, revolutionizing, or conquering American culture; and it is not even a straightforward exportable material commodity from which Japan is guaranteed to benefit economically or politically. Objects may have some form of agency, but in the case of manga, they do not act alone. These three stories miss the mark in that they do not account for the many people, like the woman depicted above, who are actually responsible for what has occurred and what, precisely, they have done—and continue to do—to make it occur. Only by taking them seriously, I argue, can conclusions about manga in America whether or not any of these popular takes on its global consequences have any redeeming merit can be drawn.

In search of a word

However, this claim immediately begs two obvious questions: (1) What exactly are these people actually doing? (2) How precisely are they organized to accomplish it? Unfortunately, the answers are not nearly as straightforward as the questions. When asked during fieldwork about the subject of this research project, I typically said I was studying "the American manga publishing industry" or, if my interlocutor, an academic colleague, say, was unfamiliar with the word manga, "the part of the publishing industry that publishes Japanese comics in English translation." While either of these two explanations, truthful as far as they went, usually satisfied casual inquiries, they functioned, in reality, to conceal far more than they revealed. Take the phrase, "American manga publishing industry." Manga, in this rhetorical formulation, is just another category of print, as different, perhaps, as literary fiction is from magazines, but no more exceptional. Nothing about the particular transnational organization, relationships, and labor processes required to make manga American is anywhere implied. The second formulation is a little better in that it captures the necessary acts of symbolic transformation in the word "translation." Yet, translation is only one small aspect of the real work required to get a volume of manga onto a bookstore's shelf. To publish a polished English-language edition of a volume of manga, it must also be licensed, adapted, and re-lettered. Interior art may need to be retouched or censored. The finished product must be marketed, manufactured, sold, and so forth. The bulk of transnational relationships and labor processes are, once more, hidden by the limitations of language. The role of non-Japanese and original manga titles in the industry is likewise omitted. And this only scratches the surface of the problem. How am I going to draw any conclusions about what the case of manga has to teach us about the transnational production of culture in the twenty-first century if I cannot even begin to express with a sufficient level of analytical—and succinct—precision what sorts of actors, groupings, actions, processes, and behaviors are involved in that production?

It is, in fact, extremely difficult to achieve rhetorical clarity about what, precisely, the manga industry does. There is no universally agreed upon word, technical or vernacular, which fully encompasses it. When asked what a good word for what they do might be, some of my informants were entirely stumped. "Repurposing," "shepherding," and "evangelizing" were among the creative answers supplied and, while each is well worth unpacking, none were ever suggested by more than one individual. The only answer receiving more than one mention, particularly from employees of one of the oldest US manga publishers, was "localizing," from the term "localization," which originates in the field of business translation and consultancy (Brienza 2012). However, while more expansive and open-ended than "translation," localization implies a unidirectional social process, taking a cultural object already manufactured abroad (in this case in Japan) and then tailoring it to local (in this case American) tastes. As a concept, it does not take into account the possibility of bi- or multidirectional processes, the possibility, in other words, that being published in English might come to affect manga at its initial moment of production in Japan. Indeed, this lack of clarity, I would suggest, is why the stories about manga's commercial success in the United States, even within groups of people actually doing the work resulting in that success, so readily devolve into accounts about the autonomous agency of the medium itself.

Therefore, being absolutely clear in the context of this research is absolutely critical. But how to go about achieving such clarity? The standard stories fail, and industry professionals themselves cannot even agree upon an appropriate verb for what it is they do. Can sociology do any better? Can the sociological literature on publishing and cultural production reveal anything useful about what these people are doing and provide any frameworks or theoretical interventions to help conceptualize their actions? Yes, in my view, it can. In the following sections, I review the scholarship on the production of culture, focusing in particular upon manga and other categories of trade book publishing. I begin with studies of manga publishing, both within and outside Japan, and continue on to contemporary trade book publishing, including the strengths and weaknesses of the theories used to undergird them. Then, by synthesizing my analysis of Pierre Bourdieu's theory of fields and Gary Gereffi's global value chain framework, I map out the structure of the American manga publishing industry as it will be understood subsequently throughout this text. Finally, I develop a conceptual vocabulary for the labor of the transnational production of culture that is both expansive and precise enough to suit the subject of my research. The word I choose to represent this collective labor and its constituent components is "domestication."

Past research on manga publishing

Previously published scholarly accounts in English of manga publishing focusing upon the industry in Japan are few and far between. The tone unquestionably has been set by Frederik L. Schodt (1983, 1996, 2007), a freelance Japanese to English translator and personal acquaintance of the now-deceased Osamu Tezuka, Japan's most revered creator of manga. Schodt's writings, though, however influential and at times evangelical in their own right, are broadly historical, descriptive, and impressionistic, lacking in critical, interpretive rigor. Beyond that, within the social sciences broadly, the publishing of entire genres of manga are represented by a single monograph: Sharon Kinsella (2000) writes about yaoi doujinshi and seinen manga, Jennifer Prough (2011) about shoujo manga, and Kinko Ito (2011) about ladies' comics. The shortage of material is in part due to the logistical difficulties of working across language barriers, but Kinsella in her introduction also notes that she does "not believe that it would be possible to enter the manga industry and the amateur manga world again today in quite the way that circumstances made it possible in the early 1990s. The culture industries as a whole are notorious for their secretive tendencies. The manga industry has shown the same reticence exhibited by the culture industries in general" (2000, 15). Prough, who conducted her fieldwork nearly a decade after Kinsella, commends her for her "prescience" and recounts frequent difficulties she had gaining access to informants for her own publishing industry research (2011, 14). It comes as no surprise, then, that Ito relies primarily upon archival and textual sources for her research. Nevertheless, taken together, they paint an important portrait of a mainstream commercial industry, embedded within and sustained by its particular national context.

Given the rather impoverished state of the research outlined above and the researchers' own interests in contemporary Japanese society, studies of transnational manga publishing, especially outside of the Asian region,[1] are

---

[1] I confine myself in this chapter to cases of transnational manga publishing that include at least one country outside of the East and Southeast Asian regions. As Iwabuchi (2002) argues, compellingly in my view, cultural flows between Japan and other countries within these areas are governed by different social forces.

unsurprisingly rarer still. Nevertheless, their orientations range similarly. The research firm ICv2 has covered the US manga industry extensively since 2002 both in print and on its website, and there are several interesting accounts of the industry written by industry insiders themselves (Blanchard 2015; Clements 2010; Donovan 2010; Erik-Soussi 2015; Hayley 2010; Thompson 2007a, 2007b). These naturally vary in quality but at their best constitute rich, historical accounts structured around firsthand experience. Jason Thompson (2007a; 2007b)'s histories of the manga industry, aimed at a general audience of US manga fans, are excellent in that they capture the key structuring transformations of the field, and Magda Erik-Soussi (2015), working as a freelance manga adaptor and editor with the pen name Lianne Sentar, tells an impassioned tale of simultaneously growing up while growing into her role as a manga publishing professional. The explicit feminism of her account both anticipates and explicates the feminization of the manga field (Brienza 2011). Emma Hayley (2010) tells the story of the Manga Shakespeare line of global manga as no one else can because the books were her idea in the first place, and the candid account by David Blanchard (2015) of his own modest career as an artist and publisher is important for the way it documents failure in the business. While rarely discussed in the open, failure is ubiquitous, and the persistence of the industry even in the absence of success is in itself a matter of significance.

In addition to the professionals' accounts, aficionados who have cobbled together a career based upon published textual commentary and criticism on the industry periphery have also included brief treatments of the North American industry in their publications (Gravett 2004; Kelts 2006; McCarthy 2009; Schodt 1983; Schodt 1996; Yadao 2009). As these writers are primarily interested in the properties of manga as a cultural object, these are cursory, afterthoughts for the most part, signaling the existence and success of manga publishing outside of Japan but little else. Manga blogger Melinda Beasi (2013), in collaboration with a six-member team of manga-focused journalists, librarians, and publishing professionals, spearheaded a pamphlet-length publication with Dark Horse for the Comic Book Legal Defense Fund, introducing Japanese manga to American librarians and discussing preemptively the sorts of defenses which may be invoked should they face public objection to problematic, for example, overtly sexualized, manga content.

Apart from these works, scholarship in this nascent area has thus far been entirely short form, comprised of essays scattered about numerous journals and edited collections. There is no authoritative journal publication venue, so instead research on manga publishing in particular national territories tends to be monopolized by a single scholar who becomes recognized as an authority on the subject by those with interest in it. For example, Jean-Marie Bouissou (2006) writes about manga publishing in France and Paul Malone (2010b) about manga publishing in Germany. Along with Marco Pellitteri, who wrote his doctoral thesis on the reception of manga in his native Italy, these authors also write, sometimes collaboratively, about manga publishing in Europe and elsewhere (Bouissou 2000; Bouissou, Pellitteri, and Dolle-Weinkauff 2010; Malone 2010a). In the English-speaking territories, Leonard Rifas (2004) and Roger Sabin (2006) have written about *Barefoot Gen*, the first manga ever published in English, and Dru Pagliassotti (2008, 2009) about boys' love manga publishing and reading in the United States. Due to the abbreviated length of all of these pieces, they are either broad, general overviews of an entire field or highly specific, niche case studies of one genre of manga publishing or, at the most extreme, the publishing history of a single, significant title.

The most important observational insight of this literature is made by Malone (2010a), that the successful establishment of manga in France, Spain, and Italy all trace their beginnings to Marvel/Epic's American release of Katsuhiro Otomo's *Akira* in 1989. This speaks quite directly to what Koichi Iwabuchi (2002, 38) terms, the "Americanization of Japanization," whereby American cultural power and distribution channels are necessary to bring Japanese popular culture into the global arena. In a separate case study of the global success of the *Pokémon* franchise (which, of course, included *Pokémon* manga, though this is not explicitly discussed), Iwabuchi (2004) further argues that, far from upending the global political hierarchy, it just reinstantiates it because the *Pokémon* that was seen by the world beyond Asia was the American-adapted version. The facts, therefore, seem to contradict one of the standard stories already discussed of a manga invasion, conquest, or revolution.

Though she does not write about manga specifically in this context either, the scholar to think most deeply about the relationship between the global flow of popular culture and cultural power in the context of Japan and the United States is cultural anthropologist Anne Allison. In her early writing on this topic, she sees Japanese cultural goods as circulating globally "in a form that de-couples characters and stories from manifest signs of geographic place and identity" (Allison 2000, 88), but as she studies the *Pokémon* phenomenon more closely, she comes to believe that particular forms of uniquely Japanese cuteness provide new opportunities for different sorts of interaction between children and media and observes that local media industries in the United States no longer attempt to conceal their products' Japanese origins (Allison 2004). Yet, Allison nonetheless becomes implicitly critical of Japan's soft power ambitions: "American kids can love *Pokémon* and know, even fetishize, its origins but associate Japan in all this less with national power or a cultural lifestyle than with a consumer brand that can be collected and customized as one's own" (Allison 2006b, 262). Bluntly put, "American kids do not see *Pokémon* as Japanese, even though most are fully aware that the property originated in Japan" (Allison 2006b, 246). This is, in her view, a highly personalized, apolitical, narcissistic relationship with Japanese popular culture, not a horizon-expanding one. Later, though, Allison changes her mind and instead strikes an optimistic note, arguing that "ideas, images, information, and trend-making [are] becoming decentered away from any single place, including the United States" (Allison 2008, 107) and holding out hope that American youth will emerge from "within the shell of their own ethnocentrism" (Allison 2008, 110). These are conclusions drawn upon her study of Americans' reception of Japanese popular media, so it should come as no surprise that Allison's normative conclusions differ depending upon whom she observes. The jury is still out, in my view, as long as there is no real clarity and specificity about how and under what sorts of new transnational, decentered conditions these "ideas, images, information, and trend-making" are being produced. The one takeaway point here is that so-called cultural exports may make Japan money—although interestingly *Pokémon*, the grist of so much research and debate, did not the first time (Tobin 2004)—but they do not necessarily also transform Western sympathies toward Japan as a nation or reorient global cultural hierarchies. Furthermore, while symbolic materials may be culturally promiscuous, circulating quite readily through authorized as well as unauthorized channels, accompanying substantive material benefit, particularly for cultural producers, is far harder to identify and measure, let alone guarantee.

Although all of the literature I have covered thus far is important for understanding the particularities of the lived experience of manga in America for its producers and consumers, it is ill-suited for providing in-depth, critical accounts of how transnational cultural production is organized or what, precisely, actors are doing to accomplish it. Fortunately, there are several scholars who have sought to account specifically for the explosive growth in the manga market in the United States in the beginning of the 2000s, which has become known in the industry as the "manga boom" (Brienza 2009a, 2009b, 2011; Goldberg 2010; Lopes 2009; Matsui 2009). Each of these scholars understands manga's American success as a complex phenomenon, supported by new, formalized organizational configurations. My own and Lopes's, taken together, are the most compatible, as we both draw upon the social theory of Pierre Bourdieu. Although, as discussed in the previous chapter, his use of "Manga Revolution" as a rhetorical device may be problematic, any analytical distinction between us is primarily one of emphasis; he argues that manga succeeded outside of the comics publishing field—and in fact it is quite possible that sequential art *can* only ever succeed commercially on the outside (Lopes 2009)—whereas I argue that manga publishing migrated from the comics publishing field to the book publishing field, where the logic of this new field fueled the manga boom (Brienza 2009a). While I would revise the argument of that paper slightly in a manner discussed in more detail in the next chapter, both accounts have the advantage of being at once historically specific as well as theoretically situated.

Given the breadth and quality of this writing on this particular question (and only this question), I am convinced that why manga became popular in the United States has already received sufficient treatment, and the source of this transformation was not an underground subculture of fans or pressure from Japanese government or business. The source was, rather, locally situated publishing companies and imprints, often owned by some of the largest multinational media conglomerates in the world. Furthermore, although all of this research is based upon the field as it was prior to the financial crisis which rocked the global economy at the end of 2008 and continues to affect the manga market years later, any changes to this landscape have been changes of degree, not of kind. In a very real sense, the arguments made by myself, Goldberg, Lopes, and Matsui still apply; publishing houses have come and gone, but those that remain, along with a handful of new companies, still play by the rules of the book publishing field. Hundreds of new titles are still being published each year, and, despite significant contraction, the market, worth $120 million in 2010 when I commenced fieldwork, remains twice as large in terms of revenue as it was a decade ago. Manga was definitely not just a fad. Something happened that has not been undone. And yet, the mystery remains: What are these people actually doing, and how exactly are they organized to do what they do? Answering these questions requires both in-depth inspection of the lived, day-to-day practices of manga publishers *and* a clear-sighted understanding of the wider sociological context in which they act. The latter must necessarily come first, so as not to misattribute exogenous social forces to the particularities of manga.

Book publishing and theories of cultural production

Although the literature on manga publishing is sparse, unable to conceptualize cultural production on a transnational scale, and, for the most part, not theoretically rigorous, all of the published literature, either explicitly or implicitly, makes one absolutely crucial point: American manga publishing today most closely resembles American trade book publishing. Therefore, I have chosen to confine the scope of this section to studies of book publishing. Other print media, such as magazines and newspapers, will be excluded. So, what sorts of insights and theoretical interventions can the scholarly literature on trade book publishing and cultural production provide to the study of American manga publishing?

Since the classic Frankfurt School critique of the culture industries (Adorno and Horkheimer 1947), the nature, operation, and distribution of the power of the media and its producers have been matters of much scholarly debate. But to suggest that they retain no significant amount of power whatsoever would, in my view, be unsustainable, and no rigorous analysis of the tug of war between employer and employee, copyright and piracy, East and West, and so forth in the context of manga would be complete without a comprehensive knowledge of the inner workings of the manga publishing industry. However, despite being the oldest of the modern mass media industries, dating back to the fifteenth century with Johannes Gutenberg and his Bibles, the field of contemporary English-language book publishing is sorely underresearched, particularly when compared with film, television, news, and new media in English-language territories. It is therefore rather hard to know the extent of the influence of book publishing today. As is the case with manga publishing, much current knowledge about the industry originates not from the university sector but rather from veterans of industry itself and from research consultancy firms, published in journals such as *Publishing Research Quarterly* and *Logos* and written up in book form as first-person, and often highly critical, memoirs (e.g., Epstein 2001; Schiffrin 2001). This work typically focuses upon how to do good business in a rapidly changing environment or, alternatively, the impossibility of doing good work under intense economic pressure. In-depth descriptive accounts also emerge from business schools (Greco 1997, 2009; Thornton 2004) and from ambitious book history projects which trace all aspects of the book trade from its origins to the present day (e.g., Munro and Sheahan-Bright 2006; Nord, Rubin, and Schudson 2009; Suarez and Woudhuysen 2010).

Sociological and cultural research, meanwhile, sometimes mirrors the preoccupations of the publishing industry itself, particularly with regard to the fate of books in the digital age, albeit from different theoretical perspectives (Fitzpatrick 2011; Carter and Galligan 2007; Greco, Rodríguez, and Wharton 2007; Thompson 2005; Striphas 2009; Whiteside 1980). Precisely, this issue comes directly to the fore in Chapter 6. In addition, the classic comprehensive study of the American publishing industry by Lewis Coser, Charles Kadushin, and Walter Powell (1982) produced an enduring scholarly preoccupation with the tension between art and commerce, also prominent in studies of bookselling by Laura J. Miller (2006), of screen adaptations of literary fiction by Simone Murray (2012), of literary prizes by James English (2005), of book clubs by Janice Radway (1999), of marketing literature by Claire Squires (2009), and of the literary side of the business by John Thompson (2010). There are, moreover, several excellent studies of particular niche areas, most notably romance novel publishing (Radway 1984) and feminist publishing (Murray 2004). Roger Sabin (1993), Jean-Paul Gabilliet (2005), Paul Lopes (2009), and Bradford Wright (2001) have all provided excellent scholarly accounts of the American comics publishing industry through lenses of cultural studies, sociology, and history. Eva Hemmungs Wirtén's doctoral thesis *Global Infatuation* (1998) explores the activities of the Swedish subsidiary of the Canadian publishing house, Harlequin Enterprises and, in the attention given to the work of editors and translators and the production networks linking two national territories, is the closest antecedent in the field of publishing studies to my own research. Gisèle Sapiro's work on translation (Heilbron and Sapiro 2007; Sapiro 2008, 2010; Sapiro and Bustamente 2009) is likewise particularly useful for thinking about publishing beyond the national. Unfortunately, this body of literature does not add up to any one particular research agenda or question going forward, except to underscore abiding tensions between art and commerce and, more recently, the impacts of digitization upon the business. Of course, both of these topics are usually understood from the perspective either of those who read and love books or of those whose livelihoods in some manner depend upon them. But while an important set of issues that this book will address, and their importance cannot be understated, the field of English-language manga publishing is too specialized for these to be my sole, let alone primary, focus.

Bourdieu and cultural fields

Fortunately, a consensus *does* emerge about what sort of theoretical framework is most appropriate. Given the manner the industry has been portrayed in the discourse as strung up in a spider's web of tensions between cultural value and economic imperatives, it perhaps comes as little surprise that much of the modest corpus of sociological research on American, as well as British and transnational, publishing written in the years since Coser et al. (1982) have drawn upon the social theory of Pierre Bourdieu (Brienza 2009a, 2010; English 2005; Hemmungs Wirtén 1998; Lopes 2009; Murray 2012; Sapiro 2010, 2014; Squires 2009; Thompson 2005, 2010). Bourdieu himself never wrote about the modern English-language industry, but his writings on the field of cultural production, or the cultural field, and the formation of the French literary field in the nineteenth century have had a profound influence (Bourdieu 1993, 1996). They draw upon some of the key concepts of his social theory, most notably *field* and *capital*. The field, in Bourdieu's own words, is a "network or configuration of objective relations between positions" (Bourdieu 1993, 97). It is, in other words, a space for social action both structuring and structured by relations between discrete social actors. These actors cooperate and compete for resources, called capital. Capital comes in various forms, among them economic capital (money), cultural capital (skills), social capital (who you know), and symbolic capital (prestige). Different authors privilege different typologies of Bourdieuan capital, and Bourdieu himself added new forms of capital in his own writing throughout his life. The distinction between autonomy and heteronomy is, quite simply, the degree to which any cultural field is autonomous from the economic field, or the market. For example, the popular novel is a product of the heteronomous field, while symbolist poetry a product of a field with a high level of autonomy (Bourdieu 1993). A final concept from Bourdieu's social theory, that of *habitus*, while underused in the context of the study of book publishing, is also important in that it provides the theoretical link between the individual and the collective. Habitus, according to Bourdieu, is "a system of durable, transposable dispositions, structured structures predisposed to function as structuring structures, that is, as principles which generate and organize practices and representations" (Bourdieu 1990, 53). It may thus be understood as set of tacitly learned, taken for granted dispositions and ways of acting. The discursive emphasis here in both cases is on social practice, on actual lived actions and experiences in the world, and taken to their logical endpoint, such theories also reject a Platonic separation of mind and body. Social theories of practice, in other words, understand social phenomenon as a blend of the physical and the mental (Bourdieu 1990; Wacquant 2004).

So, following an ample tradition of scholarship in book publishing that draws upon the work of Bourdieu, I too have chosen to use the three concepts described above in my own work on American manga publishing as a case of transnational cultural production. Habitus and capital can be easily appropriated in the terms outlined by Bourdieu himself. The cultural field, however, is deeply problematic on two levels. The first is the distinction between autonomous and heteronomous fields. While there may have been a historic basis for this distinction in nineteenth-century France, for my purposes it cannot be sustained. John Thompson (2005) provides a persuasive critique in Anglo-American terms in *Books in the Digital Age*, and Simone Murray's (2012) work on Hollywood blockbuster adaptations of contemporary literary works demonstrates time and time again how interpenetrated symbolic value and the market actually are. For this reason, I am not fully convinced that Wendy Goldberg (2010), who proposes four models of cultural production used by US manga publishers today, makes an appropriate or sufficient distinction between the "Bookstore and Library Model" and the "Literary Model," given that many trade publishers release both literary fiction and mainstream bookstore bestsellers simultaneously and often rely upon the latter to support activity in the former. Her account also lacks historical perspective because she does not recognize the different temporal horizons of these models. Furthermore, I would note that the publishing industry in Japan is even more highly integrated, both across categories of books and across different media forms, than American publishing. One of Japan's "Big Three" publishers Kodansha, for example, publishes not just literary fiction but also scholarly monographs *and* magazines *and* manga. Several other major firms, including Shueisha, Shogakukan, and Kadokawa Shoten, also have their own television and film production divisions. And finally, in my own fieldwork, I encountered several industry informants who wanted to publish bestsellers precisely because that would guarantee their creative autonomy (both because bestsellers relieve financial pressures and deflect scrutiny from investors and/ or parent companies which might be otherwise inclined to interfere).

The second problem with the concept of field is that they are commonly presumed to be national fields. When Bourdieu (1996) writes a book subtitled the "Genesis and Structure of the Literary Field," he is actually writing about the genesis and structure of the literary field *in France*. Indeed, the empirical work of classic books on cultural production by sociologists of culture such as Howard Becker (1982), Pierre Bourdieu (1993, 1996), Richard Peterson (1997), and others are all confined to particular national, or local, contexts. Some of this is surely due to the practical geographical and spatial limitations of their methods, but in other cases the national as analytical framework is simply taken for granted. Comparative approaches, for example, Thompson (2005, 2010), have since come into fashion, but these too—if only by implication—break out national contexts as the starting points of analysis. Specifically, in terms of studies of book publishing and literary culture, there has also been some tendency to conceptualize fields in terms of linguistic, as opposed to purely national, boundaries. Murray (2012, 21), for example, focuses upon adaptation in the Anglophone world, primarily the United States and the United Kingdom, but also "historically 'periphery' English-language cultures such as Australia, Canada, New Zealand, South Africa, Ireland and—increasingly—India." She does not, in my view, ever fully justify this choice. However, given that literary adaptation is intimately tied to intellectual property rights acquisition and, as Sapiro (2010, 423) observes, "English, American, French and Spanish publishers tend to demand exclusive rights for the whole language speaking area—all the more since the development of sales through the Internet, which solves the problem of local distribution," the choice is not surprising.

The fact of the matter is that there are few sociologists who study book publishing, never mind across national or linguistic boundaries. Of those who do *and* who have drawn upon field theory, there are two tendencies. The first is epitomized by Sapiro (Heilbron and Sapiro 2007; Sapiro 2008, 2010; Sapiro and Bustamante 2009), who, despite the transnational dimension to her work on literary translation, either reverts almost immediately back to comparing national fields or, alternatively, focuses on the global. The initial statements of translation being a transnational function seem promising:

> Considered as a transnational transfer, translation first presupposes a space of international relations, this space being constituted by the existence of nation-states and linguistic groups linked to each other by relations

of competition and rivalry. [...] [T]he flow of translations should then be re-situated in a transnational field characterized by the power relations among national states, their languages, and their literatures. (Heilbron and Sapiro 2007, 95)

Unfortunately, instead of then proceeding to give further attention to the particular properties of this transnational field, this is where the paragraph ends. The next explicates the so-called "global system of translations" (Heilbron and Sapiro 2007, 95), and in that book chapter and elsewhere Sapiro expends much effort transposing all of the characteristics of Bourdieu's French cultural field onto the entire world, theorizing a *global* cultural field of translation comprised of a host of national fields with all of the features and functions of the national field intact but scaled up. Her most interesting innovation is to map large-scale or commercial production onto translations from English and small-scale or restricted production onto a greater proportion of books translated from languages other than English (Sapiro 2010). In other words, some examples of literary fields specializing in translations are more autonomous than others on the basis of the works' language of origin. This may or may not be a valid comparative point, but I struggle to credit the logical conclusion about American publishing which could be drawn here: That the part of the field in the United States publishing works translated into English from other languages has a higher than average level of autonomy. After all, even Sapiro (2010, 430) admits that "translations are not distinguished from original works in English" in "the American publishing market," so why should they operate according to an entirely different logic? Besides, the case of Japanese manga in America aligns much better to Thompson's rejection of the distinction between autonomous and heteronomous fields.

This then points to a related tendency, which is to accept the premise that fields of cultural production are national and that the "transnational" is a sociological property of something other than the field itself. In my own earlier work, I framed manga publishing as a "subset" of the American cultural field (Brienza 2009a, 105), ascribing only the content to Japan, with the rest of the organizational characteristics and social processes of American manga publishing, meanwhile, to the national field. While sufficient for my analytical purposes then, it outright ignores cultural production which proceeds transnationally. Eva Hemmungs Wirtén (1998) is the only other researcher to my knowledge besides myself to use Bourdieu specifically to study a case of transnational cultural production—across linguistic as well as national boundaries—in the publishing industry. However, her research site was a single multinational firm, not an entire field of cultural production, and she too implicitly assumes that the national, in her case Swedish, cultural field is the primary space of social action. Instead, she coins the term "transediting," a collective interpretive process where "translators edit and editors translate" (Hemmungs Wirtén 1998, 126) to explicate the transnational dimension of her research. Broadly speaking, Hemmungs Wirtén uses this term to acknowledge that neither the set of actions captured in the word "translation" nor the role of the translator is alone sufficient to make a Harlequin romance written in English succeed in Scandinavia. What is actually involved in moving culture across national boundaries is an issue to which I will return later. But for now it is enough to observe that transediting, in Hemmungs Wirtén's view, may be understood as a locally taken action oriented transnationally.

The great limitation of these two ways of adapting Bourdieu's concept of the field to transnational publishing organizations and processes is that they do not actually attempt to theorize the transnational as a thing in and of itself. This does not make sense. "Transediting" would not occur in a national or linguistic field in closed conditions of isolation; it is, rather, a relational social process which links two fields. Similarly, while transnational relations between different national or linguistic fields may be a necessary condition for a "global system" of literary publishing, the opposite does not necessarily follow. One might easily hypothesize a cultural field comprised of networked relations across national boundaries without assuming a fully unified global field. What, then, about a transnational field? What would it look like? The simplest model for the transnational field might be presented in terms of Figure 2.1. However, this visualization, while promising, does not seem quite right. The transnational field in this view exists where two national fields overlap, the sum total of all of the relevant properties of two national fields. While analytically distinct, the transnational is still contingent upon the national and is not a thing in and of

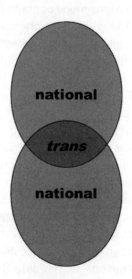

FIGURE 2.1 *A flawed model of a transnational field.*

itself. Furthermore, any actor embedded in the transnational field must, by definition, also be embedded within both national fields simultaneously. That simply does not square, for example, with Hemmungs Wirtén's observation that "editors in Stockholm seem to think about their own work as autonomous and unconstrained by the parent company in Toronto" (1998, 114).

So, Figure 2.1 is unsatisfactory. How can it be improved? In their chapter on "Constructing Transnational Studies," Sunjeev Khagram and Peggy Levitt (2008, 26) suggest that from a transnational studies perspective, "the world consists of multiple sets of dynamically overlapping and interacting transnational social fields that create and shape seemingly bordered and bounded structures, actors, and processes." This is a productive start, and I particularly like the idea that transnational fields can effect transformation upon those other fields with which they are linked, including, presumably, national ones, but it is rather difficult to visualize. It is worth at this juncture to return to Heilbron and Sapiro (2007) and their all too cursory comment that any transnational transfer presupposes a separate space of social action constituted by the relations between nation-states. This separate space, I argue, could be a transnational field. I would therefore propose the model of the transnational field shown in Figure 2.2. This better, improved model conceives of a transnational field that is simultaneously overlapping with and distinct from its constituent national

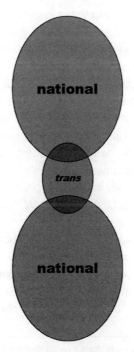

FIGURE 2.2 *A better model of a transnational field.*

fields, while preserving the view that national fields can in turn be influenced by the presence of the transnational. Within this transnational field, it is also possible for actors to be positioned within one, the other, both, or neither of the two national fields. This is meant to reflect how connections between fields produce positions which would not exist in the absence of those which serve to link up two fields, such as the role of the "transeditor."

Gereffi and value chains

So if, as stated at the beginning of this chapter, one of my aims is to understand how the people who publish Japanese manga in the United States are organized, I can now assert this as: They represent the core positions and activities of a transnational field of cultural production. They exist in order to link up the Japanese and American national cultural fields and would not exist in the absence of this linkage. Unfortunately, this model still lacks any real specificity about what actors in the field are actually doing out there in the world, and field theory alone is ill-equipped to provide it.

In the context of the publishing business itself, the textbook term would be "publishing value chain," the sum total of the activities "undertaken in order to take the author's text and make it available as an attractive product that consumers will want to buy" (Clark and Phillips 2008, 67). The precise number and description of the links in the chain differ,[2] but activities in which most publishers take direct control include "the acquisition of intellectual property, editorial, design and production, marketing, and sales" (Clark and Phillips 2008, 67). As these activities, taken together, are what is implicitly meant by "publishing," it should come as no surprise that manga publishing in the United States may be mapped onto analogous functions. Rights to titles must be negotiated, pages must be retouched, logos and covers must be designed, people working on projects must be managed, finished products must find their way into the hands of readers, and so on. "Translating," "editing," or indeed even Hemmungs Wirtén's "transediting," alone cannot fully encapsulate what is actually involved in producing manga transnationally and connecting two national publishing fields. Within the transnational cultural field, in short, is a transnational value chain.

In sociology, the most comprehensive and prolific theorist of the value chain which crosses national boundaries is Gary Gereffi who, with his collaborators, has developed a framework for the analysis of "global value chains," or "GVCs." This research has its origins in a book chapter by Gereffi (1994), which coined the term "global commodity chain" to link the concept of the value chain,

---

[2]Sample diagrams of the publishing value chain may be found in Clark and Phillips (2008, 67) and Thompson (2010, 16).

the activities required to design, produce, and market a product, to that of the global organization of manufacturing industries. The central insight of this early chapter is to underscore the disproportionate impact large retailers can have upon production, and this insight is certainly applicable to trade book publishing in the United States and Britain (Thompson 2010) as well as manga publishing (Brienza 2009a). In subsequent work, a broader typology of the governance of global value chains was developed, with the retailer-centric model termed "captive value chain" (Gereffi, Humphrey, and Sturgeon 2005).

In any case, according to Gereffi and Karina Fernandez-Stark (2011, 5), "the GVC framework allows one to understand how global industries are organized by examining the structure and dynamics of different actors involved in a given industry." A comprehensive analysis in this framework requires that the researcher (1) identify the main activities/segments in a global value chain and (2) identify the dynamic and structure of companies under each segment of the value chain (Gereffi and Fernandez-Stark 2011). This is excellent advice, and I will discuss both the structure and main activities of manga publishing later. The strength of GVC analysis for my purposes is that it does not presume the chain of production to be situated within a single locale or company and acknowledges that exogenous factors such as national policy or social mores can affect the organization of a value chain. Furthermore, the GVC literature has also been focused on the concept of "upgrading," the trend in global value chains for particular actors in the chain to transition from lower-value to higher-value activities through participation in global production, thereby increasing their national standing in the global arena (e.g., Humphrey and Schmitz 2002). I have witnessed upgrading in the course of my own research, for example, in the ways in which manga publishers went from acquiring content from Japan to developing their own content. This is described in detail in Chapter 6.

There are also limitations to the GVC framework, and I will discuss two of these. The model represented by Figure 2.2, with its clear distinctions between two national fields and the transnational field connecting them, points to the first limitation—the use of the word "global." For a framework purporting to be interested in specifics actors, functions, and relations, the word global is nearly meaningless. None of the value chains analyzed in Gereffi's work are truly global in the sense that they literally implicate every single space in the world simultaneously. Yet to Gereffi, the sum total of everything it takes to get a volume of manga from the first moment of its creative genesis in Japan to an English-speaking reader would be a global value chain. Precisely how the various links in this chain might relate to the other publishing value chains of Japan and the United States is virtually impossible to theorize, and for my purposes this is crucial. I know, for example, that the first links in the chain are functions of the publishing chain in Japan; indeed, in some cases, everything right down to a printed and bound copy of the book bought from a store in question is necessary to produce manga transnationally. There are also links in this global value chain which are not just analogous to but an unequivocal part of the American national publishing chain; these include printing, storage, distribution, and retailing. The only way to isolate the transnational from the national and the global is not to use the GVC framework but rather to return to field theory—any and all positions which would not exist if it were not for the linkage in the first place. This is, in my view, a severe limitation.

The second limitation of the global value chain is its lack of focus upon individual actors and the potential for unequal and/or competitive relations between them. The value chain, by its very formulation, is defined by the social activities of each of its links and only by implication by those people who are actually performing those functions. Moreover, it theorizes the workings of power, termed governance, as only being relevant to the structure of the chain as a whole, not to one or a limited set of links within the chain. None of the five forms of governance, in fact, of global value chains (Gereffi, Humphrey, and Sturgeon 2005) can be related to the outsourcing to freelancers of many of publishing's core functions. Empirical work would be needed to illuminate the particular microinteractions between individuals and groups within the field.

Still, from the discussion of publishing chains in this section, it soon becomes clear that something has thus far been missing from my model

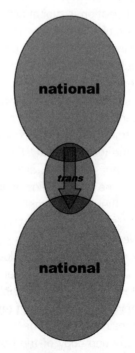

FIGURE 2.3 *Directionality of the transnational field.*

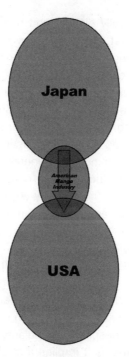

FIGURE 2.4 *The American manga industry as a transnational cultural field.*

of the transnational field as represented by Figure 2.2. That something is a feature which I will refer to as "directionality," and by directionality I mean that transnational cultural fields develop for movement *from* one national field *to* another and not—at least necessarily—the reverse. This should make eminent practical sense; far more books are translated into other languages from English than are translated into English from other languages, for example (Sapiro 2010). It also explains the apparent paradox of why a transnational field of cultural production such as the one which publishes Japanese comics in English should be known in the vernacular as "the American manga industry." As it turns out, the designation "American" does not signify a national field. Instead, it signifies the directional orientation of a transnational field from Japan to the United States. I would therefore revise one final time my model of the transnational field to Figure 2.3, with the site of my own research represented in the center of Figure 2.4.

Domestication as transnational cultural production

In the previous section, I have conceptualized the transnational cultural field as a field which connects two national cultural fields and is characterized by positions which are analytically distinct and directionally organized along a value chain of production. Yet, although I now have a name for the field in question, the American manga industry, I still do not have a word for what it does. As already noted, its core activities are analogous to the core activities of a national publishing industry when described in terms of the links of a value chain, yet in their specifics they are not precisely identical. Simply to uncritically write "publishing" in both contexts is not sufficient, and to say that this field is publishing and distributing Japanese manga in English does not in any manner identify a unique yet generalizable, collective action verb. And although the reality of production is far more complicated and blurry than a step by step, assembly line "commodity chain" (Gereffi 1994) that has a concrete origin point in Japan and end point in the West, at least in principle there must be a way to talk about it in a way that eliminates, as much as possible, obvious sources of confusion.

Unfortunately, the academic literature is not especially helpful, either. Some of the most obvious "unit-ideas of sociology" (Nisbet 1966, 3) current in the common parlance, such as "globalization" and "hybridity," have been so often used (and overused) that they have been emptied of any specificity of signification. "Localization," despite its popularity with my informants, does not seem satisfactory either, as it implies a straightforwardly unidirectional process whereby a fully constituted object from one locale is reconstituted for another by local actors. It does not take into account the ways in which manga's success overseas has had a subsequent impact upon the genesis of new product in Japan or the ways in which transnational cultural production can be unevenly, even irrationally, constrained by the nation of origin. Indeed, as noted previously, the term "localization" is popular with the employees of one publisher in particular, and it is no coincidence, in my view, that these people reported some of the lowest levels of professional autonomy and satisfaction in their business relations with Japan. Another possible term is "intermediation," which incorporates the word "media"—a convenient synergy given that I assume manga to be a medium—and the similar term "remediation" has been used to describe the traces of an older medium in a newer one (Bolter and Grusin 1999). However, the term "cultural intermediaries," first used by Bourdieu (1984) to talk about those working in advertising, and appropriated in the literature by numerous others (Cronin 2004; Hennion 1989; Negus 2002; Nixon and Du Gay 2002), creates an unproductive distinction between the artists on the one hand and the publishers, the marketers, advertisers, and so forth on the other. All of these people are links in the same value chain and do not exist in isolation. The publisher is no longer merely the gatekeeper as described by Coser et al. (1982) but—and this is particularly the case in the comics publishing industry, where all intellectual property belongs to the publisher, not the artist—will on occasion itself orchestrate the production of creative content like the director of a film. After all, to quote Howard Becker (1982, 1), "All artistic work, like all human activity, involves the joint activity of a number, often a large number, of people."

Of course, people both within and without the industry would refer to published English-language editions of manga as "translations" or "adaptations" of Japanese content, even though translating and adapting are only small parts of what manga publishing houses actually do. As such, applying translation theory or adaptation theory to the study of manga in the US context might, on the surface, seem to be the two theoretical rubrics most self-evidently suitable to describe and comprehend the sort of texts the US manga publishing industry produces. However, adaptation theory studies adaptations (where "adaptation" is typically understood as intellectual property that is converted from one medium into another, such as a popular novel that gets adapted into a feature-length Hollywood movie) at a textual level of analysis (Murray 2008), though there have been recent calls from within the fields of communication and media studies to rectify this with more production- and industry-centered analyses (Clarke 2009; Murray 2012). As discussed above, theories invoking translation likewise understand it in terms of the textual analysis of cultural objects. Traditionally, the objective is perfect communication (Benjamin 1936), however defined, which of course is a longstanding human ambition but not possible, or at least not yet, and perhaps not a wholly desirable an achievement anyway (Peters 1999). While both perspectives are interesting theoretically, it has little to contribute *per se* to questions of how meaning is produced and practiced collectively. Translation theory, so-called, is dominated by debates about praxis and the relative merits of "formal" versus "transparent" styles of translation (Venuti 1995, 2000). While it might well be interesting to discuss which of these two styles various actors within the manga industry subscribe to and why, neither of theories related to "translation" or "adaptation" strike me as particularly applicable methodologically to sociological research.

Clearly, what the American manga industry does cannot merely be called "translation," "adaptation," "intermediation," or "localization." There is, in my view, a much better word than any discussed thus far. The one I have chosen for this purpose is *domestication*. The *Oxford English Dictionary Online* provides the following four-part definition for the verb, "to domesticate":

1. *trans.*

    a. To make, or settle as, a member of a household; to cause to be at home; to naturalize.

    b. *transf.* and *fig.* To make to be or to feel "at home"; to familiarize.

2. To make domestic; to attach to home and its duties.

3. To accustom (an animal) to live under the care and near the habitations of man; to tame or bring under control; *transf.* to civilize.

4. *intr.* (for *refl.*) To live familiarly or at home (*with*); to take up one's abode. *Obs.*

This definition points to the term's many advantages as a make-ready yet precise concept. As a verb, it may signify both action and ongoing state of being, which allows me to discuss domestication in terms of both the production of new social practice and its maintenance across time and space. It is also transitive, which means that one can domesticate as well as be domesticated, and the sense in which humans exert their will on other living, often non-human, things, in order to domesticate them for specific instrumental ends, allows me to think about asymmetrical configurations of power, the manifestations of deliberate force, and the desire to control. This is a causative construction (i.e., made to domesticate or be domesticated). Naturally, it may also be used reflexively (i.e., domesticating oneself), and domestication, unlike localization, need not be a unidirectional process. One can be simultaneously domesticating the object, oneself, and the nation of origin. Last—but certainly not least, in my view—the word is aesthetically and intuitively pleasing; domestication is linked to the home, and publishing companies are often referred to as "publishing houses" or, colloquially, just "houses." The home, furthermore, is stereotypically thought of being the domain of women, and manga as a category of books has become feminized in terms of its content, as well as its target readership and production (Brienza 2011; Prough 2011).

The term "domestication" has also appeared in both Japanese studies and media studies and thus may be used to link these two fields. In the context of Japanese studies, Anne Allison (2006b), Millie Creighton (1991), and Chie Yamanaka (2006) all use domestication to talk about cultural flows in and out of Japan, but never with much analytical precision. And although he does not use "domestication" in any systematic critical fashion either, Joseph Tobin (1992), who writes about counterflows of culture from the West into Japan, reflects upon his use of the term and argues that it signals an active human process in which ideas are actually changed in the encounter. I appreciate his sense of domestication as an active human process, though of course I would deemphasize the way in which he limits the word to the transformation of ideas. It should be noted that Ian Condry (2006) critiques Tobin for seeming to assume an essentialist conception of national culture, but I see no logical reason why particular fields of cultural production might not, purely from an empirical standpoint, be distinct from each other in terms of their functions, even if this is neither a necessary nor permanent state of affairs. In any case,

Tobin himself believes that the word's complex range of possible meanings is a distinctive advantage and points out that none of these meanings are bound up in the activities of particular nations.

Media scholars, in contrast, have been more precise in their use of "domestication," and by their definition it refers to the process through which objects of the media become ordinary and everyday (Berker et al. 2006). Drawing upon the theoretical work of Roger Silverstone (Silverstone and Haddon 1996; Silverstone and Hirsch 1992), they investigate what, precisely, consumers do with media inside the home and how it comes to find a place within it. Like the wolf that becomes the domestic lap dog, domesticated media objects can even become a beloved part of the family. Yet this process is never complete, and "just as young puppies (and older dogs) can cause damage in the household and arguments between family members" (Berker et al. 2006, 3), the media may well occupy the home simultaneously as taken-for-granted fixtures as well as sites of continual renegotiation and struggle. Once again, the sense in which the word refers to an ongoing process is productively underscored, and their invocation of Anthony Giddens's (1984) recognition of the household as the site of the formation of ontological security is well taken. But because these researchers understand the object of the action to be the media object and not, as it were, the human object, they rather miss the point—it is the people and their relationships with the media that change and are made to change.

In sum, it is worth sustaining the literature's use of domestication as a social process. However, the rest of the admittedly rudimentary debates about domestication and nation, and an exclusive preoccupation with what consumers do with media without an equally keen eye on its producers, are not particularly useful for my purposes, and I will not belabor their arguments further. Instead, in keeping with the spirit of the previous section, I would define domestication as the sum total of those social positions and functions which reside exclusively within the transnational cultural field. Put simply, domestication is the transnational production of culture, and a transnational value chain is a domestication chain.

So what exactly does this terminology allow researchers to do? First, domestication provides a way to think clearly about what makes transnational cultural production different from national *or* global cultural production. This is particularly important in a research context where all production is called "publishing" and there is no one word to describe those particular activities which are distinct to the American manga publishing industry. Otherwise, it is all too easy to descend into confusion; as Beth Luey (2009, 34) notes, "In the postwar era, the definition of 'American book publishing' had expanded to include companies owned by American stockholders operating globally as well as companies owned by foreign corporations operating in the United States and abroad." If her definition of "American" includes all that, what counts as transnational?! The great advantage of my concept of domestication is that by focusing not just on who cultural producers are or where they reside but rather upon what they *do* (intentional and unintentional), I am able to detach transnational cultural production from geographic locality of the actions taking place or corporate ownership. Thus, when I call the industry I study "American," this is to describe the national territory into which it is instantiating new content and practices, not the nationality of the industry itself or its individual and/or organizational actors. In short, to study domestication is to study an entire transnational cultural field and to see that what it does is not merely textual translation from one language to another or straightforward importation of objects from one country to another—but rather a complex, organized, collective process.

Second, domestication when understood as a generalized process of transnational cultural production gives researchers a way to bring together disparate strands of empirical research and weave them together into a comprehensive account of how culture travels globally. As previously discussed, other studies of the transnational cultural production of manga do exist, but they are written for different academic disciplines and do not speak to each other theoretically. Although this is but one more such piece of the proverbial puzzle—I do not claim to explain how the transnational production of culture works everywhere, in every field, or culture industry—I strive to situate it in the broadest possible theoretical terms. So, although I am writing about manga, Japan, and the United States, nothing about domestication in and of itself requires one to know about these two countries or about manga. This cannot be said for "transediting," for example, which only makes sense in the book publishing field and only accounts for one small part of the entire process of production. By speaking to and building upon some of the most important social theory of the past century, I am confident that domestication as a concept invites further research on a wide range of cultural topics, publishing and otherwise, in a diversity of national territories.

So, to be absolutely clear, when using "domestication" throughout this book I refer simultaneously *both* to the overall macro-process of making manga American as well as the individual labor components and practices of that process, such as translating, editing, lettering, and so forth, in the same way that "playing baseball" involves, among other things, swinging the bat, catching the ball, and running the bases. While each component can and, indeed, be described in great detail in its own right, none cannot be understood in their appropriate sociological contexts as anything other than a single collective social process which is, while constituted and shaped by the realities of those individual parts, more than the sum of those parts. Returning once more to the ballgame metaphor, swinging a bat is an integral

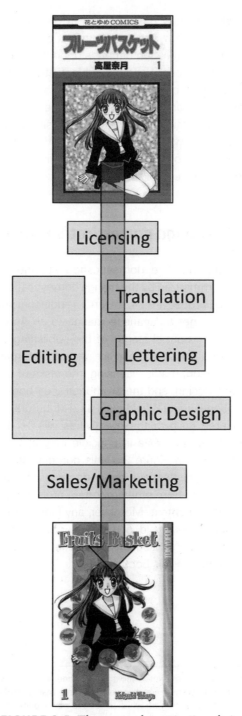

FIGURE 2.5 *The manga domestication chain.*

part of what it means to play baseball, and at the same time one simply cannot play baseball without swinging a bat. So, on the one hand, the success or failure of domestication depends upon the peculiar properties of its individual parts of the process and the subjectivities accompanying them. And on the other, it is only by recognizing that each of these geographically dispersed and disparate parts are a unit can it be most clearly seen that domestication is in fact multidirectional, acting simultaneously upon the manga object, and upon two national contexts. While it would be difficult to argue that the practice of translating or localizing manga has the social force to transform Japanese publishing, the practice of *domesticating*, I will demonstrate, certainly does.

The manga domestication chain

To conclude, then, the core domestication activities of the American manga industry are summarized by the manga domestication chain graphically illustrated by Figure 2.5. These are the minimum additional publishing activities required to legitimately get a Japanese manga to an American reader that exist *on top of* all of the normal stages of the publishing value chain within a single national field. Links in the chain include international intellectual property rights negotiation, that is, licensing, the tasks of translation, editing, lettering, and graphic design, and the promotion their books to other players in the American national cultural field such as distributors, retailers, libraries, and individual readers.[3] Each of these activities will be discussed in detail in subsequent chapters, and while in principle they can be arranged neatly on a flowchart, as shown in Figure 2.5, this domestication chain is actually oversimplified. First, the distinctions between many of the tasks cannot be so neatly drawn or isolated from other important professional actions taken in one or the other national context. Moreover, any hint of the broader network impacts of the transnational field of the American manga industry upon adjacent fields is absent. This issue will become an especially salient one throughout the remainder of this book.

---

[3]While the industrial manufacturing of printed books is, as a general rule, no longer done in-house by trade publishers, and manga publishers are no exception, some manga publishers have developed their own smartphone and tablet apps from which to sell and view e-book editions of domesticated manga. I have chosen not to include this "virtual manufacture" on the manga domestication chain at this stage, but such activities are discussed in detail in Chapter 6.

3

Book Trade: The History and Structure of American Manga Publishing

A diner would not have been my first choice of restaurants in Midtown Manhattan, but the two manga industry professionals accompanying me for dinner were from out of town. Over greasy French fries and milkshakes, they told me about their ever-eccentric boss's "Four 'Fs' for 2007." "Film" and "Fashion" they understood as part of their company's long-range media-mix strategy. And as for "Fun"? Who was going to argue with that? The fourth F, though, was "Food." "Food!" they exclaimed, their tones mocking. "What does publishing manga have to do with *food*?!" (from the author's field notes)

The first Japanese manga ever published in English was Keiji Nakazawa's *Hadashi no Gen* [Barefoot Gen]. A semiautobiographical account of the author's childhood experiences of the nuclear bombing of Hiroshima, the story was serialized in a number of manga anthologies from 1973 to 1985, including Shueisha's *Weekly Shonen Jump*. In 1980, the small press EduComics began publishing a translated edition as *Gen of Hiroshima*. Ultimately, the company was able to release approximately one-hundred pages of the first volume, along with the forty-eight page prequel *Ore wa Mita* [I Saw It] in three issues. *Hadashi no Gen* was subsequently republished in English in graphic novel form by New Society Publishers and again by Penguin in the United Kingdom and Last Gasp in the United States through the late 1980s and early 1990s (Rifas 2004; Sabin 2006). None of these endeavors were commercially successful; in fact, Last Gasp's first print run of the first volume of *Barefoot Gen* was 3,000, less even than EduComics 5,000 copy run of *Gen of Hiroshima* #1 (Rifas 2004; Sabin 2006). Reflecting upon its repeated commercial failure in the West, EduComics founder Leonard Rifas remarks that for years he blamed his own lack of business acumen and the near-exclusive fixation of the comics market upon the superhero fare of Marvel and DC. However, given the poor performance of the title in far more experienced hands than his own, he now feels forced to conclude that a lack of public interest in antinuclear peace movements must be responsible. He cannot bring himself to believe that it was due to some flaw in the artistic work itself (Rifas 2004).

Rifas is absolutely correct, in my view, to find fault with the comics market, and I am surprised that he does not see the failures of other presses to sell *Barefoot Gen* in any appreciable numbers as the fault of that market as well. After all, he himself notes that by 1980 "comic books were no longer a true 'mass medium' in America, and the fan base was only able to support press runs of a few hundred thousand copies of a title. Further, the underground comix movement had peaked seven years earlier, and had never been strong enough to distribute any regularly-scheduled comic books" (Rifas 2004, 144–145). It would be naïve to think that Last Gasp, a "venerable comics publisher, with roots in the underground" would be able to do much better under such conditions in the comics market, or that a trade book publisher like Penguin would be able to make a comic work when the only other precedent in either the United States or the United Kingdom, the only other comic to have been published by a major trade house to date, was Art Speigelman's *Maus* from Pantheon.

Manga was simply not, in short, something that was ever going to work in the comics publishing field, and likewise in the late 1980s sequential art was simply not, categorically, something that players in the book publishing field knew how to make work either. These two national fields did not overlap: each had different major industry players, different distribution and retail networks, and different target audiences. Both were the same only inasmuch as they had little connection to manga publishing in Japan. As such, other small press attempts to start publishing Japanese manga as pamphlet comics by Viz (partnered with Eclipse Comics) and First Comics in 1987 garnered, at best, niche interest. In 1988, the University of California Press published a complete English translation of Shotaro Ishinomori's *Japan, Inc.*, and while this book is still nominally in print today, it appears to have been all but forgotten by history.

Indeed, although manga has been published in English since 1980, and since 1987 at least a handful of new licensed titles have been published reliably each and every year, sales were modest. Domestication was a time-consuming and labor-intensive process, involving reversing pages so that they would read in a left-to-right Western-style orientation and retouching artwork to remove and replace Japanese sound effects. At times, even the characters' names were changed. New releases were few and far between; multivolume series such as *Dragon Ball* were a decades' long prospect. Presses had to be run by idealists or hobbyists who were poorly socialized into the practices of any publishing field, whether comics, books, or magazines. By their own individual accounts they might say that they did not have good business sense, but the outcome cannot be chalked up solely to personal failure. Though they tried to get a foothold in these fields, their efforts were largely rebuked by their structural characteristics (Brienza 2009a). And since nobody was making much money, few in Japan or the West even knew—let alone cared—that manga translated into English existed at all. In some cases, not even the manga artists themselves knew that their works had been translated! Manga publishing in the United States (and other English-language territories) did not begin to take off until the late 1990s, when ongoing transformations in the American field of contemporary trade book publishing opened up a new space for manga as a category of trade books. So, while manga was not successful as a comic, and comics were not usually successful as books, by constructing the medium as something distinct from American comics, manga was able to become a book—and some manga series have gone on to sell millions of copies in the trade book market (Brienza 2009a, 2009b). Through this success, I will argue here, manga publishing companies and their employees became self-identified with the field of contemporary trade book publishing and this now defines and constrains the direction they will take manga in the future. Or, as Pierre Bourdieu (1977, 169–170) famously puts it, "[T]he manifest censorship imposed by orthodox discourse, the official way of speaking and thinking about the world, conceals another, more radical censorship . . . the fundamental opposition between the universe of things that can be stated, and hence thought, and the universe of that which is taken for granted." Yet, it cannot be overemphasized that this opportunity was specific to a particular point in history, and it is at this point that the American manga publishing industry as it is today truly traces its roots. While manga had been published in English before then, there was until relatively recently no manga publishing field. Therefore, at the very start of its formation is where I too will begin the history of American manga publishing. Before proceeding, however, brief accounts of publishing in Japan and in the United States are in order.

The manga publishing industry in Japan

From certain angles, the manga medium's eventual integration with the trade publishing field in the United States seems entirely predictable and logical. Manga is, after all, one of the most important categories of trade publishing in Japan, and unlike comics in the United States, which have, until recently, been quite separate from the circuits of production and distribution of trade books, it developed that way right from the beginning. However, the book trade in these two countries are quite different from each other in terms of historical formation, structures, and practices, and many of the transnational struggles over the domestication of manga discussed in this and subsequent chapters have their roots in the differences between the two fields. In this section, therefore, I will provide a brief overview of the structure of the Japanese manga industry with particular attention to those of its practices which differ.

Estimates of the number of publishing houses active in the production of manga in Japan vary, and the precise number fluctuates year to year, but about thirty collectively constitute the largest part of the market and produce the majority of the titles published. Arguably the most important of these are the so-called Big Three, Shueisha, Kodansha, and Shogakukan. The largest trade publishers in Japan, period, they also publish magazines, academic books, and some of the largest global brands in manga. *Naruto*, *One Piece*, and all other *Shonen Jump* series, for example, are published by Shueisha. *Sailor Moon*, *Fairy Tail*, and *Negima!* are published by Kodansha. *Inuyasha* and the rest of Rumiko Takahashi's manga are published by Shogakukan. Other mid-sized publishers highly active in manga publishing include Akita Shoten, Kadokawa Shoten, Ichijinsha, and Shinshokan. Hakusensha, a prolific publisher of famous shoujo manga such as *Fruits Basket* and *Vampire Knight* in the magazines *Hana to Yume* and *LaLa*, is owned by the same conglomerate as Shueisha but is organizationally discrete. Square Enix, best known for its video games, is also an important manga publisher, serializing titles such as *Fullmetal Alchemist*, *Black Butler*, and *Soul Eater* in its *Gangan* line of shounen magazines. Small manga publishers tend to specialize in particular genres, such as josei (Shodensha) or boys' love (Libre, Houbunsha, Aqua Shuppan, Taiyo Tosho). The boys' love genre is particularly popular, with both mid-sized publishers such as Kadokawa Shoten, Hakusensha, and Shinshokan and over a half-dozen smaller, specialty publishers such as Libre publishing new content since the 1990s. Sales overall for manga peaked in the mid-1990s, and since that time, while book sales have held steady, periodical sales have declined a few percentage points each year (see Table 3.1), leading to an overall contraction of the industry over the past decade and a half. Manga sales represented approximately 22 percent of all publishing sales and 37 percent of all volumes published in Japan, a domestic market which was worth ¥481 billion (approximately $6 billion) in 2006.

Manga publishing in Japan resembles book publishing in the United States in that creators—not publishing companies, as is the case of superhero publishers Marvel and DC—typically own the copyright to their works and retain nominal control of the intellectual property associated with those works. However, the *actual* control any artist retains is very much on a case by case basis; manga publishers, particularly the largest houses, engage in the practice of what cultural anthropologist Jennifer Prough (2011, 57) calls "raising readers" in order to transform them into creators. This can lead to

TABLE 3.1 Manga sales in Japan

Year	Total Sales (billions ¥)	Sales of Books (billions ¥)	Sales of Periodicals (billions ¥)	Percent of Total Publishing Sales	Percent of Total Volumes Published
1995	586	251	336	22.6	39.3
1996	585	254	331	22.0	38.5
1997	570	242	328	21.6	36.7
1998	568	247	321	22.3	37.4
1999	534	230	304	21.8	36.8
2000	523	237	286	21.8	37.0
2001	532	248	284	22.9	38.2
2002	523	248	275	22.6	38.1
2003	516	256	261	23.3	37.8
2004	505	250	255	22.5	37.2
2005	502	260	242	22.8	37.4
2006	481	253	227	22.4	36.7

Source: Japan Book Publishers' Association

an unequal, filial relationship between author and publisher, with the author as the metaphorical child and the publisher the parent with authority over the direction of the author's entire creative career. Thus, the literary agent is far less of a presence in Japanese manga publishing, and talent is sourced directly by publishers, through regularly scheduled manga-drawing contests or by scouting amateur artist gatherings such as the twice-annual Comic Market, for example. Editors employed by their publishing houses to work closely with artists can therefore exert tremendous creative influence on a work. Anecdotes abound of editors who have vetoed or even ghostwritten entire storylines. *Manga Manga!* recounts an incident of an editor who booked his artist charge into a hotel room with a guard stationed 24/7 at the door to ensure the recalcitrant, procrastinating artist did not escape and would meet his editor's deadline (Schodt 1983).

Tight deadlines, in fact, structure the successful manga artist's entire professional life, particularly for shounen manga creators whose serials are published weekly. New weekly serials are typically finished between two to three weeks before going to press, though in extreme cases they may be done only a week ahead of time (Kinsella 2000). While those on monthly schedules are perhaps somewhat less pressured, the vast majority of manga begin their life as a rapidly produced magazine serial. Manga magazines are typically published weekly, biweekly, or monthly, and can range from 300–

500 or more pages per issue. Unlike magazines in the United States, which depend primarily upon advertising revenue, Japanese manga magazines have very few advertisements, and most of those ads are for the publisher's own products. Magazines are sold through stores and newsstands, and there are no subscriptions. Consumer prices for magazines are kept extremely low (e.g., ¥250 for an issue of *Weekly Shonen Jump*), with profits on magazines razor thin—they are best understood as loss leaders for manga publishers. It is only when popular series are reissued in tankoubon form do publishers realize a sizable profit. They may make enough on manga, in fact, to support otherwise unprofitable publishing programs.

In keeping with the fast production of magazines, even the release of tankoubon is on a tight schedule, and there is a greater churn of printed content than there would be in an American retail environment. Street dates may be decided only a few months in advance, and as a matter of fact, publishers do not even produce their own catalogs; this is the job of the wholesalers. Furthermore, bookstores in Japan receive a 22 percent discount margin on books, approximately half customary in the United States, and for all intents and purposes are told what to stock and where to put it. In short, then, even large retail chains like Kinokuniya are not the kingmakers of particular creators and/or categories that Barnes & Noble in the United States can be, and the discount explains, far more than any other factor, including print run, why a book priced at ¥400 in Japan is $10.99 in the United States (over twice as expensive). The digital distribution of manga has also taken off in Japan in recent years. The manga e-book market was worth ¥35 billion (approximately $438 million) in 2008 (Anon. 2010b), with over eighty percent of that for the hybrid medium of keitai, or cell phone, manga.[1]

The field of contemporary trade book publishing

In order to truly understand the history of manga publishing in America, it is important to provide some background context about the US national publishing field. If it was within the field of contemporary trade book publishing that manga became commercially viable, what sort of world, precisely, is it? What sorts of opportunities does it provide? What are its limitations? To this end, I take a brief detour into the history of trade book publishing in the United States since the 1980s through to the mid-2000s.

---

[1] Manga specially formatted for the cell phone are broken up into individual panels programmed to scroll automatically, sometimes with limited animation and special effects. The most popular genre of keitai manga is boys' love.

At the same time that Rifas was failing to make *Gen of Hiroshima* the next *Maus*, two important books about the structure and transformation of American book publishing in the twentieth century were being published: *Books: The Culture and Commerce of Publishing* by Lewis A. Coser, Walter Kadushin, and Walter W. Powell and *The Blockbuster Complex: Conglomerates, Show Business, and Publishing* by Thomas Whiteside. As the titles of these books imply, both take as their subject the tensions between publishing books as the dissemination of art and knowledge with which humanity improves itself and the commercial pressures to achieve and maintain a profitable business. As Lewis Coser et al. (1982, 7) explain, "The industry remains perilously poised between the requirements and restraints of commerce and the responsibilities and obligations that it must bear as the prime guardian of the symbolic culture of the nation." But if to Coser (1975) publishing houses are the "gatekeepers of ideas" with keys to the public domain of discourse, Whiteside, far more critical, believes that those manning the watchtower have already turned traitor. He writes scathingly, "[T]he frenzied pursuit of Number One which the book-publishing industry has turned to as a central and universal tool is in its very essence anti-art, even anti-thought" (Whiteside 1980, 193). And Whiteside's criticism continues to echo decades later in the work of critics such as Ben Bagdikian (2004) and Robert McChesney (1999, 2004), who view the concentration of media ownership in the hands of a select number of multinational corporations as bad for the free circulation of ideas and spirited debate necessary for a healthy democracy.

John Thompson (2010) has undoubtedly written the most comprehensive account of American trade book publishing to date. He rejects the distinction between autonomous and heteronomous fields in publishing as well as the assumption that an orientation toward the market must necessarily result in the corrosion of literary merit or the censorship of ideas. In a footnote in the earlier *Books in the Digital Age*, he writes, "Even in publishing fields where agents are more concerned to produce work of intellectual or cultural value than to pursue commercial goals, questions of economic value are never altogether absent and they may, at certain moments, become critical" (2005, 39). However, this is not to suggest that book publishing has not changed in profound ways over the past thirty years—because it has. Drawing upon past scholarship, I will describe some of these changes, focusing on the ones which are most important for understanding the history of the American manga industry.

The first of these changes, to which I have already alluded, is consolidation of ownership of publishing houses. There are a variety of reasons for this, which I will not discuss here, but by 2007 five publishers, Random House, Penguin, HarperCollins, Simon & Schuster, and Hachette, accounted for nearly half of all trade book sales in the United States (Thompson 2010). Their parent companies are the multinational corporations—many with large, well-known stakes in other sectors of media production—Bertelsmann, Pearson, News Corporation, CBS, and Lagardère, respectively. However, at least for book publishing, corporate concentration is not accompanied by evidence of monopolistic activity, and indeed the number of books published and in print now has never been greater (Greco, Rodríguez, and Wharton 2007). Furthermore, the presence of these book publishing behemoths has allowed a multitude of independent, niche presses to sprout up in their long shadows; "this world of small presses exists as a parallel universe to the world of the large corporate publishers...because the gulf between them, in terms of the scale of resources they have at their disposal, is just too great" (Thompson 2010, 155). Although I am not convinced that the worlds of the small and large presses are quite as segregated as Thompson suggests,[2] it is certain that the trade publishing field is comprised of a handful of very large corporate presses and a large number of small ones, with very few occupying the hard-going, midsized middle ground.

Another important change is the rise of the book-retailing chain superstores. While hypothetically there are numerous ways to get books from publishers to readers, in practice in the twentieth century most of that selling has not been done directly by publishing houses but rather through a network of intermediaries. By the beginning of the 1980s, the chain mall store was ascendant, with companies like B. Dalton and Waldenbooks leading the charge. These stores made books accessible to a mushrooming suburban market that had never had ready access to bookstores when they had been concentrated solely in urban centers. And this was not a matter of mere geographical convenience; they also "lessened the elite aura that had formerly encircled the bookshop by bringing the bookstore down to the level of the supermarket across the parking lot or the teen jeans outlet next door" (Miller 2006, 91). The mall store encouraged recreational reading and hailed women and their children on their home turf. However, by the 1990s the mall store was being supplanted by the chain superstores Borders and Barnes & Noble. These new retail environments, instead of being located within shopping malls, tended to be big box stores built along commercial

---

[2]While small presses do not ordinarily have the resources to compete with large presses, large presses can and do compete aggressively with small presses in the areas which small presses consider their specialty. If a new category of books, such as manga, emerges in world of the niche presses and starts making money, the large corporate presses are eager to jump onto the bandwagon (Brienza 2009a). They do this, according to some informants, not because they have any particular interest in the content of this new material *per se* but rather because they are of the general management view that, as large presses, they ought to be active in every category of trade publishing. The outcome of this activity for particular individual firms is never certain, but when successful they can and do muscle out small presses from the field entirely.

strips or on the outskirts of enclosed mall complexes. So-called "category killers," a single one of these stores averaged some 25,000 square feet of retail space, and by 1997 the two chains together had seized 43.3 percent, nearly half, of all bookstore sales in the United States, altering the balance of power between publisher and retailer (Miller 2006, 2009). The superstores extended the bookselling innovations pioneered by the mall stores by making them not merely accessible but also attractive destinations in their own right, pleasant places to hang out, drink coffee, and socialize (Miller 2006).

A third change is the growing dependence of the field upon short-cycle bestsellers. Of course, there is always a level of uncertainty in the book publishing enterprise, and no matter how certain a press may be that a book will sell once it is published, they are on occasion disappointed. Despite this uncertainty, there are a number of principles by which a press might choose to operate. They might attempt to publish only books which they expect to be moderately successful, building a list of books hoped to sell in roughly equal numbers, or at least above a set minimum number of copies. They might rely upon books which have long shelf lives, slowly but surely earning back their initial investment over a period of many years. However, publishers now rely increasingly on short-cycle bestsellers, titles which sell a lot of copies immediately after they are released and then after a few weeks or months exhaust the market and fall off the radar. Thompson calls this the "six-week rule" for new books: "Today a book has just a few weeks—typically no more than six, and in practice often less—to show whether it's going to move" (Thompson 2010, 266). This transformation is due to a number of factors, the most important being the rise of the chain superstore described earlier. These stores have a monopoly on the space of the visible for trade books, and buying premium real estate in that space represents a tremendous financial burden to publishing houses. If they are to spend money on it, they must see returns quickly. Additionally, the large, corporate-owned houses are under intense pressure from their parent companies to report year-on-year growth, and backlist sales alone generally account for less than half of their annual revenue (Thompson 2010). These two factors together, then, mean that making new bestsellers on a regular basis is of paramount importance for many actors in the field.

Big box bookstores, short-cycle bestsellers, and corporate consolidation are by no means an exhaustive list of the recent transformations which have occurred in the trade book publishing field. Other changes include the rise of the "super-agent" and the emergence of online book retailers such as Amazon. But these have not been as important for the history of the American manga publishing industry specifically, and so I do not discuss them here. Nothing, in any case, has had such a far-reaching impact upon the field as the changing retail environment. In the next section, I will provide an account of the history of the American manga publishing industry. I begin, appropriately, with the chain bookstore.

A history of the American manga publishing industry

Mall stores and magical girls

I begin with Waldenbooks, to be precise, and the newly formed independent manga publishing company called Mixx Entertainment. Mixx was founded by Stu Levy and, with financial support from Mitsui Ventures and Nippon Venture Capital, began publishing the manga magazine anthology *MixxZine* in 1997. This magazine featured four titles licensed inexpensively from the Japanese publishing giant Kodansha, *Magic Knight Rayearth*, *Ice Blade*, *Parasyte*, and *Sailor Moon*. In every respect, from the trim size to the paper stock to the fonts that were used, *MixxZine* did *not* look like an American superhero comic. This was intentional—Levy was smart enough to recognize that he would not be able to compete with the likes of Marvel and DC on their own turf. But where do you go and what do you do in the late 1990s if you want to publish a comic book that is not a comic book? The manga, which ultimately pointed the way forward for all other manga in America, proved to be *Sailor Moon*.

To understand the history of the American manga industry, Naoko Takeuchi's *Bishoujo Senshi Sailor Moon* [Pretty Guardian Sailor Moon] is key, although it would not have seemed so when it debuted in 1997. Published in a Japanese shoujo manga magazine aimed at elementary school girls called *Nakayoshi* from 1991 to 1995, the story featured a team of teenage, sailor-style uniformed superheroines who battle successive waves of evil forces threatening the Earth. Combining the magical girl and superhero team action genres into what proved to be an irresistible formula, the series found tremendous crossover appeal beyond its core audience of young girls and attracted a devoted following of boys and adult men and women as well. Nonetheless, it is important to point out that most shoujo manga creators, particularly those writing for the younger magazines like *Nakayoshi*, are rookies, barely older than children themselves (Prough 2011). Takeuchi was no exception, and the manga was produced with a high level of editorial input and interference at every step of the process. In a way, the ostensible author credited on the cover of these books was but one small cog in an enormous—and lucrative—multimedia industry which spawned a long-running televised anime adaptation, theatrical films, live-action spin-offs, and boatloads of merchandise. *Sailor Moon* was a hit in Japan, and investors had high hopes for America as well. Unfortunately, the anime's first North American broadcast in 1995 failed to attract viewers and was quickly canceled.

The sources of this commercial failure have been explored in detail by others (Grigsby 1998; Allison 2006b), and I will not revisit them here. The key point is that when Levy was acquiring licenses from the firm, Kodansha had no reason to place much hope in the *Sailor Moon* manga's American prospects. They were, though, facing down the end of unlimited growth of profits in manga publishing in Japan and were happy to take whatever they could get. Interestingly, at this time Kodansha had a well-regarded international book division called Kodansha International, the only major Japanese publishing house with any venture of this sort. However, most of that imprint's publications in the United States were dictionaries, Japanese-language study guides, and hardcover editions of Japanese literature in translation, and they did not have the resources or the distribution networks to publish translated manga in the United States, nor did they have much interest in doing so. Kodansha was under increasing pressure at home to find new sources of revenue, though, and selling off rights to manga it had no reason to be optimistic about was a welcome boost of what must have felt like easy, unearned income.

Levy and Mixx Entertainment got very lucky. Two things happened in 1998 that saved *Sailor Moon* and *MixxZine* from an ignominious end at the bottom of the recycling bin. The first was the revival of the anime; despite the failure of its original syndication, it was picked up for cable television by USA Network in 1998. With a summer schedule and a better time slot than it had been granted previously, viewers actually started tuning in. Based upon its popularity, new episodes would subsequently be commissioned for adaptation and picked up for premier broadcast by Cartoon Network, another cable network. In her ethnographic research, Susan Napier (2007) notes that most of the female anime and manga fans she has surveyed reported becoming interested in the two media through their exposure to *Sailor Moon* on television. The second thing that happened, and by far the most important, in my view, was the installation of long-time comics and manga fan Kurt Hassler into the position of graphic novel buyer for the mall-based chain Waldenbooks. Starting in 1998, Waldenbooks was the first to distribute Mixx's titles, collaborating extensively with the young publishing house as it struggled to professionalize the production and quality of its domesticated manga. Getting collected graphic novel editions of *Sailor Moon* into the mall stores meant that the teenage girls to whom the series most appealed were far more likely to find out about this strange new thing called manga through a recognizable brand for sale in a familiar environment. After all, the mall, and most definitely *not* the forbidding, male-only terrain of the comic bookstore (Wolk 2007), was where they were hanging out already. Access to this market was a financial windfall for Mixx, and it was this particular historical moment of association between the two men and their companies—and not, I would argue, Levy or Hassler as individual actors alone—which began manga's shift toward the trade book field. Levy knew that Japanese manga was designed to make its real money as a book, not as a periodical; Hassler gave his company access to the bookstore market and helped teach Mixx what they needed to do to be a successful trade publishing house.

When the Borders Group, which owned both the Borders and Waldenbooks chains, began to streamline its operations, Hassler rose quickly up the ranks to become the national-level buyer for all Borders and Waldenbooks stores in the United States in January 2000. His ability to influence the visibility of manga in the quasi-public retail space therefore increased exponentially, and along with manga publishers, who were eager to capitalize upon the opportunity afforded by his position, he soon took advantage of it.

Chain superstores and "100% Authentic Manga"

At the dawn of the twenty-first century, manga had found a welcome outpost on the margins of the field of trade book publishing, but it had not yet become unequivocally linked to it. There were several reasons for this. Most importantly, in my view, manga publishing companies did not yet see themselves as *book* publishers. In fact, they did not, I would argue, envision themselves primarily as publishers—of comics or of magazines, let alone books—at all. Levy's love–hate relationship with printed matter has been the subject of much rumor (much of it vicious) over the years, but the company's Los Angeles location and *MixxZine*'s tagline, "Motionless Picture Entertainment," certainly hints at Hollywood aspirations from its earliest days. Viz, which had been publishing manga since the late 1980s, was originally called "Viz Communications" and was as much, if not more, involved in periodical publishing, direct-to-video anime localization, and merchandising, as it was in book or comics publishing. Based in San Francisco, it too was a continent apart from New York City, the center of the American publishing world in the United States, and its parent company Shogakukan, one of the three major book publishing houses in Japan, was literally an ocean away. They were, in the words of one industry veteran, the "forgotten outpost." A few other companies, primarily active in other fields of cultural production, were publishing the occasional manga on the side, such as Dark Horse (comics) and Central Park Media (anime). These companies, however, were quickly relegated to bit parts in the act to follow.

Also, the modest numbers of manga available for sale were still small enough that independent comic bookshops were able to keep up with new releases if so inclined, and collectively they remained an important retail venue for manga, which publishers ignored at their peril. Yes, graphic novels were becoming increasingly important, sold widely in both independent comic bookshops and chain bookstores alike, but it was still standard to publish manga as either pamphlets, colloquially called "floppies," or magazine serials first. This practice was first derived from manga publishing in Japan, which is heavily oriented toward periodical publishing, and from American comics publishing, which is also traditionally periodical based. The effect was to position manga in the United States uncomfortably between comics, trade book, and magazine publishing. So, while in theory monthly manga periodicals might be distributed through newsstands or bookstores, due to limited distribution in practice, these, more than the graphic novels, remained under the near-exclusive retail purview of selected comic bookshops, and a significant proportion was sold through individual direct-by-mail customer subscriptions handled by the publishers themselves because so many Americans had no local comic bookstore anyway. In short, manga publishers were dabbling in a number of different publishing fields, primarily comics, but had not settled decisively into any particular one, and their corporate identities and organizational structure were not yet wedded to publishing "manga."

With the success of *Sailor Moon*, though, it must be noted that shoujo manga became an increasingly visible category in these periodicals. Viz began publishing *Animerica Extra*, the all-manga sister publication to its anime-focused magazine *Animerica*, and *PULP*, a magazine intended primarily for that mature male comics field audience. Both magazines included selected shoujo manga, and *Animerica Extra*, which serialized fan-favorites *Fushigi Yûgi* and *X/1999*, had a readership up to 70 percent female. In canny response to the realities of its readership, *Animerica Extra*, before it finally folded in 2004 following the demise of *Animerica*, had ultimately become an all-shoujo manga magazine. Mixx even attempted publishing monthly floppies of magical girl shoujo manga series *Sailor Moon*, *Miracle Girls*, *Saint Tail*, *Cardcaptor Sakura*, as well as its Korean horror manhwa title *Island*. *MixxZine*, meanwhile, was split into two publications, *Tokyopop* and *Smile*, the latter of which was positioned as a magazine "For the Next-Gen Girl." *Smile*, too, eventually became an all-shoujo manga magazine, serializing *Peach Girl* and *Paradise Kiss*, among other titles, but it was discontinued in 2002 once its publisher had decided that a different sort of strategy was necessary to best reach the *Sailor Moon*-loving female audience key to its commercial viability.

By 2001, moreover, manga publishers were in danger of becoming the victims of their own unexpected commercial success. The popularity of *Sailor Moon* had peaked, and Mixx, having renamed itself Tokyopop, was in pursuit of the next big thing. Viz, too, was awash in cash as never before in its short history, having capitalized on the American success of *Pokémon* with a blitz of spinoff merchandise and a distribution deal with Toys R Us.[3] Both were seeking new opportunities to further grow their business and sustain the organizational expansion that these blockbuster properties had fueled.

Tokyopop was the first to make its move. In April 2002, working in close collaboration with Hassler, the firm rolled out a new graphic novel format and began an aggressive "100% Authentic Manga" marketing campaign, aiming to please Japanese licensors that wanted less overt alteration of content, bookstores that wanted more stock, and readers that wanted a faster release schedule in a single swoop. "100% Authentic" ostensibly referred to the preservation, unprecedented in the United States, of the Japanese right-to-left presentation and to various other textual quibbles, such as leaving sound effects untranslated and not changing the names of characters. Because these changes made preparing manga for American release less labor intensive and expensive, Tokyopop was able to speed up the release schedules of all of its series to one volume per month. Also, because a lighter editorial touch made it easier to secure publishing rights from Japan, the first volumes of a large number of new series debuted in April or very shortly thereafter, including: *Initial D, Marmalade Boy, Kodocha: Sana's Stage, GTO, Cowboy Bebop, Real Bout High School*, and *Love Hina*. Series that had begun prior to 2002, such as *Harlem Beat, Peach Girl*, and *Cardcaptor Sakura*, were gradually changed over to the new format as new volumes became available. Incidentally, the first run of the "100% Authentic Manga" manga arrived in Borders (and only Borders) adorned with plastic obi, called *bandes* in France, a knowing homage to Japanese books, which are also customarily sold wearing obi. Knowledgeable readers took the obi as a demonstration of Tokyopop's stated commitment to authenticity, and for those who did not recognize the cultural allusion, the self-explanatory "100% Authentic Manga" logo and "Done the RIGHT (to LEFT) way" slogan of the publisher's marketing campaign were printed prominently on them.

Yet, ironically, other changes that Tokyopop made to its graphic novels were *not* particularly authentic. The publisher already had a penchant for experimenting with different trim sizes, and for these new, "authentic" manga, it split the size difference between its "Pocket Mixx" (4.5 × 6.75 inches) and "Mixx Manga" (5.5 × 8 inches) imprints, and began to use a 5 × 7.5 inch

---

[3] Despite the comparatively vast amount of scholarly research on *Pokémon* beyond Japan, little attention has been paid to its impact on the manga industry. None of the contributions to *Pikachu's Global Adventure* edited by Joseph Tobin (2004), for example, make any mention of manga. Yet it was not, in my view, any contribution the brand may have made to the global visibility of Japanese popular culture *per se* that made it especially important in the context of manga. Rather, it was the capital, economic, cultural, and symbolic, which *Pokémon*'s success supplied to Viz. Viz, despite having been the longest-operating manga publisher in the United States, would not have otherwise been anywhere near the same position of strength to compete with Tokyopop.

trim size.[4] All volumes were then priced uniformly at USD $9.99. The books' 5 ×
7.5 inch trim size and $9.99 price point had no particular precedent in any other
sector of the trade publishing industry, either in Japan (which uses standard
metric sizes and yen denominations, anyway) or North America. But although
the trim size was novel, it did have the distinct advantage of being easy for
American printers to produce. In any case, these two characteristics, along
with the right-to-left orientation, made Tokyopop's lineup distinctive from other
American graphic novel editions of manga, as well as instantly recognizable
as manga to everyone, from casual readers to industry professionals. Under
the right circumstances, brands can constitute powerful signifiers of both
individualization and conformity (Baudrillard 1988; Bourdieu 1984; Simmel
1997), and what came to be known in the industry as the "Tokyopop (trim) size"
in this case proved to be a powerful agent of change, simultaneously making
this thing called "manga" distinctive at the same time as it was standardized
to a specific—and easily reproducible—physical form (see Figure 3.1).

FIGURE 3.1 *Twelve volumes of manga, one published
each year from 1996 to 2007 (left to right).*

---

[4]Actually, the very first 5 × 7.5 inch, USD $9.99 book available from Tokyopop predates the
"100% Authentic Manga" campaign by a few months. This book is *Island Vol. 1* by In-Wan Youn
and Kyung-Il Kang, a comic of Korean origin. The original Korean edition of *Island* is B6 size

Because the greatly accelerated release schedule was meeting heretofore unmet demand among preexisting consumers, the "100% Authentic Manga" campaign was a resounding success for Tokyopop and an all-out crisis for competing manga publishers that would draw manga rapidly and decisively into the book publishing field. Viz, until 2002 the largest publisher of manga in the United States, was knocked down to second place virtually overnight in terms of number of new books published each month by release schedules fully *six times* faster than its own—and they were not about to take this challenge sitting down.

Viz responded within the year by accelerating its publishing schedules and mimicking Tokyopop's format and price point, and the companies became each other's main competitors. Both had a bestselling series, *Naruto* for Viz and *Fruits Basket* for Tokyopop, which industry informants have told me sold in almost exactly equal numbers in the mid-2000s. In 2007, although having put out only 384 volumes compared to Tokyopop's 510 (Goldberg 2010), Viz definitely had an advantage in terms of bestsellers; ICv2's list of "Top 50 Manga Properties" includes twenty-eight Viz titles but only nine Tokyopop titles (Anon. 2008). The company would reassume its unchallenged position at the top of the US manga industry in the run-up to Tokyopop's collapse, and as of 2012 it is the largest publisher of graphic novels, of any sort, not just manga, in the United States, and many of its current employees bring their experiences in trade and textbook publishing to the professional practices of the company. Viz has always been very conservative, waiting for someone else to blaze new trails for it to follow, and in the early 2000s, it had yet to establish itself firmly in any one publishing field. But by responding to two particular historical moments—and competing with those who seemed to be on the cusp of making that history—Viz was ultimately pulled definitively and irreversibly into the field of trade publishing.

The first of these moments in history was the establishment of Gutsoon, the American arm of the Japanese publishing company Coamix. Coamix was founded in 2000 by former *Weekly Shonen Jump* editor-and-chief Nobuhiko Horie along with a handful of manga creators from that same magazine. Prominent creators included Tsukasa Hojo and Tetsuo Hara, whose famed manga *City Hunter* and *Hokuto no Ken* [Fist of the North Star] headlined the magazine in the 1980s. The existence of Coamix infuriated Shueisha—the defection was taken as a personal slight—and Gutsoon's announcement of the first ever English language weekly manga anthology was but additional insult, for the magazine, called *Raijin Comics*, had also acquired the rights

---

(approximately 5 × 7 inches), nearly equivalent to Tokyopop's American edition. Because resizing pages of manga, by making them either smaller or larger, can lead to a perceptible loss of detail in the final product, the similar trim size was chosen in this case to best preserve the visual quality of the illustrated pages.

to *Slam Dunk* by Takehiko Inoue, one of *Weekly Shonen Jump*'s all-time bestselling manga titles in Japan. As the copyright holder, Inoue was able to take his work to whomever he pleased, and the deal cut out *Slam Dunk*'s Japanese publisher entirely. Shueisha, despite having published the lion's share of the most popular manga properties under its *Jump* brand, had never before expressed interest in seeing its manga published abroad and had until that point rebuffed most overtures. But now, faced with Coamix's American ambitions, the publishing house was having a sudden change of heart—and this represented the opportunity of a lifetime for Viz, which was casting about frantically for the next *Pokémon*. Viz, as a wholly owned subsidiary of the rival house Shogakukan, would not have been a particularly attractive partner for Shueisha under less extraordinary circumstances. However, these were extraordinary circumstances, and to settle scores back home, Shueisha partnered with Shogakukan to buy an equity stake in Viz. The company later reformed in 2005 as Viz Media, LLC and is currently co-owned by Shueisha Inc., Shogakukan Inc., and Shogakukan-Shueisha Productions, Co., Ltd.

Although Gutsoon and *Raijin Comics*'s ill fortune in the American market was all but a forgone conclusion,[5] Viz, awash in *Pokémon* money with which it could reinvest into new projects and newly partnered with Shueisha, was very well positioned to respond to the Tokyopop tsunami of new titles. And respond Viz did, with what was the second of two turning points in the history of manga in America. Viz's American edition of *Shonen Jump*, a monthly magazine serializing selected titles, some dating back to the 1990s, from the Japanese magazine, debuted at the end of 2002 with an issue date of January 2003. Akira Toriyama's *Dragon Ball Z* was its headlining title. Other serials included *Yu-Gi-Oh!*, *One Piece*, *Yu Yu Hakusho*, and another short series by Toriyama titled *Sandland*. Masashi Kishimoto's *Naruto*, the series that would become Viz's bestselling title, and the all-time bestselling manga series in America to date, began serialization in the second issue of the magazine. Viz also began to accelerate its new graphic novel publishing schedule, and by late 2003 the company had stopped flipping pages, co-opted the Tokyopop trim size, and lowered its list prices to $9.95 or $9.99 for almost all of its new releases. It would subsequently lower many of its prices even further, to $7.95 or $7.99 for shounen manga titles bearing its Shonen Jump (SJ) and Shonen Jump (SJ) Advanced imprints and $8.99 for shoujo manga titles bearing its Shojo Beat (SB) imprint. Some of these prices ticked back upward to $9.99 in 2009.[6] These books, too, were available in chain

---

[5]For more on this topic, see Brienza (2009a).

[6]Viz's decision to price its titles below $9.99 was quite controversial in the manga industry at the time. Japanese manga, which are typically priced at approximately ¥400 for NPB sizes, are significantly less expensive than English-language editions. This price difference is partly a difference in economies of scale but mostly due to the much smaller discount that bookstores in

bookstores throughout the country, and as the volume of titles available increased rapidly, comic bookshops with their limited space and specialized clientele, could not keep up. The local Borders, Waldenbooks, and to a lesser extent Barnes & Noble became the main game in town for those wanting to buy manga, and fortunately the chains were everywhere. Manga had, in short, become a book sold in bookstores, governed by the logic of the field of trade publishing, and for those publishing manga there was no going back.

Category colonization, expansion, and standardization

No one has reliable data on total American manga sales prior to 2002 because among other things, suffice it to say, it was not important enough to measure. But the growth since then, whether quantified by independent research firm ICv2 (350 percent from 2002 to 2007, the year the market peaked) or as the lived experience of radical spatial changes occurring at every chain bookstore in the nation as they made room for the flood of new volumes, was undeniable. The explosive growth of manga sales, often colloquially referred to as the "manga boom" in the publishing industry, was not just a two-way arms race between Tokyopop and Viz; new players also fueled growth. Drawn to double-digit growth in an industry otherwise infamous for growing at roughly the rate of inflation, other cultural producers began to colonize this nascent field and release graphic novel editions of manga of their own. This dramatically expanded the total number of Japanese manga available in English. Furthermore, because these new manga publishers were in way too much of a hurry to parse out systematically exactly what was actually responsible for Tokyopop's success, they preferred not to take any chances and began reproducing as much as possible Tokyopop's "100% Authentic Manga" strategies, particularly that of trim size, even if strictly speaking, it was not necessary to do so. Figure 3.1 illustrates this phenomenon well; every book in the image after Tokyopop's *GTO* in 2002 is by a different publisher.

The following are just a few of the most important examples of this flood of newcomers: ADV Films, an anime localization company based in Houston,

---

Japan normally take. Japanese executives, misunderstanding the economics of book publishing and selling in the United States, assume that these list prices are too high and put pressure upon those companies with whom they have the most leverage, such as their subsidiary Viz, to push prices down. Retailers, meanwhile, saw no difference in sales of $9.99 manga versus $7.95 manga and reacted angrily at presses for unnecessarily undervaluing their products and losing money for the entire sector. If anything, they were convinced prices could go slightly higher, and as such US-based and American-owned companies such as Del Rey Manga and Yen Press were far more likely to set their prices baseline at $10.95 or $10.99.

Texas, whose first video release dates back to 1992, began a manga line called ADV Manga in 2003.[7] Random House, the world's largest trade book publisher, began publishing manga under the Del Rey Manga imprint in the spring of 2004.[8] DC Comics, one of the two largest publishers of American comic books in the United States, also began publishing manga under the newly formed CMX imprint.[9] Yen Press, a division of the newly formed Hachette Book Group USA, came relatively late to the game, yet five out of the seven Yen series published in 2007 were 5 × 7.5 inches and priced at $10.99. Because most of these publishers were book publishers new to manga or comics publishers new to books, they were also basically content to follow Tokyopop's lead in the particulars of format, price range, and use of the word "manga" to describe their products. Interestingly, whereas doing so in 2003 might have been a sort of irrational imitation, within only a couple of years imitation had become quite rational because it demonstrated knowledge of the rules and standards of the new field and thus one's rightful place in it. In fact, when publishers choose to publish manga in a different trim size, they do so now with keen awareness of how these books will look shelved alongside the standard collection of 5 × 7.5 inch titles and will sometimes pick larger trim sizes for books for which they want to command greater visual space and attention. Digital Manga Publishing (DMP), for example, does this for most of its releases to help compensate for the company's—and its offerings'—relatively lower industry profile.

It was only when manga in graphic novel format had become standardized into a particular trim size and price point and had, indeed, become synonymous with it, I would argue, that all of the companies publishing this content began to see themselves as part of a cohesive social group. In other words, while there were certainly companies publishing manga prior to the 2000s, there was no such thing as a manga publishing industry back then. Yes, many early manga pioneers had a shared personal history, but they had no ready, preestablished market and were publishing books primarily for themselves. The industry proper did not begin to form until the late 1990s with *Sailor Moon* and the mall stores, and its future was not guaranteed until Tokyopop and then Viz and others standardized the format of this thing that through collective consensus came to be called "manga." Obviously, it is impossible to pinpoint the exact moment when American manga publishing finally became a structured field of

---

[7]ADV Manga released a large number of series in its early days in a variety of different trim sizes. Titles included *Full Metal Panic, Azumanga Daioh, Gunslinger Girl, Those Who Hunt Elves,* and *Demon City Shinjuku.* All books, though, were initially priced at $9.99.
[8]Del Rey Manga began modestly with four series: *Negima!, Gundam Seed, Tsubasa,* and *xxxHOLiC.* All of these books are 5 × 7.5 inches and priced at $10.95.
[9]Early CMX titles include *Madara, Land of the Blindfolded,* and *From Eroica with Love.* All of these books are 5 × 7.5 inches and priced at $9.99.

transnational cultural production in its own right, but for the purposes of this book I have chosen the year 2005. By 2005, manga publishers saw themselves as producing a common product, and the people working for these publishers saw themselves not just as fans but also as manga industry professionals with compatible knowledge sets, shared modes of labor practice, and skills which could be transferred by leaving one manga company and taking up employment with another. This identification began to define their actions and became justification to do—or *not* do—particular things. "We're book publishers," one manga executive exclaimed, when asked why his company did not branch off into anime licensing. "We don't *do* that." Employees of various companies also reflexively invoked their primary role in publishing to register disapproval of decisions higher up to venture into new cultural fields, such as video games or, as in the case of the anecdote used to open this chapter, food journalism. Yen Press launched its monthly magazine *Yen+* because, as a print medium, they deemed it a natural extension of their business.

Furthermore, 2005 was the year that Borders made "Manga" an official category in all of its stores, complete with permanent dedicated shelf space and signage, advertising the popularity of these books from Japan to anyone who might come into the store and wander by (see Figure 3.2). Barnes & Noble followed suit, although their manga stock was divided between shelving near

FIGURE 3.2 *The manga section of a Borders bookstore (December 2007).*

the area dedicated to adult science fiction and fantasy and the young adult section in many stores through the mid-2000s. In any case, because publicizing a book often comes down to "the battle for eyeballs in the bookstores and other retail outlets" (Thompson 2010, 257), for manga publishers, who cannot ordinarily afford to buy space for their books right in front of the store's main entrance, their own dedicated bank of bookcases was the next best thing. Even being shelved spine out under such conditions was not an automatic death sentence; many titles are published over many volumes, so a single manga series might occupy a foot or more of shelving and thus plenty of visible space.

The American manga publishing field today

The financial crisis of 2008 and in particular the Borders bankruptcy of 2011, along with the rapid transition in other areas of trade publishing to digital formats and delivery, have hit the American manga industry very hard. Publishers large, medium, and small have gone out of business one after the other, including Tokyopop, ADV Manga, Go! Comi, CMX, DrMaster, Aurora Publishing, Broccoli, and Bandai Entertainment. Anime licensors and American comics publishers have all but exited the field. Trade publishers have, unsurprisingly, given that the new manga field is structured primarily by the logic of trade book publishing, fared better; nearly all of the manga publishers now left standing are formally affiliated with trade book publishing houses, whether as imprints, wholly owned subsidiaries, partners, or as recipients of investment. Manga sales, which peaked in 2007 at an estimated $210 million, have been in decline (see Figure 3.3 and Table 3.2). ICv2 reports in its 2011 White Paper annual sales in 2010 at $120 million but notes that the multi-year drop appears to be slowing in the first half of 2011 (Anon. 2011a).

By the end of 2011, the free fall seemed to have eased up. As of this writing in 2012, none of the presses extant at that time have since gone under, and

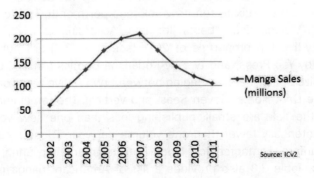

FIGURE 3.3 *Annual North American manga sales.*

TABLE 3.2 Annual North American manga sales by market value and volumes published

Year	Estimated Sales	Volumes Published
2002	$60,000,000	–
2003	$100,000,000	–
2004	$135,000,000	–
2005	$175,000,000	1088
2006	$200,000,000	1208
2007	$210,000,000	1513
2008	$175,000,000	1372
2009	$140,000,000	1115
2010	$120,000,000	996
2011	$105,000,000	695

Source: ICv2

those remaining have begun to fill niches left vacant, with Viz, for example, partnering with Japanese independent Libre to publish boys' love. The Del Rey Manga imprint, meanwhile, was reorganized with a near identical profile under Kodansha USA as Kodansha Comics. A handful of presses, such as Penguin in 2011 with *Gandhi* by Kazuki Ebine, have even begun to dabble in the publication of single volumes of manga, and others, such as Fantagraphics, have developed a coherent and growing list of manga. JManga and other new players based in Japan are promoting digital manga reading platforms with some of their own licensed content.

Yet, as Table 3.3 shows, in the second decade of the twenty-first century the industry leader remains, without question, Viz Media, averaging over twenty new releases each month. Both in terms of sales and number of volumes published, they are, in fact, the largest graphic novel publisher of any kind. Kodansha Comics, Yen Press, and Digital Manga, meanwhile, all publish between six to ten new volumes per month. The former two, along with Viz, dominate bestseller lists. According to ICv2, fifteen of the twenty-five top properties of 2011 (see Table 3.4) are published by Viz, eight by Yen Press, and two by Kodansha Comics (Anon. 2012a). The medium-sized publishers, averaging between two to five new volumes per month, are Dark Horse, Seven Seas, and Vertical. The remaining presses active in the field are small, publishing less than one new volume per month—potentially fewer than one volume per year. These small players include Fanfare, Fantagraphics, Udon Entertainment, Top Shelf, and ALC Publishing. Table 3.3 also provides a list of American manga publishers along with their parent companies (if applicable) and North American

TABLE 3.3 American manga publishers (active as of the end of 2011)

Manga Publisher	Parent Company	Trade Distributor	Size
Viz Media	Shueisha Shogakukan	Simon & Schuster	(Extra-)Large
Kodansha Comics	Kodansha	Random House	Large
Yen Press	Hachette	Hachette	Large
Digital Manga	N/A	Diamond	Large
Dark Horse	N/A	Diamond	Medium
Vertical	Kodansha Dai Nippon Printing	Random House	Medium
Seven Seas	N/A	Tor/Macmillan	Medium
Fanfare	N/A	Midpoint	Small
Fantagraphics	N/A	W.W. Norton	Small
Top Shelf	N/A	Diamond	Small
Udon Entertainment	N/A	Diamond	Small

trade distributor.[10] The extent to which the field as a whole is connected to both the largest Japanese *and* US houses is evident, and these ties have become closer as well since 2007.

The particular genres of manga that are most popular and sell best have not changed significantly since the industry's 2007 peak. Shounen manga, especially from Viz's female-friendly *Shonen Jump*, and shoujo manga are mainstays. ICv2's "Top 50 Manga Properties" for 2007 listed thirteen shounen titles and nine shoujo titles in its top twenty-five (Anon. 2008). Its "Top 25 Manga Properties" for 2011 lists fifteen shounen titles and seven shoujo titles (Anon. 2012a). Nine properties (*Naruto, Bleach, Vampire Knight, Fullmetal Alchemist, Negima!, Death Note, Ouran High School Host Club, Yotsuba&!,* and *D.Gray-man*) are in the top twenty-five of both lists. If anything, shoujo manga are moving up the list, with only *Fruits Basket* (now out of print) in the top five in 2007 and both *Sailor Moon* and *Vampire Knight* in the top five in 2011, along with *Black Butler,* which despite being nominally shounen targets female readers near-exclusively.

Despite its narrower range of stock, Barnes & Noble remains the single most important retail venue for manga. Online sales of print books have increased post-Borders, with Amazon now representing over 10 percent of the market. Independent bookstores, comic bookstores, and retail giants such as Walmart also continue to sell manga. There is, however, concern in the industry that none of these outlets have fully replaced the sales potential of

---

[10]Presses which have published only one manga or have not officially closed but have been inactive since 2008 are not included. Also not included are digital-only publishers, such as JManga.

TABLE 3.4 "Top Manga Properties" for 2011

Rank	Title	Publisher
1	Naruto	Viz Media
2	Bleach	Viz Media
3	Vampire Knight	Viz Media
4	Sailor Moon	Kodansha Comics
5	Black Butler	Yen Press
6	Blackbird	Viz Media
7	Fullmetal Alchemist	Viz Media
8	Rosario + Vampire	Viz Media
9	Soul Eater	Yen Press
10	One Piece	Viz Media
11	Blue Exorcist	Viz Media
12	Maximum Ride	Yen Press
13	Bakuman	Viz Media
14	Yu-Gi-Oh!	Viz Media
15	Negima!	Kodansha Comics
16	Death Note	Viz Media
17	Pandora Hearts	Yen Press
18	Dengeki Daisy	Viz Media
19	Ouran High School Host Club	Viz Media
20	High School of the Dead	Yen Press
21	Spice & Wolf	Yen Press
22	Yotsuba&!	Yen Press
23	Higurashi When They Cry	Yen Press
24	D.Gray-Man	Viz Media
25	Otomen	Viz Media

Source: ICv2

Borders, which boasted a market share peaking at 40 percent, falling off to 20 percent at the time of its closure (Anon. 2012b), and this concern has accelerated the development of new publishing models covered in more detail in Chapter 7. Even so, Nielsen BookScan's weekly sales numbers[11] for

---

[11]BookScan rankings represent sales at bookstores, that is, Barnes & Noble and Amazon, but do *not* include sales at discount retailers such as Walmart or Costco or to the library market. They also do not capture sales at comic bookshops and other key retailers specializing in manga and anime such as Right Stuf, which have different market demographics. As such, they are potentially less reliable sources of information about manga sales numbers and trends than about other categories of trade publishing, for which it captures an estimated 75 percent of the market (Anon. 2011b).

TABLES 3.5 Manga on *Publisher's Weekly* Graphic Novel Bestseller List for the week ending 27 May 2012

Rank	Previous Rank	Weeks on List	Title	Author	Publisher	List Price	Publication Date	Units	Year to Date
2	2	4	*Sailor Moon 5*	Naoko Takeuchi	Kodansha Comics	$10.99	May 2012	1,031	7,200
3	3	4	*Naruto 56*	Masashi Kishimoto	Viz Media	$9.99	May 2012	1,014	6,348
11	26	2	*Soul Eater 9*	Atsushi Ohkubo	Yen Press	$11.99	May 2012	530	979
14	22	2	*Omamori Himari 7*	Milan Matra	Yen Press	$11.99	May 2012	453	921
15	11	7	*Black Butler 9*	Yana Toboso	Yen Press	$11.99	April 2012	405	5,028
16	37	2	*Puella Magi Madoka Magica 1*	Magica Quartet and Hanokage	Yen Press	$11.99	May 2012	395	702
17	36	2	*Pandora Hearts 10*	Jun Mochizuki	Yen Press	$11.99	May 2012	394	745
19	14	10	*Sailor Moon 4*	Naoko Takeuchi	Kodansha Comics	$10.99	March 2012	388	12,384
21	18	12	*Naruto 55*	Masashi Kishimoto	Viz Media	$9.99	March 2012	322	12,963
24	21	36	*Sailor Moon 1*	Naoko Takeuchi	Kodansha Comics	$10.99	September 2011	319	8,466
25	29	20	*Sailor Moon 3*	Naoko Takeuchi	Kodansha Comics	$10.99	January 2012	306	16,398

Source: *Publisher's Weekly* via Anime News Network

TABLES 3.5 Manga on *Publisher's Weekly* Graphic Novel Bestseller List for the week ending 3 June 2012

Rank	Previous Rank	Weeks on List	Title	Author	Publisher	List Price	Publication Date	Units	Year to Date
3	3	5	*Naruto 56*	Masashi Kishimoto	Viz Media	$9.99	May 2012	990	7,338
5	2	5	*Sailor Moon 5*	Naoko Takeuchi	Kodansha Comics	$10.99	May 2012	865	8,065
9	–	1	*Bleach 40*	Tite Kubo	Viz Media	$9.99	June 2012	495	507
10	–	1	*Black Bird 14*	Kanoko Sakurakoji	Viz Media	$9.99	June 2012	472	488
12	11	3	*Soul Eater 9*	Atsushi Ohkubo	Yen Press	$11.99	May 2012	462	1,441
13	–	1	*Bleach 41*	Tite Kubo	Viz Media	$9.99	June 2012	448	460
14	–	1	*The Tyrant Falls in Love 6*	Hinako Takanaga	Digital Manga Publishing	$12.95	May 2012	444	455
17	16	3	*Puella Magi Madoka Magica 1*	Magica Quartet and Hanokage	Yen Press	$11.99	May 2012	412	1,114
21	14	3	*Omamori Himari 7*	Milan Matra	Yen Press	$11.99	May 2012	349	1,270
22	19	11	*Sailor Moon 4*	Naoko Takeuchi	Kodansha Comics	$10.99	March 2012	345	12,729
23	24	37	*Sailor Moon 1*	Naoko Takeuchi	Kodansha Comics	$10.99	September 2011	343	8,809
24	17	3	*Pandora Hearts 10*	Jun Mochizuki	Yen Press	$11.99	May 2012	341	1,086
25	21	13	*Naruto 55*	Masashi Kishimoto	Viz Media	$9.99	March 2012	335	13,298

Source: *Publisher's Weekly* via Anime News Network

in mid-2012 show that new volumes of popular series such as *Sailor Moon* and *Naruto* can still sell in excess of a thousand copies per week for the first few weeks of their release (see Tables 3.5 and 3.6), with total sales in excess of 100,000 copies for individual volumes quite rare but not unprecedented, according to industry informants.

Manga's impact on the trade book and comics publishing fields

So, within a few short years, manga publishing went from being a nonentity bumbling gamely along at the margins of the American cultural field to the overnight success story that everyone working anywhere in comics or books was talking about. "No one had seen anything like it before," remarked one well-placed industry informant, and naturally, they did more than just passively observe. In Chapter 2, I theorize that the transnational field can transform a national field, and indeed, manga was to have a profound influence on both the trade book and comics publishing fields—it brought them closer together.

In 1997, the same year Mixx Entertainment was founded, Rich Johnson joined DC Comics as its VP of Book Trade Sales. With his experience in chain bookstore retailing, he too had success getting DC's graphic novels, particularly those published under its Vertigo imprint, into bookstores. He also helped pave the way for comics of all sorts, including manga, in libraries, which for the most part have been reactive and not proactive in the development of the manga publishing field. On his LinkedIn profile, he writes:

> At DC Comics I was at the forefront in establishing graphic novels in the bookstore market. Under my watch, DC Comics achieved their first *New York Times* Bestseller with Neil Gaiman's *Sandman: Endless Nights*. Additionally I was a driving force in institutionalizing graphic novels in the library market, partnering with the American Library Association to create READ posters of DC Comics properties as well as initiating talks with the OCLC to create a Dewey Decimal number specifically for graphic novels. I was responsible for sales of graphic novels to all outlets, except for comic book shops. [...]I also developed new product for DC and worked with other divisions, including one of the first OEL manga titles...(Johnson n.d.)

Johnson, in other words, was a book person working for a comics company. Nevertheless, he clearly owes a part of his success in this position to the bookstores' newfound interest in manga because the manga boom made stores eager to acquire more manga-like content, and this in turn helped spark a renaissance in graphic novel publishing. Certainly, the Original English Language, that is, OEL, or what I term original global manga (see Brienza 2015) he produced for the *Sandman* franchise, mentioned above, would not have happened without it. Published in 2003 in the Tokyopop trim size and priced at $9.95, *Death: At Death's Door* featured a female protagonist drawn in a cute style by a female artist and targeted the *Sailor Moon* demographic. Johnson ultimately left DC for Hachette to help found its manga imprint Yen Press with former Borders bookstore buyer Kurt Hassler, and it would be hard not to conclude that he made this move in part because the social and organizational context of a trade publishing house was more to his liking. After all, no matter how impressive Johnson's achievements for DC, he was just one person for one publisher, and DC, despite being one of the most important players, does not equal the comics publishing field as a whole. There were very real limits to how much change he could personally effect, particularly if he was already more sympathetic to the business practices of trade publishing.

Diamond, the only distributor to independent comic bookstores in both the North America and the United Kingdom, branched out into trade book distribution in 2002. The sudden expansion of sales of manga threatened an end run around Diamond's monopoly, not to mention bad news for comics publishers who did not have the know-how to get their titles into the chains. Thus, the establishment of a book distribution arm was in explicit and direct response to the bookstore-fueled manga boom, and by hiring Ku Liang, an Asian-American who had previously worked for Random House, to head the newly formed Diamond Book Distributors, they chose someone whose professional and personal background ought to help him understand both American trade books *and* Asian content. Through this new operation, Diamond now represents comics publishing companies to the bookstore market, and they distribute their books to consumer retail outlets such as Barnes & Noble and Amazon as well as other trade book distributors such as Ingram and Baker & Taylor. One of their most important manga-publishing clients is Dark Horse.

Another example of a company which has benefited from the manga boom is Oni Press, which publishes the *Scott Pilgrim* series. Drawn by Bryan Lee O'Malley, a Canadian of Korean and French-Canadian descent, this ongoing series began publication in 2004 and was adapted into a feature-length Hollywood film titled *Scott Pilgrim vs. the World* in 2010. There are six volumes as of 2011. The artist himself calls his work "manga-influenced comics" (McAlprin 2006), and certainly his press has, in its presentation of the book, made it look like a manga. The pages are monochrome, individual volumes are trimmed to approximately the Tokyopop size, and first printings of some volumes included Japanese-style *obi*. In fact, though *Scott Pilgrim* has been published by a so-called "indie," "underground," or "alternative" comics press, part of a movement that two decades ago "had never been strong enough to distribute any regularly scheduled comic books" (Rifas 2004, 145), it is so book-like that it was licensed for publication in virtual facsimile in the United Kingdom and Australia not by a comics press but by the Fourth Estate imprint of HarperCollins.

Indeed, any attempt by actors in the comics field to become important players in books as well is dwarfed by the actions of trade publishers. The large trade publishing houses are of the general management view that, as large presses, they ought to be active in every category of trade publishing, and as manga and other graphic novels became increasingly visible in bookstores, they too jumped onto the bandwagon. Some, such as Random House, established "manga" imprints, and these have been discussed above. Other presses, though, spun off successful graphic novel imprints that do not publish manga *per se* but would never have existed if the manga boom had never happened. Among the most notable of these is First Second, an imprint of Roaring Brook Press, part of Holtzbrinck USA. It began publishing graphic novels in 2006 and immediately made a big splash with the bestselling *American Born Chinese* by Gene Luen Yang. Scholastic also began publishing graphic novels, and its *Amulet* series by Kazu Kibuishi, serialized since 2008, was one of its first and has become a banner property. Note how these books, like the *Scott Pilgrim* series, (1) have a connection to Asia through the ethnicity of the authors and (2) are targeted to teenagers or children.

Furthermore, as comics, philosophically, became something that book publishers "do," there was a tremendous learning curve within trade publishing itself. Children's picture book editors who had never been confronted with a sequence of panels before had to learn what worked visually and narratively and what did not. Marketers who had previously specialized in genre prose fiction novels had to learn about direct market sales and distribution. Of course, their take on this content was their own. Even so, *American Born Chinese* and other works produced in trade publishing went on to be sanctified by the Eisner Awards, the comics industry's most prestigious honor, yet they look nothing like anything that had ever come out of the comics industry before. To be absolutely clear here—although it is impossible to know for certain what might have been had the manga boom not happened, I would argue that graphic novels like *American Born Chinese* and *Amulet*, by and for Americans, would not have been published by Marvel and DC under different conditions. They would, rather, have not existed at all.

However, to suggest that manga had the effect of pulling comics and book publishing closer together is emphatically *not* to suggest that the results were symmetrical. By 2009, over 60 percent of all retail sales of comics (i.e., graphic novels and manga) were realized through the *book* retail circuits (Reid 2009). This meant that the cost of not knowing how to get on well in the field of trade book publishing was higher than not knowing how to get on well in the field of comics publishing. And even with Diamond Book Distributors on their side, collectively comics presses were never going to win trying to beat trade presses at their own game on their own turf. Already established trade houses thus had the upper hand, and that only accelerated the pull of graphic novels away from the comics field and toward that of books. It would not be too much of an exaggeration, therefore, to conclude that the book field has colonized the comics field and started to remake it into its own image.

This colonization has had two important effects upon the production of comic books in both fields. The first is that it has dramatically increased the competition for market share and resources. Comics presses need to publish graphic novels as books to promote themselves and have become increasingly dependent upon bestsellers to prosper in the long run. If that does not work, increasingly the best option is to get out of the business altogether. Marvel and DC, the historic heavyweights of the American comics industry, for example, look more like Hollywood studios today than publishing companies (Anon. 2009; Andreeva 2010; Kimbell 2011). Movies and merchandising, not short-cycle bestsellers, currently fund their publishing operations (Last 2011). Yet, even as some comics presses are feeling the heat, others like First Second, firmly entrenched in trade publishing, are doing well. The second effect has been to dramatically increase the number and variety of books being published, and this further translates into more would-be artists and other publishing people from around the world finding work in the profession. Whether or not these jobs are well paid, or "good" jobs in any sense of the word, it is an open question to which I will return. Nevertheless, the content widely available, as well as the sorts of people involved in producing it, has never been more numerous or diverse.

Opportunities past, constraints to come?

I have argued in the past that manga owes its commercial success to its migration from the comics field to the book field (Brienza 2009a). While on one level this is true as far as it goes, I would further clarify this argument now to suggest that when manga was being marketed and sold primarily according to the structure and logic of comics publishing, the actors themselves did not identify themselves primarily as comics people. Professional self-identification was not widespread until the mid-2000s, when they came to identify with trade publishing. Thus, as it became analogous to the structure and logic of the field of contemporary trade publishing, manga publishers internalized its rules as taken-for-granted. As one informant from a large company with a long view of the industry's history put it:

The early company was bringing in people from the fandom who would learn editing on the fly. Later ones were people with journalism degrees or whatever who were learning comics on the fly, and that gives you a different product. It's a case of, "What's your focus?" If now it's all about the books and this certain kind of marketing mindset, I think it gives you a different kind of company, a different type of product.

These people have, in short, become conservative, doing the things well-socialized book publishers do, and are now far more likely to be affected by changes to the field than they are to effect dramatic change in the trade publishing sector as a whole themselves. This means that what was once an opportunity is now a very real constraint that is likely to have a profound impact upon the ways manga is domesticated for the American market in the future.

The first of these new constraints to manifest itself is the manga industry's new fixation on bestsellers and bestselling series. This began during the expansion of the field in the 2000s and became enshrined in 2009 when the *New York Times* began publishing a weekly bestselling manga list on its website. Bestsellers have become a way of placating parent companies who expect to see annual profits, and having one bestseller moreover raises the expectation that a press will have more in the future. Yet, success in the market, contra Bourdieu, provides publishers with creative autonomy: If a company is making enough money to keep investors or corporate parents happy, no one looks too closely, and they are left to get on with what they feel must be done. Also, a bestseller provides the funds necessary to finance the sorts of projects which will never be commercially successful but without which manga industry people would not feel like their jobs are worthwhile. There is growing concern that there is no next American bestseller incubating in Japan, and that the sorts of books popular in Japan now are not surefire hits across the Pacific.

This sentiment, in turn, has effects which will be analyzed in more detail in Chapter 6, and it is just one example of the many issues now confronting the American manga industry. It is hard not to conclude that manga publishers, who once found a new opportunity linking themselves to the field of trade book publishing, are now constrained by it. Furthermore, the problems which continue to confront the field as a whole are felt in particular ways within the manga industry. This is due to their complicated relationships with such groups as original Japanese rights holders and digital pirates, both of whom reshape and limit the range of possible action. For publishers, in other words, domesticating manga is a constant struggle between competing interests which structure the process at every step.

In subsequent chapters I will explore the process of domestication of manga in detail, focusing upon the struggles between different stakeholders and the effects of this conflict upon the final outcomes. I will also delve deeper into the ways in which the field of contemporary trade book publishing has been rapidly transformed since 2007 and how these changes both affect and, to a much lesser extent, are affected by the transnational field of American manga publishing. Ultimately I will show that, by making Japanese manga ordinary in an environment of new constraints, the industry runs the risk of erasing it from the field altogether. The next chapter, then, provides an account of how manga companies are formed and how they decide what they choose to license for English-language publication.

4

A License to Produce: Founding Companies, Negotiating Rights

Rhetorical question being asked in the wake of today's announcement [of the demise of Tokyopop]: Would you rather be a personality or a publisher? (from the author's field notes)

I've never viscerally disliked anybody so much. [This particular founding father] seemed to find everybody utterly contemptible but himself. Said he hated Shueisha and that Kodansha was nice and outward looking at first, but then they became, well, he used some expletive or another to describe them. He lost licenses because he refused to renegotiate contracts; a deal was a deal and that's the way it *should* be, he said. And when he decided to liquidate [his company's] assets while he was still ahead, he said he figured his former employees would whine about how it's all so unfair. Not the case, I must say, but where there's smoke there's fire; no wonder so many manga industry people hate the executive types! (from the author's field notes)

Tokyo summers are hot and humid, and while it would be customary for those seeking escape from the heat to retreat indoors, in the summer of 2011 the heat seemed to follow people everywhere, straight into their homes and offices. An earthquake, among the worst in Japanese history, had ravaged the Tohoku countryside and knocked out a nuclear power plant in Fukushima back in March. Anticipating power shortages in the coming months, the government imposed mandatory restrictions on electricity consumption in the Tokyo area. Office buildings were required to reduce their use by 15 percent—and this meant turning the thermostat up and the air-conditioning down.

Under such conditions dress codes began to loosen; coming to work in ordinary business attire meant risking heat exhaustion. Even so, my interviewee for the day, whom I will call Shinsuke, may well have been the worst-dressed employee in the building, the headquarters of one of Japan's three largest publishing companies. Now granted, most of the time it is not his job to be seen. Responsible for representing the company's domestic interests abroad, advising and corresponding with the many foreign presses around the world releasing the company's manga titles in their own countries, his business contacts are likely to know him primarily as a disembodied voice over the telephone or a block of prose in their email inboxes. Nevertheless, his faded jeans and wrinkled t-shirt set him apart from his copresent colleagues...and of course he knew it, though he feigned ignorance.

"So why are you dressed so much less formally than everyone else?" I asked.

"I don't know what you're talking about," Shinsuke deadpanned and refused to elaborate further.

To be perfectly honest, I did not need him to elaborate. Our interview was over by the time I asked that question, and already I understood exactly why his clothes looked the way they did: He did not think he fit in with Japanese corporate culture, and he was signaling his feelings of alienation. In fact, Shinsuke had told me a lot about himself during our interview and at times seemed more eager to talk about race and ethnicity in American culture than about his career in transnational cultural production.

Although he was fluent in Japanese and had lived in Japan for the entirety of his adult life, a childhood in the United States meant that this young Japanese man might as well have been a foreigner in his own country. Of course, he was deeply critical of American culture as well, but his criticism was of the sort commonly encountered among Americans of Asian descent. For example, Japanese people usually do not see themselves as part of an Asian racial group, whereas Shinsuke clearly thought of Asia and people of Asian descent as a single unit with a shared disadvantaged, minority status. Assuming, perhaps, that I am Asian-American and therefore empathize personally with his grievances, he regaled me with his frustrations with white America and what he perceived to be its prejudice against Asians. As one of the few kids of Asian descent in his peer group, he had apparently had a hard time in his American public school. American culture, in his view, treats Asian boys like they are emasculated, feminized. They never, to use the vernacular, get laid. "I would not use the words Cool Japan until a scrawny little Asian kid in Knoxville, Tennessee can get laid with, like, ten blonde, blue-eyed soccer team girls. If that happens then I would say Cool Japan...or Cool Asia. It's not happening yet," he affirmed.

Eventually, I was able to nudge the discussion back on topic. I told him how many of the people I had interviewed in the United States had no end of complaints about what it was like dealing with the large Japanese publishing houses. No one, in fact, had any positive remarks about their experiences at all. So what, I asked him, was Shinsuke's side of the story?

"Well, we enjoy being nasty!" he replied.

Obviously, this was meant in jest, and he immediately went on to say, "I really sympathize with them because, at the end of the day, we're just telling them what to do. Those guys out there—they're actually printing the books, they meet the fans, they do the promotion—they have to do a lot more than we do."

Nevertheless, in light of his remarks about American racism, it was impossible for me to dismiss his joke out of hand. Were the headaches reported by some manga industry professionals more than just a symptom of bloated Japanese bureaucracy, as I would have otherwise presumed? Was Shinsuke, on some subconscious level, taking his position of power over the American manga industry as an opportunity to get back at a country that had once made him feel powerless? What, precisely, is the connection between race and ethnic relations and the domestication of manga in the United States?

In this chapter, I explore the conditions under which American manga publishing companies are established and how they go about securing the rights to material to publish. I show how relationships forged across national boundaries are structured by both opposing economic incentives and high emotion, which together undermine, over the long term, any renegotiation of relations of power between Japan and the West. Ultimately, I conclude that the growing number of transnational partnerships and the presence of subsidiary companies in the United States have the effect of redistributing material financial risk back to Japan while still providing American manga readers with ready access to the content they crave.

Founding fathers

One would be forgiven for thinking that maybe Shinsuke was directing his personal grievances at the wrong group of Americans. Surely, anyone who would bother to try to make a living by publishing Japanese comics in English would not be exceptionally racist. Unfortunately, it is best not to make assumptions. At the management level, manga companies are disproportionately white and male, and the most uncomfortable interview I ever conducted for this fieldwork was with the founder and head of a small manga publisher whose explanation for all of his troubled dealings with Japan could be understood through a lens colored by the grossest stereotypes: Why don't the Japanese honor contractual agreements like Americans do? Because they are culturally and racially homogenous! (His Asian spouse sat quietly across the table the entire time.) Another informant employed at a different company, one of the largest, was convinced that upper management was racist and made a point of volunteering a tale of deep shame and regret about a time she was forced to lay off an intern. There had been some recent thefts of computer equipment in the office, and although there was no concrete evidence against any employee, the intern, a black man, struck her boss as the obvious culprit, and he told her that either the intern was going—or she was instead. "I should have quit right then and there, but I was a coward," she lamented.

Of course, people who found and run manga companies are just people, and people are after all flawed. Perhaps, one might argue, these sorts of attitudes emerge as they would anywhere. However, I do not think the explanation is quite so simple. In fact, to be a founding father of American manga—and nearly without exception[1] all founders to date have been men— is decidedly not about a modest tolerance of difference. It requires, rather, a strong belief in one's own exceptionalness, a conviction that *he*—and not anyone else, certainly not the Japanese on their island archipelago an ocean away—knows best. I spent many an afternoon interviewing manga industry people who, like nineteenth-century armchair analysts, would nod sagely and inform me, *sotto voce*, they have long ago concluded that their boss is a complete narcissist. In any case, broadly speaking, I have identified three types of founding fathers, the Evangelist, the Opportunist, and the Specialist. Naturally, my typology is to some extent a generalization, and some founders exhibit characteristics of more than one type, but it provides a neat way of thinking about the sorts of people who want to domesticate manga and why. It also maps onto the history of the formation and expansion of the manga industry, with Evangelists in the early days, Opportunists to fuel the boom, and Specialists in the field's current mature phase. I will now discuss these three types in turn.

The Evangelist

"We were like cultural evangelists in the old days," a management-level professional for a manga publishing company which predated the manga boom

---

[1] There are three exceptions to date. Go! Comi was founded by husband and wife team David Wise and Audrey Taylor. ALC Publishing and DramaQueen were both founded by women. All three companies are, as of the end of 2011, either inactive or out of business.

confided. "Every time I wrote 'manga' for any publication I'd automatically add in parentheses, 'comics from Japan.' You never expected people to know, so you had to keep on telling them." My first type of founding father, the Evangelist, is as this industry veteran described—the person who wants to be the bearer of the good news of Japanese manga to the West. Leonard Rifas of EduComics, described at the beginning of the previous chapter, is a good example of this type, as is Seiji Horibuchi of Viz, the Japanese immigrant turned Bay Area hippie described by Jason Thompson (2007b). And of course, Stu Levy of Mixx Entertainment and Tokyopop is widely thought to be of this type as well. His formal letter of farewell read, in part:

> My dream was to build a bridge between Japan and America, through the incredible stories I discovered as a student in Tokyo. [...] Fourteen years later, I'm laying down my guns. Together, our community has fought the good fight, and, as a result, the Manga Revolution has been won—manga has become a ubiquitous part of global pop culture. I'm very proud of what we've accomplished—and the incredible group of passionate fans we've served along the way (my fellow revolutionaries!). [...] Together, we've succeeded in bringing manga to North America and beyond. (quoted in Johnson 2011)

This excerpt typifies the self-perception of the Evangelist. Manga is important to him because it had a transformative effect upon him during a critical life stage, and he believes that it will have the same effect upon other people. At his best, he is a revolutionary fighting the good fight, a builder of bridges between different cultures. He introduces a new product to the market not because he thinks it has an audience but because he believes that it *should* have an audience. An industry veteran with over a decade of experience put it this way: "Really, it came down to guys who liked comics and thought, 'Why not? Let's try releasing them in English and see if anybody likes it.' I think that was the really driving force for a very long time. They would bring over titles they personally liked and see if anybody bought them." Although sometimes the Evangelist will merely throw proverbial content to the wall to see if anything might stick, he is also committed to finding other people who will enjoy it. But since any market for the Evangelist's new content must be built painstakingly from scratch by the Evangelist himself, financially speaking publishing manga is usually a money-losing proposition. One Evangelist heading a small press even admitted nearly taking out a second mortgage to fund the English-language release of a favorite property (and only the 2008 recession led to a change of heart). Cultural production, therefore, is made to become fundamentally pedagogical in the hands of an Evangelist. The person who coined the moniker "cultural evangelist" in the previous paragraph explained: "[We were] trying to expand peoples' perceptions of what manga was. It wasn't commercially-driven. It was evangelism." In other words, people must be taught about manga in the first place before they can be remade into the Evangelist's image, into avid manga readers. Previously, I have argued that transnational cultural production is a distinct set of organizational processes and practices which link two national fields. The Evangelist takes upon himself the hardest task, the *creation* of these brand new sets of social practice across national territories. Without him, there would be no break with continuity, and he is, I would argue, needed for domestication to ever occur in the first place.

However, his is an uphill battle, and because he is not motivated primarily by money, the Evangelist is not usually a good businessman. He publishes the manga which interest him personally, not those with the best commercial prospects. At times, in fact, his eccentricities can actually interfere with the day to day execution of his chosen mission. One full-time editor described with considerable humor how her boss had insisted that the office be "feng shui-ed," and while that may have been conductive to the unimpeded circulation of natural energy through the space, it was most definitely not convenient for production workflows. Another freelancer for this same company swore up and down that they used to arrange their new publication release schedules according to astrological charts. Indeed, the longevity of manga publishers founded by an Evangelist seems ultimately to depend upon whether or not investors, parent companies, and/or other stakeholders are able to sideline the Evangelist when and if his company ever becomes commercially viable. Then they must try to keep him safely contained in "the rubber room," as one former marketing director for a medium-sized, independent press put it, and sometimes they literally move him into an office in a building in another part of town away from the rest of the company. After all, newfound success must be maintained, but the Evangelist, with his restless creativity (the less generous might call it "attention deficit"), would rather keep on investing in new, untried things instead of devoting the necessary resources to what is certain to work. The Evangelist has instead become wont to assume that success in manga publishing will bankroll his ambitions in other fields, such as video games and films. Unfortunately, he is always sorely mistaken, for the profit margin on books is very low overall; becoming overextended in other fields of cultural production is usually how independently run manga publishing companies go bust.

There is another hazard to being run by an Evangelist as well. Because the Evangelist's company was founded in order to bring knowledge of Japanese popular culture to the United States, he runs the risk of conflating any commercial success with his own personal virtue and the righteousness of his chosen cause. Evangelists sometimes build cults of personality around themselves and come to see the value of their company stemming not the quality of their product but rather from the exceptional brilliance of its founder. This, in the view of more modest industry players, is a dire mistake. It can, for one thing, damage relationships with Japanese licensors who, while amenable to a high-minded mission of cultural exchange, are far less impressed by self-aggrandizement. One industry insider, commenting on Tokyopop's announcement that it was shuttering its publishing program in the United States, saw the company's—and by extension Levy's—hubris as an important contributing factor in its downfall:

> [T]hey got too full of themselves. They really thought that the brand Tokyopop was selling their product. That was their first major mistake. They really thought it was not the books that they were not making, *that they were licensing from other people.* That stupid little Robofish or whatever the hell they called it, they really thought that that was what was selling the books—huge mistake in a variety of ways. One, massive ego that was then projected onto the people in Japan. They didn't appreciate it. [Two], massive mistake to think you can just put a logo on something to make it sell. People don't buy by imprint.

Too full of himself or not, there would be no American manga industry without Tokyopop, and there would be no domestication without the Evangelist. Only he has the passion and commitment to effect cultural transformation for its own sake, even though he may look foolish. Felipe Smith satirizes the Evangelist in *Peepo Choo*, the first serialized story manga commissioned for publication in Japan to be both written and drawn by an American.[2] At a nominally fictionalized anime convention in Chicago, the founding father of a manga company, in fact based upon Stu Levy, gets up on stage in front of a crowd of young people and, well, *testifies* for manga: "I was unhappy, lonely and utterly lost./I was at the end of my rope./Until I discovered JAPAN!/A country full of people just like me!/Nerds and geeks who love comics and cartoons!" (Smith 2010, 2: 195–196) He raises his arms up into the air; his eyes glow. The teenage audience, initially skeptical, soon becomes so touched by his oration that they burst into tears...and then they cannot run fast enough to buy, buy, buy his "Japa-Tastic" wares.

The Opportunist

Smith's portrayal of a poorly disguised Levy also proves to be a satirical portrait of the second type of founding father, the Opportunist. After his impassioned speech to the convention attendees, the character named "Sir Dog Milk" (a

---

[2]For more about Felipe Smith's creative output of original global manga, see Brienza (2013).

parody of Levy's chosen *nom de plume* DJ Milky) retreats back into the inner sanctum of his company's futuristic exhibit booth. Away from prying eyes, he tears off his geek costume to reveal a demonic villain in a well-tailored suit, greedily counting his money and celebrating the gullibility of the fans on whom he has just foisted his third-rate manga series. Now, obviously this is also exaggeration for comedic effect, and some might dismiss the Opportunist as purely a conspiracy theory cooked up by manga fans oversuspicious of corporate power. However, my research proves definitively that there is a grain of truth to be found here—and the Opportunist is entirely real.

Naturally, all founding fathers have identified an opportunity and exploited it, but this alone does not make them an Opportunist. The Opportunist, rather, is motivated solely by the notion that there is value to be extracted from publishing manga in America. He does not seek to build bridges between cultures or to achieve legitimation as a professional in this field. He certainly does not care about manga as art for its own sake. His first, second, and only reason for getting into the manga business is profit and personal financial gain; he doesn't care, in the words of someone acquainted with Opportunists, "if he's selling manga or...lamps." In exceptional cases, he is actually corrupt. As such, Opportunists proliferated during the rapid expansion of the number of manga titles being published first by Tokyopop and then by Viz in the early 2000s; this was a period of dramatic increases in revenue for manga that the Opportunist was eager to exploit.

The Opportunist comes in two varieties. The first is closest to the sort portrayed in *Peepo Choo*, the man who builds his own manga publishing house from the ground up. They are rather rare; there are better entrepreneurial bets out there, after all, than books. But they were the among first to recognize the importance of the female market for manga, and because they did not care whether or not they were publishing books which suited their own personal tastes, companies founded by Opportunists were among the first to publish shoujo and boys' love manga, two genres which have quickly come to shape the contours of the whole category. The second type of Opportunist is already at the helm of a large corporation and, seeing an opportunity, wants a piece of the manga action too. The corporation could be American or Japanese. In fact, it is probably better to think of the corporation as a collective organizational entity, and not any one individual bean counter *per se*, as the Opportunist. Random House (with Del Rey Manga), DC Comics (with CMX), and Oozora Shuppan (with Aurora Publishing) are among the most prominent examples of this variety of Opportunist. One editor hired to spearhead the short-lived manga imprint of an Opportunist conglomerate was blunt about the experience:

> [The parent company] told [their comics publishing division] that you must be the leader in every field, and one of those fields is now manga. You

must start doing manga. I did not know that when I went in; I might not have gone in if I'd known that. [The division forced to form this new imprint] didn't want to do manga; they had nothing to do with manga. I don't know whether [the boss of the division] was behind the project or not. I don't think he was particularly against it, but he didn't care about the project so much. The staff definitely didn't want to be doing it, so I had people around me who didn't want to do be doing this project.

US manga publishers founded by Opportunists have not, as a rule, survived past 2009. Their founding father's profit motive meant that they were likely not to be awash in resources or broad-based organizational support even when times were good, and once times became bad there was absolutely no reason for the company to continue. Whereas the Evangelist might see setbacks as a proverbial test of faith and soldier onward, the Opportunist merely sees a one-time opportunity fading away, victim to bad times. His company then folds abruptly and ignominiously, its employees out of a job, its licensed series unfinished, and the licensors feeling shaken, angry, and betrayed. The great majority had fallen into the red before the end; only one founding father boasted to me that he had gotten out of manga in time to take his money and run. Nevertheless, whatever his motives, the Opportunist added fuel to the fire at a critical time of expansion in the mid-2000s, thereby increasing the visibility of the manga category. Equally important, he also provided a crucial training and proving ground for the final type of founding father.

The Specialist

Specialists are the third and to date the rarest type of founding father, as they do not usually appear from "the outside," as Evangelists and Opportunists do. They are publishing industry professionals, and they have already learned the rules of the game, laboring in the lower ranks of the American manga industry. As such, the industry must have reached its mature phase to have founding father Specialists, and they are therefore unusual in large part because the field is already crowded with competitors. Nevertheless, no one understands manga better than they, and if there is a viable niche, they will find it. Yen Press' cofounders Kurt Hassler and Rich Johnson are both of this type. An interviewee working in licensing on behalf of a Japanese company describes a Specialist this way:

Whenever I see him, specific titles just pop out of his mouth, you know? [He will talk about] titles I don't even know that are doing very well in his country, like the boys' love series, which I won't even touch with a pole, and the original work that they publish. [He will] immediately link these titles to the ones we publish, which means in his head he knows that this reader who reads that series will also like some title of ours. I think that's a really great skill.

At the time, I was quite surprised by this comment. Comparing a book one might publish with other successful titles deemed somehow similar— publishing, say, *Fairy Tail* because it's a lot like the bestselling *One Piece*—is a standard publishing industry practice. When I pointed this out, my interviewee agreed but stuck to his original point: "You know," he said, "It's surprising how few people there are that are actually capable of doing it!"

Superficially, the Specialist resembles the Evangelist; he, like the Evangelist, has a personal, irrational reason for getting into the manga business. Usually he will say that he is doing it for love (a standard explanation found throughout the manga publishing field delivered like a knee-jerk reflex), although one exceptional Specialist told me that he was motivated by a quest for "revenge":

> I want to beat up the big companies [in Japan]. No, I mean it. We've been treated so poorly by those big companies just because they have the brand, they have the money, they have more resources. They really look down on us. This is almost like my revenge. I've been telling [the small Japanese publishing houses] that you're small but we're gonna beat up the big companies together. Let the people know that small can beat big.

Founding fathers were not, needless to say, normally so forthcoming in their personal sentiments. "When did the anger towards the big companies start?" I asked him, surprised.

> Oh, from day one, when I started going to Japan and try[ing] to license titles, and all the big companies said, "Who are you?" The Japanese custom is that if you don't have an introduction from another big company's president or vice-president, [they won't even look at you].

He then described a business meeting at one of the big Japanese companies. He had come with a man I will call John, the CEO of a well-respected American comics press which had been publishing selected manga titles since the 1980s and with whom this Specialist's company was planning to co-publish manga:

> They looked at John first, of course. "Here's [So-and-So from Some Such Small Manga Publisher] and we're working very closely together." "[Some Such Small Manga Publisher]?! Who are you?!" That kind of look. I could tell. And then later red carpet for [John], and they always looked at [John]

when they talked and completely disregarded me. That really pissed me off. [John] is a white American, and I'm a typical Japanese—those Japanese are *stupid*! They look down on their own people and look up to all the Americans. I've gone through those situations so many times, so I said, "Someday, I'm gonna kill you." You know? My motivation is twofold. One, making money, of course. And the second, revenge.

He concluded his story emphatically: "You can write that. I hated those big companies because they have no respect towards their publishers in America. None. *None.* I hated it." This Specialist's account is an intriguing, evocative counterpoint to the feelings of cross-cultural victimization I found within the self-same big Japanese publishing house, and this is a conflict to which I will return. But for now I note that this Specialist's vendetta means in practice that he is focused upon generating a better publishing business model than all of his competitors. He must, in other words, out-professionalize the professionals. Generally speaking, however, the difference is most clearly evident not through the Specialist's account of himself but rather how he is perceived by others. Those who have worked in manga publishing can immediately recognize a Specialist. There is, according to one small press's editor, a distinctive "smell" about them; they are the sort of people, according to a marketing specialist, "who have never done anything else with their lives." In short, they have, using the language of Bourdieu's social theory, habitus. The Specialist's strength, then, is the *maintenance* of these new social practices of domestication.

Through this description of the three types of founding fathers, the internally determined conditions for success in the manga industry become clear. Commitment to the medium is important but not in and of itself sufficient. To succeed, a prospective manga publisher must know how to make and sell books, and in many cases a well-organized, professionalized division of labor is preferable to an inexperienced but driven amateur. Yet, even companies with a very top-down management structure must be led by someone with an abiding, deeply felt reason—whether it be a love for the medium or a quest for revenge—for wanting to make those books sell. Books do not, after all, sell themselves, and getting them onto the market requires a lot of effort and intelligently allocated resources. Since there are much faster ways of getting rich quickly, neither the passion of the Evangelist nor the greed of the Opportunist are enough to keep a manga publishing house going. The Specialist's commitment to the work itself is also necessary. The Japanese licensor quoted at the beginning of this section summarizes his views on the three types of founding fathers thusly:

If there's one person who really knows manga, has a love for the product, has the authority to do what he wants to do, and if the company's financially stable, we don't have to think to complain. The worst case scenario, I think, is when the company has no interest in manga but they just want to do it because they think it should be a part of their portfolio, or they think it could sell. And when you go to book fairs, like Frankfurt Book Fair, and you meet a lot of publishers from many countries—you know, you don't have to be a brain surgeon to tell that a person is just out to make money. I meet a lot of those people, who just come to our booth and say, "Hey, can you show us a good series? We're a very big media conglomerate from wherever, and we want to do manga! So, uhh, what is the difference between anime and manga?" We have to start from there. But when the guy is good, you can tell immediately that he knows the difference between anime and manga, that he actually reads the stuff, and that he actually cares for the quality. See, the otaku just stops there; he just wants to do what he likes. But what we seek in a licensee is a person who actually sees joy in selling these things.

Although he obviously prefers Specialists above all other options, this is not to imply that the interests of an American manga publishing company, even one run by a Specialist, and the interests of stakeholders in Japan are perfectly aligned. Quite the contrary, in fact. Yet, while it's easy to see why Japanese companies might not be interested in the Evangelist's proselytizing and incipient narcissism, why would there be any material conflict with the Specialist or even the Opportunist, for whom selling manga is of paramount importance? In the next section, I explore how the rights to publish manga abroad are secured and why the process of licensing titles for English-language publication pits Japanese and US publishers against each other.

How licensing works

Although my informant quoted above talks about attending international book publishing industry events, such as the Frankfurt Book Fair, the American manga industry's participation in such events is a relatively new phenomenon, and book fairs remain at best a marginal part of the deliberation and negotiations about what to buy or sell that are otherwise happening all throughout the year. Even though the process of securing the rights to publish manga in other countries is not geographically situated in any one country, as befitting a transnational field, the procedure is guided by its own provisional, make-do sets of often-unspoken rules and tacit guidelines. In fact, rights contracts in and of themselves between Japanese and American publishers can reveal only so much about the way manga licensing works. At its most extreme, a contract may be no more than a polite fiction. Although the explicitly defined contours of negotiations are important, even more important are all of those features of manga publishing rights deals that are never put to paper. To truly understand what is going on, serious attention must be paid to the relationships between actors in the field and conditions upon which those relationships are built.

A brief history

In Japan, manga creators ordinarily retain the rights to the works they produce. It is the same state of affairs as in American trade book publishing but differs from the American comics industry, where publishers, not writers or artists, retain all intellectual property rights. Thus, while DC owns the character of Batman as well as the copyright to all *Batman* comics, even those penned by luminaries like Frank Miller, Naoko Takeuchi, not Kodansha, her publisher, owns the character of Sailor Moon and the copyright to the *Sailor Moon* manga. It should come as no surprise, then, that the process by which the contractual rights to publish manga in other countries is secured has, over time, come to take its cues from the practices of Western trade book publishing.

Although there are particular manga artists who deal with overseas publishers directly, they are relatively rare and tend to be either at the top or at the extreme margins of their chosen profession. Thus, the all-female quartet known as CLAMP has its own management company and does not deal with licensing in the usual manner. Self-published creators such as Rica Takashima also typically represent themselves, and of course any company publishing a particular artist with whom it is personally connected is likely to be another exception to the rule. For the most part, however, licensing deals between American presses and Japanese artists are handled by an intermediary who splits any licensing revenue with the artist. This intermediary may be one of two parties: (1) an international rights department or division of the artist's Japanese publisher or (2) another third-party company like a literary agency. Whether literary agency or international rights division of a large publishing house, however, intermediaries see themselves as representing and defending the best interests of the artists. "At the end of the day, I think, who's really important for me? The readers abroad or the artist? At the end of the day, what we have to do as licensor is stand up for the artist—that's our job," said one licensing intermediary.

There are two third-party companies handling manga licensing to the United States, Tuttle-Mori and Tohan. Both are based in Tokyo, Japan. Tohan is primarily a distribution company selling books and other media to retail stores in Japan and abroad with a licensing agency business on the side. The Tuttle-Mori Agency is a literary agency specializing international rights management between Japan and other countries. It is the oldest and biggest literary agency in Japan and traces its roots back to a department for literary agents founded in 1948 within the Vermont-based publishing house Charles E. Tuttle and Company (now Tuttle Publishing). It became an independent company in 1978 and has been handling manga licensing since 1992. Tuttle-Mori is currently the most important player of this sort in the manga business; many manga publishers have licensed titles through Tuttle-Mori over the years, including Yen Press, Tokyopop, Go! Comi, and even Viz.

Japan's three largest publishing houses, Kodansha, Shueisha, and Shogakukan, prefer to handle licensing on behalf of their artists themselves. Shinsuke, whom I introduced at the beginning of this chapter, is employed in such a role for one of these companies. However, the formalization of licensing activities is relatively new and only happened once it became clear to these publishers that the manga that they were producing for Japanese audiences had global appeal. They then took their professional cues from literary agencies like Tuttle-Mori; in fact, the Tuttle-Mori office is located just down the street from both Shueisha and Shogakukan. One veteran literary agent tells this story about the first time she—or her employer—had ever been asked to handle manga:

In 1991, November, there were faxes coming in from Barcelona asking for the rights to [a popular shounen manga series]. So I had to answer those faxes. We didn't think that there would be a market for manga outside of Japan—it was still '91, '92. [Those faxes] became a manga division, and now it's 20 percent of the agency after 20 years and a department of six people full time.

She also then outlined in detail the dramatic changes she had seen in her field over the years:

In the beginning there were no rights divisions in the Japanese publishers. So I'd just call the editor, and whoever was very unlucky that day took my call. And you can tell! You can tell, can't you? You've hit on the unlucky person, and you just have to try to explain. As all these offers began to pile up, then there would be a first contact. They just found this person who didn't have anything to do, and so they appointed this person to handle the rights. So my first contacts were very unhappy people because they didn't know why they were asked to look after these foreign rights. They had a kind of history in their company and were very unhappy to have been asked to deal with this. But then this unhappy lot grew happier because they started to make a lot of business and gained internal recognition. Some of these people got President's Awards in the company because, you know, the growth rate is really rapid if you start from zero! So all these unhappy people, they turned out to be very happy people.

You have no people in the beginning, just editors who are totally annoyed. Then you have your first person, unhappy, but then the person turns happy and then you start to get more people. And then the fourth stage is that you have a rights division, and it's called an "International Rights Division." Then they have computers and software made to get this all calculated. That's one, two, three, four, five stages, and then you have a really nice department. And also the *right* people, from manga editorial, the brightest people. After 20 years, you can get answers very quickly.

This informant was furthermore particularly keen to point out the following, for the record:

All of those faxes coming in from Barcelona actually symbolize how no one went out from Japan to sell [manga]. Period. No matter what the [journalistic] press says today—we have such and such a market abroad—when it gets reported it sounds like, you know, hey, we went out to get all this market share, etc. But if you had been there...I still make a point of making this clear to people that there wasn't a market. No Japanese publishers went out to find a market. So it was all very passive.

The early history of licensing manga is, in short, one of foreign interests actively seeking out less-than-receptive Japanese rights holders. Japanese publishers were reactive, not proactive; while some may today have their own agendas for international manga publishing, this odd history reverberates through the ways in which licensing deals do—and do not—go down.

Choosing licenses

There is no one way of deciding what to license. Many prospective licensees start off in the simplest of terms, securing the rights to titles that they themselves enjoy. This was certainly true in the early years of Viz and their selection of classic titles such as *Mai the Psychic Girl* and *The Legend of Kamui*, and editorial taste continues to have an influence over what gets published even at large, corporate-owned companies. Since in many cases, the favorites are not the titles most likely to become bestsellers, presses will attempt to balance their list with manga which are not necessarily popular in-house but are likely to pay the bills, along with manga likely to lose money but deemed to have artistic merit. Associate Publisher Dallas Middaugh, addressing a crowd of fans at a convention, said that Del Rey Manga published the award-winning *Mushishi* not for its commercial potential but rather for "the readers of the future."

In other cases, a publisher may have a special relationship with a particular artist or sets of artists. This is particularly common when companies are just starting out, but it can remain an important factor for the success even of mature companies. Examples of this include Fantagraphics' publication of Moto Hagio's *A Drifting Dream* and Takako Shimura's *Wandering Son*, through their connection to former Kyoto Seika professor and professional translator Matt Thorn, Go Comi's publication of Higuri You, Dark Horse's reprints of CLAMP's backlist, and CPM Manga's publication of several of Tomoko Taniguchi's shoujo manga titles. Many of the manga published by Gutsoon were penned by parent company Coamix founders Tetsuo Hara and Tsukasa Hojo. These relationships may even allow companies to publish titles that they would not have been able to otherwise. One VP of a small independent press told me how a much larger house had wanted a particular vintage manga series because they knew it was to be made into a new live-action film in Japan. The VP, who had cultivated a good relationship with the deceased manga creator's estate, was immediately offered the rights to the title that the other company had wanted. That other company may have had the bigger reputation as a publisher and been better capitalized, but to the creator's estate, they were an unknown commodity, and therefore the small indie press got the rights to the property.

Personal preferences and relationships, however, go only so far. Manga publishers also research new potential licenses. This research may be as simple as heading to the nearest Japanese bookstore and checking out what is on the shelves. The editor of a press that was just starting out in an already crowded field reported doing just that. After explaining how they had decided upon a Japanese publisher to work with, he reported that they all "went to Kinokuniya, bought whatever [of that publisher's] books looked good, [and] checked out their magazines to see what was still running." Others may page through the latest issues of Japanese manga magazine anthologies to see if there is anything that they like. Many established presses, in fact, receive regular shipments of these magazines from Japanese publishers with whom they have worked in the past and amass considerable in-house reference libraries. Wise licensees have learned the hard way to wait and see how a title of interest evolves over time; after all, a promising storyline might peter out quickly, or a safely teen-oriented title might suddenly become decidedly adults-only. However, it may also be unwise to wait too long; many believe, as a general rule, that books older than about a decade or so, all other things being equal, do not sell well because the art looks dated. While there are numerous counterfactuals to this common wisdom, the prejudice against "vintage" manga remains entrenched, and sometimes the Japanese deflect interest in older properties, assuming that surely anything new must be better. Moreover, many publishers seem to welcome suggestions from all ranks—in one company even interns were allowed to prepare proposals. Some may also go to fan conventions in order to soak up the buzz; a press that wanted to get into boys' love, for example, but knew nothing about what was hot went to the BL-focused Yaoicon and collected lists of popular titles from attendees. Many also watch bestseller lists coming out of Japan for potential licenses, for although there is no guarantee that what sells in Japan will also sell in the United States, it is a good place to start. Properties with media tie-ins such as animated adaptations and video games are especially sought-after for the additional free publicity.

Plenty of research is also conducted online. Editors will, for example, hang out on online discussion forums to see what sorts of titles fans are talking about. The editor quoted in the previous paragraph also reported "look[ing] online to see if there was any discussion about the titles [and trying] to find out more about the creators." Some will solicit license requests on social media platforms such as Facebook and Twitter. Also, because many manga industry people cannot read Japanese, "research" in many cases is actually a euphemism for reading illegal scanlations, fan translations of manga published online.[3] It is a practice that is ubiquitous throughout the industry, from the smallest of start-ups to the oldest and largest of established houses. One editor who has worked for multiple companies remarked to me that the dependence upon scanlations to research new material is in fact greater at his current new employer than his old one because a smaller proportion of the company's employees are bilingual. In fact, some publishers will even go so far as to systematically data mine highly trafficked fan sites, including sites that aggregate information about scanlations such as Baka Updates. An editorial intern for one independent company who did just that explains the process thusly:

[In addition to copyediting], I also did some [research] in terms of going to certain manga sites, not really scanlation sites, but going through the lists that Baka Updates has and seeing how much people looked at these titles, were they scanlated, how many people read the scanlations, if they had any other media tie-ins, how old they were, if they were by artists who had previously been released, things like that. I was literally going through their rankings. I think for that particular research assignment, I was

---

[3]The word "scanlation," a portmanteau of "scan" and "translation," refers to the practice of domesticating manga for free digital distribution without having the legal right to do so. The people who make scanlations are known as "scanlators," and the verb for what they do is "to scanlate." The techniques used for producing scanlations, such as translation and lettering, are the same as those used for producing licensed manga. But instead of printing and binding finished pages, pages are simply kept as image files bundled by chapter or volume and distributed to readers via IRC, BitTorrent, and so on. Various sites index and aggregate large numbers of scanlated works. Due to their particular skill set, many people now working in the industry, as high up as vice-president in the case of one company, were themselves former scanlators. In spite of that, from the publishing industry's perspective, scanlations are blatant digital piracy, and since the economic downturn of 2008, views on scanlations have hardened considerably.

given instructions to go through the shoujo manga list starting from the top ranking. Obviously, I couldn't touch Kodansha, Shueisha, or Shogakukan titles, and I wouldn't do anything before a certain date. I think the cutoff was 1995 because, you know, they say that people won't buy stuff because it looks too old. So I went through the list, put down the various numbers that they wanted, and then my opinions—does this kind of thing look good? Is it a possibility? I don't know how they ever used that research, but I did it for them.

The general consensus from informants across multiple companies was that a title with a frequently downloaded scanlation may or may not be a prospect; the way to tell if it would sell or not in print was if there also seemed to be a lot of fan activity around the property, that is, discussion, fanfiction, cosplay, and so on. The impact of scanlations upon licensing and print sales is an issue to which I will return in greater detail in Chapter 6.

It should never be assumed, though, that any particular manga is available in English because someone believed in it and "chose" it. Manga rights holders are not merely standing attentively at the gate, deciding which bids for their intellectual property shall and shall not pass. Japanese companies also attempt to push particular titles onto American publishers, and on occasion they push quite hard. Some have been known to actively shop their catalog around, looking to form an exclusive partnership with a US company. Others will hold desirable licenses hostage, demanding that licensees also buy the rights to additional titles in order to get the one they really want. When required to purchase multiple licenses as part of a single deal, this is colloquially called "bundling." Other stipulations are more arcane: One author would not allow a company to publish his more recent works until they had completed an earlier series; another licensor would not allow a small press to publish a minor, single volume work of a famous author unless they also licensed his ongoing, 20+ volume magnum opus. There are many cases where books—along with entire new imprints—get published purely in order to appease a parent company or to otherwise cement a relationship with a Japanese company.

Such pressure can be good or bad. Within the American manga industry, it is, however, generally assumed to be negative. Several informants at other companies suggested, for example, that Del Rey Manga clearly did not have complete autonomy over the selection of titles in its catalog because they were well acquainted with the person there in charge of acquisitions, and they were sure she had much better judgment of taste than to want to publish, say, Shiki Tsukai. The implication, of course, is that Del Rey Manga knew full well that they were not publishing the best books possible. But in other cases, companies, particularly of the Opportunist sort, simply do not know any better than to take whatever deal is on offer. Or perhaps they just do not care. One informant remarked about a former employer's poor selection of licenses and explained why vintage titles are such a bad idea:

> Frankly, I think they picked some stuff that the Japanese couldn't pawn off onto anybody else. They said, "Hey, let's see if we can sell this stuff to these moron foreigners!" Some of the titles that they picked were twenty years old and in old styles that had *never* been popular in the United States. If there was any logic to it, I don't know what it was. What's the point of picking old stuff? It only has nostalgia value to people who read it twenty years ago.

In other instances, though, taking the advice of a Japanese publisher trying to push particular manga titles and genres has been profitable. The founding father of an independent press told me the following story:

> One day when I went to Tokyo to license manga titles, one publisher, the president, told me about yaoi. I didn't know anything about yaoi or boys' love, so he explained to me what it is. I wasn't sure about the genre—It's homosexual love!—but he was really strongly suggesting that I take it to America. He was an old man, like sixty-five, and he was talking about yaoi! It was kinda funny. Anyway, I came home with a bunch of the yaoi titles without knowing for sure if this genre would make the business here. But we published the first title... and it took off, like, *bang*! I think we sold 15,000 units in a couple of months. This had never ever happened in manga publishing. And we didn't even promote this title 'cause I wasn't sure!

Since he came back from Tokyo with "a bunch of yaoi titles" a decade ago, the boys' love genre has become a permanent part of the US manga publishing landscape. It quickly became an important moneymaker for small presses and has continued to help keep them afloat in hard times. Even corporate-owned imprints such as Yen Press and market leader Viz, which for most of its history shied away from this homoerotic, often quite sexually explicit genre (despite being located in San Francisco, one of the world capitals for LGBT community pride), have gotten into boys' love.

Making the deal

As described in detail previously, the history of licensing manga is, in its moment of genesis, one of Western publishers using Western-style literary agencies to make the initial overtures to their Japanese counterparts. Therefore, because the Japanese had no other experience or alternative sets of practice to go by, the financial aspects of deals typically accord with Western expectations. The importance of relationships between licensor and licensee, however, cannot be overstated, and rights contracts are most correctly viewed as being the beginning of an ongoing series of negotiations, not the final word.

The most important part of licensing is the advance, part of the total licensing fee. Also called a minimum guarantee, this is a sum of money paid to the rights holder upfront to secure permission to publish, calculated as a percentage of the gross revenue of a set number of books. A normal minimum guarantee might be 8 percent of the listed retail price for 40 percent of the first print run. For a midlist title this may be around 2,000–3,000 copies, so if the manga is priced at $10.99, then the advance is approximately 88 cents per copy, or $1,760–2,638. Coming up with actual numbers is more art than science since no one can ever be absolutely certain how many copies any book will sell, and there are many variables which may be tweaked, though naturally books perceived to have better prospects can command higher fees. The main challenge is to strike a balance; too much optimism about how well a book performs will literally cost a licensee, while one that is too low is insulting and may raise questions about a petitioner's motivations and sincerity.

In rare cases when multiple publishers are competing for the rights to the same title, they will often do so by bidding up the minimum guarantee and arguing that they, and not a competitor, are better positioned to sell more copies. Perhaps they have more name recognition and better distribution networks, or perhaps they are especially well known for publishing manga similar to what they are bidding on. Additionally, because many manga are part of a transmedia trinity which also includes light novels and anime, larger companies which are not solely manga publishers might also promise synergy with other media. To give one example, both the manga publishing arm of the North American distributor of the property's anime and the manga imprint of a multinational publishing conglomerate wanted the English-language rights to a particular fan-favorite manga series. Ultimately, the manga imprint of the multinational publishing conglomerate won the license because they were also willing to publish the novels in English translation. The novels were, in the view of the Japanese, the most important part of the franchise.

Numerous other aspects of the relationship between licensor and licensee are also negotiated at this time. Of course, the specifics vary from title to title, and from publisher to publisher, but some themes are common. Rights are typically granted for a set number of years, usually a decade, and American publishers, who are producing titles in the de facto global language, may or may not obtain rights to publish outside of the United States and Canada, though global English-language rights is increasingly becoming standard. Presses may also be obliged to keep books in print for the duration of the license, or they may automatically lose it if they let them go out of print. Furthermore, licensors typically want their licensees to immediately commit to the publication of an entire series, perhaps paying advances for a few volumes at a time in installments. But because manga series can be a dozen volumes long or more— and may run indefinitely—and total sales from one volume to the next always drop, this can be a tremendous financial burden upon licensees. With the global economic downturn, some licensors have become more lenient with this requirement, allowing companies to obtain the rights of a few volumes at a time, with deals for more volumes subject to the performance of what has already been published. The wine manga *Drops of God*, published by Vertical, is a notable example.

Restrictions upon production and marketing are often a part of the agreement as well and can be quite onerous. These may be written explicitly into licensing contracts, but they are often enforced through Japanese-style tacit relations between different actors in the field. It is standard, for example, for manga artists to be granted the right to approve or refuse cover designs. Being artists, some demand to be allowed to design their own covers; an example of this is the US edition of *Moyashimon*, with the creator Masayuki Ishikawa felt ought to have an American flag motif...in spite of being about microbiology students at a Japanese agricultural university (see Figure 4.1). Some licensors even

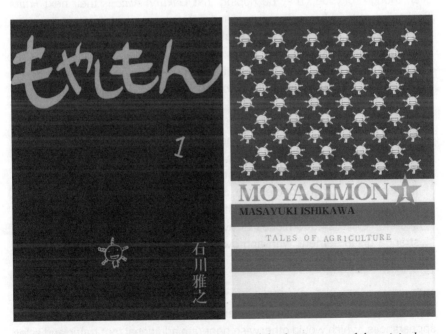

FIGURE 4.1 *A side-by-side comparison of the front covers of the original Kodansha edition of Moyasimon Vol. 1 (left) and the Del Rey Manga edition of the same book (right). The American flag on the US edition is meant to signify the country in which it is being sold and has nothing to do with the plot. The stars on the flag have been replaced with cartoon germs.*

reserve the right to approve interior pages and text. Failure to pass approvals can lead to costly delays—or in extreme cases—the outright cancellation of a project. This actually happened with at least one frontlist title; the original Japanese publisher's employee, supposedly representing the best interests of the artist, kept sending their translations back. "He thinks he knows English better than we do," confided one angry employee. There are also restrictions upon the sorts of marketing and promotional materials companies produce to advertise their wares. Common constraints include not being allowed to use interior art or to put novel words into characters' mouths. Viz cannot, for example, put the title character of the *Naruto* manga on a web banner with a speech balloon telling people to "Buy *Shonen Jump* Manga!" It is likewise common for some companies not to want art from their books remixed with art from another company's books in brochures, catalogs, tip sheets, merchandise, and so on—they may be bitter rivals back in Japan, after all. Another popular form of direct advertising in American manga publishing is to put several pages of ads for similar titles at the back of books; however, some artists have personal disagreements or vendettas against each other and may not allow the advertisements for an enemy's books to go into their own. So even though Tokyopop may be hoping that *Gakuen Alice* is their next *Fruits Basket*-like shoujo bestseller, they cannot promote it in the latest volumes of *Fruits Basket* because Natsuki Takaya does not like Tachibana Higuchi. Licensors may even have final approval over any ancillary merchandise a US company may produce to promote a particular property. A marketing intern for one of the largest manga publishers told this story:

> We had [an item] printed for [San Diego Comic Con], and the printer printed it messily. All the images were there, but it was gray on black, and the copyright could be legible but not clear. We were told to discontinue all 24,000 [items] and not use them at Comic Con because you couldn't read the label and it disrespected the original art. So we had nothing to give away, and in the end…we used them! It's not exactly an easy-to-keep secret; it's like 24,000 pieces of evidence floating around. It was a really strange disagreement with approvals that ended up getting solved with subterfuge.

Other forms of publicity popular in the trade publishing industry may be out of the question as well. Live events, such as book signings and author appearances, which would otherwise generate additional foot traffic and sales in stores as well as free press buzz for a title and a company, can be virtually impossible to arrange. In fact, companies that have been in the manga business for a long time have learned not to even bother trying; a person responsible for cultivating media industry contacts for a company which organizes fan conventions and would like help sponsoring Japanese guests described his frustration with them: "Oh, but that would take two years to arrange," they say and put him off. He persists and replies, "Okay, it's an annual convention; let's start now." Yet they just continue to dither. When I asked him where this lack of energy is coming from, he did not seem to know. But the problem, in fact, lies in the difficulty for anyone to get past an artist's intermediaries in Japan. One of these licensing intermediaries explains:

> We get a lot of requests from abroad to bring our artists to events. Let's say that a certain artist is drawing for a weekly magazine, drawing twenty pages every week. That's a lot of work, right? Sometimes we don't even really need to even ask if the person can go abroad. We have 1.5 million readers waiting out there in Japan. There's more damage that can be done by giving them a vacation to the US or wherever. To go out of the country takes at least a week of time off from work.

In other words, they do not even bother allowing artists to decide for themselves whether or not to appear at such an event, although it is possible that artists may learn about the invitation afterward from their editors.[4] Those few artists who do make appearances in the United States must be particularly self-motivated and tend not to be serialized in the most pressure-intensive weekly magazines. Otherwise, they will have to work ahead of their usual weekly deadlines to make room for a holiday, and with the manga industry's tight publishing schedules this can be very difficult. In many cases, a book signing in the United States is a last-minute opportunity which falls into the proverbial laps of manga publishers, leaving them unable to exploit the best venues, such as the San Diego and New York Comic Cons, or even most chain bookstores, which expect events to have been planned well in advance.

Interestingly, being the subsidiary of a Japanese parent company does not necessarily guarantee better—and more lenient—treatment: "We treat our subsidiary like any other licensee," asserted one informant working in licensing for a publisher in Japan. "I would say there's no favoritism." Some subsidiaries even pay advances for the manga their own parent companies publish. During my fieldwork, I encountered widespread resentment and frustration expressed by employees of manga publishers working closely with the largest Japanese companies. They felt that they were being held to a

---

[4]Typically, the intermediary explained, they would mention any invitation to the artist's editor after the fact: "Well, we got this type of offer from abroad, and we know you're very busy, but just to let you know. In case the artist finds out later. The artist probably knows he can't go anyway, but...." The exceptional authority of Japanese manga editors over every aspect of their working artists' lives is described in detail by Kinsella (2000) and Prough (2011).

higher standard by companies which, on the balance, were more demanding than mid-sized or small Japanese publishers already. Independent American publishers were far less likely to report being required to get all interior pages approved by the licensor than were US-based subsidiaries of Japanese companies, for example. One editor who had come to manga publishing with extensive experience in children's trade publishing told me that she could not believe that subsidiaries are required to pay their parent companies advances and wondered why they were not just allowed to take on any projects they wanted. In all fairness, a large part of the reason that parent companies require advances from their wholly owned subsidiaries is because they are not, as explained earlier, the exclusive rights holders to the work that they publish. They are essentially representing their artists like a literary agency and taking a cut of the artist's take.

So why aren't these intermediaries who claim to be on the side of the artists being more accommodating to American publishers? After all, they aren't protecting artists and the integrity of their creative visions for purely altruistic reasons; at the end of the day it's also about cold, hard cash for themselves. What, then, drives the many restrictions on marketing and promotions? If the US manga field makes more money, surely the Japanese stand to benefit as well? The reason for this behavior is simple: Licensors make the majority of their money upfront once the ink on the contract dries; one publishing executive told me that no more than 10–20 percent of their titles ever earned out their initial advances and began generating additional royalty payments. Furthermore, all licensing deals all around the world together account for only about 15 percent of Japanese manga publishing's annual revenues. There is little material reason, then, to go out of their way to make it easier for an American publisher to sell more books, since the payoff is really only ever going to be tiny. Besides, as the literary agency veteran explained, they never wanted the relationship in the first place. Thus, they have no motivation *not* to be, as Shinsuke put it, "nasty," taking out longstanding ethnic and national grievances on their supposed publishing partners. Why bother reining in the Japanese autocrat in charge of approvals who has been gumming up the domestication works by insisting, say, that the particle も [mo] should be translated as "too" and not "as well"? Conversely, they certainly have every motivation to focus on getting the biggest bang for their proverbial buck at home by preventing their artists from taking overseas vacations and missing deadlines. And they are likewise free to protect some ideal of creative integrity and make sure that Naruto is not telling fans to buy Viz. Licensees, meanwhile, only make their money after they have invested in producing a finished product and the books have started to sell. The stakes are much higher for them, yet their ability to promote the manga can be severely curtailed. Whenever I have asked, people in publishing will say that they actually have quite a lot of power to make books sell. For manga publishers, though, a good measure of this power has been taken away.

No wonder, then, that I encountered such deep feelings of cross-cultural resentment and victimization on both sides as I delved into the details of these often adversarial business relationships. A significant amount of what is actually going on in the American manga industry has nothing to do with the bloodless legalese of literary contracts; any one interaction may well be guided by the irrationality of high emotion. So, American publishers, who have licensors "telling them what to do," bluster, complain, vow "revenge," and engage in acts of "subterfuge." Japanese publishers, historically both reactive and "passive" in dealings with foreigners, go to great lengths to defend the text and react to any bad behavior by conflating it with their own subordinated racial and national position and taking it as opportunity to enact their own passive-aggressive forms of resistance. This is a world away from the Evangelist's dream of building bridges between East and West, yet it is in fact the outcome of manga licensing practices.

Clearly, these licensing deals are unbalanced relationships with licensors holding all of the best cards. Everyone knows this all too well, naturally, and some in US manga publishing have refused to compromise. I interviewed one head of a company who claimed that he was always adamant in his negotiations with the Japanese that he be given exclusive right to determine what a book looked like and how it was promoted. He reenacted his negotiating strategy for me: "Do you know the American market? No, I didn't think so. If you did, you wouldn't need me. Therefore, you are going to leave all of the decisions to me." He believed that those who did not do the same were gluttons for punishment and had only themselves to blame. However, I am not convinced that the situation is always as clear cut as he made it out to be; in many (if not most) cases, the choice may in fact be to accept these restrictions upon one's own actions as the necessary cost of doing business. To do otherwise would be to foment a breakdown of good relations—resulting in not being allowed to domesticate manga at all.

Alternative licensing experiments and arrangements

Given these problems, why aren't different methods of licensing manga being attempted? Actually, they are. One common strategy on the margins of the business is co-publishing, where an American company will produce a book as usual but credit the original Japanese publisher by including its logo on the spine of the book and possibly even the company president's name in the colophon. Yen Press and DMP, for example, have co-published selected titles with the likes of Kadokawa Shoten, Shinshokan, Taiyo Tosho, and Oakla Shuppan. Co-publication provides additional publicity for the Japanese publishers' brands, and in exchange American publishers negotiate a better deal for themselves, such as elimination of the minimum guarantee. This means that there is less financial risk upfront, but it is only a compelling deal for authors and presses whose work would be expected, at best, to perform modestly well on the American market but would not otherwise be worth publishing. The carrot being offered to the creator is the prestige of being published in English in the United States, which many Japanese would consider a tremendous professional achievement. Co-publications thus tend to be midlist or niche genre titles.

The Digital Manga umbrella company, which includes DMP, has, in fact, expanded upon this co-publication model with the Digital Manga Guild. DMG, as it is typically known, publishes manga from selected small publishers with whom it has partnered in e-book format, and no one in the value chain— including original creator, licensee, licensing intermediary, and everyone involved with translation, editorial, and graphic design—receives any financial compensation until the finished books begin to sell. DMG books are, like co-published books in general, niche titles, and the only way this model of licensing manga stands to be profitable is by selling small numbers of a very, very large inventory of books. Needless to say, the party which stands to benefit the most financially from such an arrangement is Digital Manga itself. All others can expect to receive a fraction of the money they would have received under a normal licensing and publishing arrangement. Indeed, because the artists of niche titles make a modest living at best, they are the ones who benefit most from the status quo system of advances. Therefore, any co-publication or revenue-sharing model in fact favors American licensees over rights holders even more so than would seem evident at first glance. Likewise, flooding the market with titles which required little investment upfront to produce is likely in the long run to hurt everybody's profits...except the company which opened the gates in the first place. Digital Manga's gambit, along with three other new publishing models, is discussed in greater detail in Chapter 6.

As noted above, US-based subsidiaries of Japanese companies do in fact pay license fees to their corporate parents. This does, however, function to keep as much of that money as possible within the proverbial corporate family, and thus working with a subsidiary as opposed to an entirely different company may also be understood at some level as a different licensing model. In July 2008, the Japanese publisher Kodansha announced that it planned to form a subsidiary based in New York City that would publish its own English-translated manga. Some of the recent bestselling manga in the United States, such as *Sailor Moon*, *Chobits*, *GTO*, *Peach Girl*, *Tsubasa*, and *Negima!*, to name just a few, had been Kodansha properties, and this way they could, at least in theory, cut out the middleman and rake in a higher percentage of the profits. This would effectively remove Del Rey Manga, Random House's US manga imprint, which had a previously arranged exclusive licensing agreement with Kodansha, from the domestication chain. Of course, journalists and online bloggers were eager to get Del Rey Manga's side of the story, and they had their chance that September at the company's panel at the 2008 New York Anime Festival. Del Rey Manga's employees were not, needless to say, particularly forthcoming and kept up an obstinately positive face, even though the common wisdom circulating among the rest of the manga publishing industry was that they must be "scared shitless" that unemployment might be looming in their collective near futures. Nevertheless, one comment on the panel about the "Kodansha situation" from the company's Marketing Manager Ali T. Kokmen struck me as particularly telling: "If there's one thing I've discovered, well, it's that this world has a steep learning curve," he mused philosophically. "And at some point, you've either climbed it or you go tumbling off of it."

"This world," of course, refers to manga publishing in the United States, and Kokmen was of the opinion that no one, not even powerful Japanese publishing conglomerates, would be exempt from learning—and playing by—its rules. The underlying implication of his words was that he considered it likely that Kodansha does not understand the logic of the transnational field of American manga publishing, and that if they do not, their overseas corporate venture would founder, and other US publishers, if not Del Rey Manga itself, with its head start on the slope of that learning curve, would emerge unscathed. After all, other subsidiaries of Japanese companies such as Gutsoon (Coamix) and Aurora Publishing (Oozora Shuppan) have not succeeded. Only Viz has survived the long haul, and it is supported by two of the Big Three. His prediction proved prescient, and Kodansha USA did not become active until October 2009, over a year later than planned. They had indeed run into problems, among them that they did not understand how trade books like manga are distributed,[5] and when they did finally land a distributor, it was, yes, Random House. The first two titles announced by Kodansha USA,

---

[5]As mentioned in a previous chapter, Kodansha does actually have a long history of English-language book publishing, the longest of any Japanese publisher, in fact. Its international subsidiary specialized primarily in dictionaries and other reference books as well as a small selection of literary fiction and serious nonfiction. These books were distributed in the United States by Oxford University Press, which, while a reputable distributor, is clearly not the obvious market leader in the distribution of manga or trade books. In fact, key Japanese prose fiction authors Haruki Murakami and Natsuo Kirino, after defecting from Kodansha America to Random House, subsequently became bestselling authors in the United States. Kodansha permanently shuttered all of its older English-language book publishing divisions, including Kodansha America,

Akira by Katsuhiro Otomo and *Ghost in the Shell* by Shirow Masamune, were previously published in the US by Dark Horse but had gone out of print, and these new editions are straight reprints of the Dark Horse books. New titles were not published until 2011, and they ended up outsourcing this labor to an all-American team, provided by Random House Publishing Services. Dallas Middaugh, once Associate Publisher of Del Rey Manga, remains employed by Random House but now heads editorial for Kodansha Comics. Although the logo on the covers of the books has changed, substantively nothing else had, not even the fonts in the text balloons, the formatting of the copyright page, or other paratextual materials. Cutting out the middleman was not nearly as easy as Kodansha's executives might have imagined from afar.

So, what does the renegotiation of the relationship between Random House and Kodansha really mean? Clearly, Kodansha has not eliminated the American organizational structures and processes which are necessary for the domestication of manga. Is the company somehow taking back control of its properties by publishing them themselves? Well, certainly, Kodansha's branded logo no longer has to share cover space with Del Rey Manga's. Yet, the format and "look" of the books is still very much a legacy of the American publisher, so there is not much difference there. Perhaps the titles being chosen for English-language publication are different? Well, inasmuch as Del Rey Manga ever had sole autonomy in deciding what to publish (which, industry insiders with other companies assure me, was never), there is not yet much difference in the teenage core target audience. The casual reader is unlikely to notice much beyond the new logo. In fact, it would be more apt to think of this not as Kodansha taking back control but rather of Kodansha being compelled by its international ambitions to assume more of the upfront financial risk. One informant with experience in marketing and publicity was blunt: "It will make them a better company," he said. When I asked him to clarify what he meant by "better," he continued, "It'll make them a better company because now they'll understand how much it *really* costs to publish manga here."

The *schadenfreude* in that informant's tone was painfully apparent, and in light of issues I have explored throughout this chapter, it should not be surprising. Founding fathers of the manga business, whether motivated by pedagogical passion, profit, or professional honor, find their objectives thwarted at every turn; the standard model for licensing manga, ironically imported from the West, means that American publishers must care far more

---

in 2011. The newly formed Kodansha USA is currently focused on manga publishing. Kodansha is no longer a player in English language academic publishing. In other words, far from driving manga's popularity itself, the commercial success of manga abroad has transformed Kodansha's overseas activities in a classic example of what the Japanese call *gaiatsu* (outside pressure).

about English-language manga's commercial success than their Japanese counterparts. Making manga succeed commercially in the United States is far more difficult than it would be for locally produced original content due to restrictions upon domestication activities, and the largest Japanese companies are, perversely, the most restrictive of their wholly owned subsidiaries. In sum, the traditional emphasis the Japanese place on good relationships and regard for their own cultural products over just making money has not always been to their own benefit. In the ongoing struggle over who gets to make his or her money when, the balance sheet, on the occasion it has tipped in the post-2008 period, has tipped in favor of the Americans, with the Japanese assuming increasing amounts of upfront risk under the auspices of alternative licensing arrangements and experiments.

What is perhaps most remarkable about these findings from my research is that the most ardent advocates of Japanese manga in the United States have, as Stu Levy put it, "fought the good fight" and won—if winning is to be defined as having achieved access to the wealth of domesticated content they wanted right from the start without having to be the ones to bankroll the projects. Having one's favorite manga titles available in American English no longer requires American business acumen and investment to drive projects forward. Like so-called Hollywood "runaway productions," where the host country pays American studios for the privilege of hosting a Hollywood film production locally (Miller et al. 2005), Americans have found ways to make Japanese manga American without having to pay for it themselves. The case of Del Rey Manga's transmutation into Kodansha Comics just exemplifies this trend; behind the scenes, the organizational upheaval and its implications for the people doing the actual work of domestication are not to be understated, but readers would have been able to continue consuming their favorite series for all intents and purposes uninterrupted. The only stakeholders to benefit unequivocally from all this, in other words, are the fans themselves.

Thus far, I have shown how the American manga industry has become professionalized and how professional honor has become a driving motivation for the founders of companies. Furthermore, I have shown how regarding one's professional expertise and autonomy as important is not necessarily compatible with what is involved in licensing manga. But professionalization is good for certain things, and of course it must not be forgotten that these different companies and stakeholders are constituted through the collective labor of a large number of people, and that to write solely about egotistical managers is but a problematic "great man" account of history. For this reason, I turn in the next chapter to the workers, the salaried, and contracted cultural laborers of the field, and ask: Why do these highly educated and often put-upon people accept long hours and low wages to work in the American manga industry?

5

Working from Home:
Translators, Editors, Letterers,
and Other Invisibles

I read this book recently that explained why you can't make a living just as a translator. The author—I can't remember his name—said it's because a translator's job is to be invisible.[1] Do it right; they forget you're there. And they're not going to pay for what they forget is there, you know? I was, like, this explains all the problems I've been having! (Interview 2011)

A booth in the exhibit hall of a fan convention can be a great way for manga industry insiders to meet readers and publicize new releases. With the number of book retail storefronts on the decline, some also come hoping to boost sales and to otherwise generate excitement for their brands with free giveaways, contests, and even author signings. Still, it can be a bit boring for those editors, marketing managers, and interns obliged to man the booth at all times, and conventions are one of the best places to trade gossip and otherwise catch up with colleagues at other companies...provided you are willing to raise your voice over the cacophony of the churning crowd of attendees.

---

[1] The book to which this informant refers is likely one written by translation theorist Lawrence Venuti. The following passage is indicative: "A translated text, whether prose or poetry, fiction or nonfiction, is judged acceptable by most publishers, reviewers, and readers when it reads fluently, when the absence of any linguistic or stylistic peculiarities makes it seem transparent, giving the appearance that it reflects the foreign writer's personality or intention or the essential meaning of a foreign text—the appearance, in other words, that the translation is not in fact a translation, but the 'original.' [...] What is so remarkable here is that this illusory effect conceals the numerous conditions under which the translation is made... The more fluent the translation, the more invisible the translator, and, presumably, the more visible the writer or meaning of the foreign text. [...] The translator's invisibility is thus a weird self-annihilation..." (Venuti 1995, 1–2, 8).

"You moved recently, right? Are your parents happy to have you a bit closer to home?" I asked an editorial assistant for one of the largest American manga publishers, whom I will call Nisha.

"Actually, they're horrified," admitted Nisha ruefully. "I don't even have a coffee table—Mom couldn't believe it."

"You *have* to see it," interjected an intern I will call Jennifer, who was seated beside Nisha at the booth. "She doesn't have any furniture; it's all books!! I think it's cool, actually."

"Why don't you stack some books up and put a piece of plywood on top? That should work as a coffee table. Or you could get a piece of glass cut to size and do the same thing," I suggested.

Nisha was, needless to say, scandalized. "No way! My parents taught me to treat books with respect!"

"Okay. Never mind."

A year later I learned from a third informant that Jennifer had moved in with Nisha. She had apparently been having problems with her prior roommate, and Nisha, although her family had helped her to pay for the new apartment, could still use the extra income (and quite possibly the addition of a roommate's furniture). Both women continue to work at the same company, which means that they now spend the bulk of their working *and* personal time together. Such arrangements are certainly not for everyone, but they are surprisingly common in manga publishing. During the course of my fieldwork, I met several sets of spouses, siblings, lovers, and friends, all of whom both work in manga and share the same living quarters.

In the end, I never did see Nisha's apartment, but many other industry insiders were generous enough to invite me into their homes, and irrespective of type of accommodation or geographic location, they all—without exception— had one thing in common: Books. Lots and lots of them. Sometimes they were shelved neatly, other times messily; in a few homes they were piled up like tottering Towers of Pisa on the floor in dusty corners or propped up against already sagging bookshelves. Shinsuke, introduced in the previous chapter, told me that he considered a clean office a bright red flag; the best licensors, in his view, always surround themselves with plenty of manga. It shows that they know their stuff, that they are keeping up with the latest trends, and that they are interested in the product for its own sake. Indeed, these collections of books were, unequivocally, the materialization, and social signal, if you will, of these people's professional identities.

One reason why these industry insiders share their living space with so many books is because many do not have a desk or cubical at their employer's office to clutter up in the first place—they are, in fact, freelancers who work entirely from home. By bringing me into their houses and apartments, they were showing me not only their most intimate spaces but also their day

FIGURE 5.1 *A manga industry professional collates a small portion of a large personal collection of manga.*

to day working conditions. This chapter is about these ordinarily "invisible" cultural laborers throughout the manga publishing industry whose work it is to contribute to each and every stage of the domestication of manga in the United States. In the following sections, I explore precisely who they are and what they do, and in so doing explain why, if they are so overworked, underpaid, and not, in many cases, given much in the way of professional autonomy, they remain so passionately committed—and why, without them and the strength of their sentiments, the process of domestication simply would not function (Figure 5.1).

Domestic laborers

While founding fathers and others in management positions are predominantly male, the gender makeup of those American manga industry employees of lower rank is quite different. Precise figures are virtually impossible to quantify, especially given the ever-shifting landscape of freelancers moving in and out of the field, but for the trade publishing industry as a whole the gender split is about 50/50 (Luey 2009), and my intuitive sense is that in manga specifically women actually outnumber men. Two of the largest, most prolific publishers included in my fieldwork were well over half female—and one these was 75 percent female. Most, in any case, are in their twenties and have at least bachelor's degrees. Translators in particular are likely to have higher degrees in Japanese language and literature; several were in PhD programs and later decided to drop out of academe. In fact, translation agencies such as Translation by Design have been known to recruit at universities, and some translators have gotten their start in the business through agencies which handle manga.

Agencies of any sort are rare, however, and have become far less common post-manga boom. Pay for Japanese-to-English manga translation is far less than that for, say, legal or medical translation, and for most agencies it just is not worth the bother.[2] Agented translators, too, are frequently frustrated by the relationship. One translator, for example, begged her agent to be allocated a particular title which she had adored when she had read it in the original Japanese and knew, through the grapevine, would soon be available, but the agency assigned a different translator to it when the time came. Moreover, many find their agency's cut of their earnings—as much as 50 percent—quite onerous. Another freelance translator explains:

> The agency takes half of the money. It's not like a literary agent where they take, like, a 15 percent commission. If you're getting a certain amount for the work, the agency is getting that amount as well. When I went full-time freelance, I made it clear to [my agent] that I was trying to make a full-time job out of this. She said, "Nobody does this full time. It's a sideline for everyone. It doesn't pay well enough." And I was thinking, "It doesn't pay well enough because *you take half the money I earned you*!" Working through an agency just became so much of a pain that I decided I'd rather not translate than translate through an agency. By that point I'd made a couple of direct editorial contacts, and you know, I'm just going to count on my ability to talk to editors directly from now on. Because it's not worth my time. I'd get like $2,000 for two months of work, and knowing that $2,000 for two months of work isn't a living wage, but $4,000 totally is, I'd rather do it for $4,000 or not do it at all.

---

[2]It is exceedingly difficult to directly compare rates for business or legal translation, where pay is calculated per character or word, with manga translation, where pay is calculated per page or project. But if, say, a legal translation is billed at $0.20 per word on average, and manga with an above-average amount of text has some 100 words per page, an entire volume of 180-odd pages might run 18,000 words. At a rate of $0.20 per word, that is $3,600, of which an agent may take half, giving the translator $1,800. In reality, pay per volume of manga *before* any agent's involvement is more along the lines of $600, often irrespective of word count—though this too ranges widely between publishers and even between individual projects at editorial discretion. At the height of the manga boom, $3 per page was considered low-end, but by 2012 veteran translators were complaining about being offered projects paying only $1.50 per page.

Needless to say, most freelance translators do not have agents, and most manga publishers prefer not to work with them because agents do not allow editors to talk to their translators directly. Any questions or concerns that arise about the translation therefore have to be fielded through the agency, and this is inconvenient. There are other risks too; "[my agent] doesn't read emails right," lamented one translator. The companies which rely upon them most heavily tend to be new players which have not yet built up a personal network of contacts. Indeed, several freelance translators I interviewed reported getting their professional break simply by approaching manga publishers at their booths at fan conventions and handing over a resume. Agencies managing recruitment for other positions are virtually unheard of. Many jobs are advertised externally in the usual places, such as Monster. com and the publisher's own website. Others are acquired less formally, through face-to-face contact with employers or word-of-mouth in industry networks. Freelancers who are approached with work that they are too busy or otherwise unwilling to take on will frequently refer clients onto other professional acquaintances. Tokyopop employees are particularly well known in the industry for passing opportunities on to each other, and as that company began to lay off its staff, several have, with the encouragement of ex-Tokyopop employees already placed in the company, found new positions at Viz. And something similar happens in those rare instances when companies attempt to poach talent from another publisher. In one case of this sort, a search for an editor, the hiring manager started by approaching one editor who did not want to relocate cross-country, was referred by her to a second who had just accepted a new position and did not want to jump ship prematurely, and was referred by this second contact a third time, finally, to someone, currently employed in children's publishing, who was suitably qualified and already living in the area.

Yet, despite their often dense networks and considerable academic credentials, a combination of youth, inexperience, and enthusiasm for manga works to keep wages very low for everyone. In this field, in fact, there is always someone waiting in the wings and willing to work for free, although the quality of that work may be less than professional. Unpaid internships and other creative schemes to extract labor without paying for it have become increasingly common. There is also universal downward pressure on rates and salaries, although the specific numbers vary considerably. The poached editor described above told me around the time she was hired that she actually accepted a pay cut to work in the manga industry. Her former employer even offered her a salary increase to try and keep her, but manga had for too long been her "dream." This editor, despite the financial hardship and many a late Sunday night in the office to meet deadlines, could still count herself lucky; many other informants told me they despaired of ever achieving even modest financial stability in this industry. One young woman, fluent in both English and Japanese, moved from one coast to the other after graduating from college in the hope of landing a job in manga. Despite arriving just on the cusp of the manga boom, she never got much past the front door; apart from some freelance translating and adapting work, the closest she ever got to working full time in the manga industry was as one company's receptionist, a "temporary" position[3] that lasted three years. After being laid off, she spent a long period without health insurance—buying into the state-sponsored COBRA would, although she was in her twenties with no history of illness, have cost her $800 per month, far beyond what she could afford. Furthermore, because the company had laid her off, she was not allowed to work for them as a freelancer for a minimum of nine months.

Even the most experienced are not immune to financial trouble. In fact, due to salary compression and inversion, which became especially pronounced during the height of the manga boom, some of the most experienced full-time employees have survived rounds of mass layoffs post-boom *because* their salaries are so low. Those who do get laid off are generally unemployed for six months or more and try to pick up casual contract work during the interval. Even some freelance informants with over a decade of experience and a constant stream of work reported pay cuts of 40 percent, from $1,000 down to $600 per project, in 2011. Precise rates for freelancers vary by company and sometimes by project within a single company. Some publishers have a standard rate, which is applied universally. For example, the translation rates of one company, now out of business, were $3 per page. At the time, this was about as low as rates went in the industry, but they have since gone lower still. Other companies leave exact amounts for any particular job to the discretion of a manga series' editor, who is given a total budget from which they can allocate funds to their freelancers as they wish, based upon how complicated they deem the jobs to be.

Conditions of low pay and job insecurity are further exacerbated by the high cost of living in the regions where work in this field is most abundant, New York, San Francisco, and Los Angeles, and these laborers of domestication have a wide variety of ways to make ends meet. Some full-time employees of manga publishers moonlight only semi-secretly for others; freelancers are often full-time students or holding down another job in an entirely different, more lucrative field, such as medicine, local government administration, or telecommunications. If they are American, as many of them are, they are likely to receive crucial financial support of some sort from a breadwinning spouse, family, or friends. Many I have interviewed receive help with rent,

---

[3]The receptionist was classified as a temporary worker, even though she worked full time for three years, so that her employer would not need to pay her retirement benefits.

health insurance, and car payments. Some live with their parents rent-free or find temporary accommodation with friends. A few are young enough to be willing to risk going without health insurance for long periods. One full-time editor reported learning, to her utter horror, that some of her company's unpaid summer student interns had been making ends meet by "freegan" dumpster diving, a technically illegal but increasingly popular practice of scavenging unsold food past expiration date from supermarket trash disposal units. Although they had assured her that they had gotten food poisoning only once from some spoiled milk, dumpster diving in pursuit of a career in the manga industry was, for this particular editor, a bridge too far.

But what, exactly, ought to be considered a bridge too far? Much has been written about exploitation, self-exploitation, and precarious labor in various sectors of the culture industries (e.g., Andrejevic 2004; Banks, Gill, and Taylor 2013; Born 2004; Deuze 2007; Hesmondhalgh and Baker 2011; McRobbie 2002b, 2014; Taylor and Littleton 2012; Terranova 2000; Ursell 2000), and to blame this effect upon a single "bad actor" company in one particular cultural field would be beyond naïve. From one perspective, youthful amateurs are stripping a profession of its ability to command a living wage to the enrichment of immoral capitalists, while from another even precarious, underpaid labor provides unique emotional fulfillment and a sense of doing good for people like oneself. Besides, those on this side may well argue, a poorly paid job is infinitely better than no job at all! To wit, is cultural labor galloping economic exploitation, an example of Marxist false consciousness in action? Or is it an important source of creative autonomy, self-actualization, and personal satisfaction?

Unsurprisingly, opinion differs. Proponents of contemporary cultural labor such as Richard Florida (2002) write of a new "creative class" which is highly educated, mobile, and contributing to economic growth at a time when industrial manufacturing is of declining importance. David Hesmondhalgh (2010), in a different but generally affirming vein, suggests that unwaged cultural labor should not be immediately equated to exploitation. I agree with him that low pay—or even no pay—for work does not alone mean that laborers are being exploited. Money is not, after all, the only form of compensation, and this is an issue to which I will return later in this chapter. In contrast, critics such as Richard Sennett (1998, 2006) decry the new flexibility and socially corrosive precarity of even highly skilled jobs, although he does continue to idealize certain forms of artisanal, hands-on cultural labor (Sennett 2008). As I am not convinced that it is possible to fully separate so-called "creative labor" from other forms of labor in the service professions, in this sense the contours of this debate are relevant to the entire world of work today. Indeed, in their recent book *Creative Labour*, David Hesmondhalgh and Sarah Baker (2011, 234) research three media industries, television, magazine journalism, and music, and conclude that there are both "good" and "bad" jobs in these industries and that any redress for the "bad" ones must be grounded in broader debates about social justice. It is therefore unsurprising that both proponents and critics agree that the social forces underpinning these transformations is the growth of "individuation" (Giddens 1990, 1991) or "autonomy" (Castells 2009) in neoliberal contemporary society. In her writings about the UK Labour government's policy toward cultural labor, Angela McRobbie (2002a, 99), for example, describes an environment where "work comes to mean much more than just earning a living; it incorporates and takes over everyday life." She also illuminates the important ways in which young people are the fast, cheap fuel which powers this creative economic engine (McRobbie 2002b). Although she does not comment specifically about manga publishing, she could have been.

Underneath these debates about cultural labor are abiding concerns about who precisely is benefiting from these social arrangements. Is it the capitalist owner of the multinational corporation enriching himself at the expense of his workers, or are the workers themselves getting the better end of the bargain, compensated for their time and effort with something other—and more precious—than money? Alternatively, could both sides be somehow partially correct in their arguments? Perhaps it is time to move the discussion beyond the all or nothing and attempt to find out how both might be right at the same time, or how both positions capture a partial picture of a complex, heretofore poorly described labor dynamic in the culture industries.

I would, it should be noted, differ from John Thompson (2010, 155) in his characterization of the mind-set of freelancers in what he terms "the economy of favors." While admitting that some are "willing to work for less (or even for free) because they need the work and experience and they don't yet have the connections," Thompson asserts that others who also do work for large corporations will accept much lower rates from small presses because "they share the ethos of the indie presses and/or they find it rewarding to do so" (156). This is certainly true as far as it goes, but it misses something fundamental about what it means to be a freelancer. By Thompson's account, skilled, in-demand workers are benevolently granting boons to cash-strapped presses, as if with a wave of their hand (or rather with their optical pointing device). This, at least in the context of my own fieldwork, was simply not the norm; it grossly underestimates the precariousness and attendant anxiety experienced to a greater or lesser degree by virtually all freelancers who were active in the field. One veteran translator who had, in the mid-2000s, aspired to organize a manga translators' union in the hope of staving off the erosion of pay rates had given up hope after the financial crisis. It was either take what you can get—or leave it. Some, of course, elect to leave it.

In any case, purely in terms of humane living conditions, my own research shows the following: The same low pay becomes more tolerable and sustainable over a long period when the worker is a citizen of a state with a strong social safety net. Several of my interviewees were Canadians, and they were able to take on some of the lowest-paid freelancing work in the business and maintain themselves for far longer without receiving assistance from their personal network than their American counterparts. They were also the only ones to report granting the "boons" Thompson describes. One informant with Canadian citizenship and chronic health problems, which made the flexibility of freelancing especially attractive but medical bills a constant concern, told me candidly that she would never have lasted so long in the business had she stayed in the United States and not moved to Canada after graduating from college.

All other things being equal, of course, the most attractive employee is one who is a well-educated American because the US market is the most important for publishers and manga is domesticated along US cultural and vernacular lines. This is the case even when books are listed for sale in multiple territories. "Australia could sink into the ocean tomorrow, and I don't think I'd notice any difference in my sales figures," said one marketing director for a small press ruefully. For this reason, among others related to geographic opportunity and proximity, Canadians were more common in the industry than, say, UK citizens who, though also supported by nationalized healthcare, cannot reasonably be expected to be fully fluent in the American vernacular. They were still very much a minority, however, and generally speaking, because the United States is one of the least robust welfare states in the developed world, it became clear to me during the course of fieldwork that working in manga, for many informants, was or was to become a de facto life stage. Past a certain point, the low pay and long hours become intolerable. This is certainly true for freelancers but perhaps surprisingly even for full-time employees with a good salary and benefits. One of the most well-regarded professionals in the industry told me a poignant story about turning twenty-five. I wrote the following in my field notes, dated September 2011, after our conversation:

A lot of her friends and acquaintances were getting married (and one is already divorced), and meanwhile her parents were getting divorced. She was confused about her personal life. Also, a lot of them were changing post-college careers around their mid-20s, either leaving grad school or entering grad school, say, and she meanwhile was ensconced in [her company] yet feeling like she had peaked in her career [there]. [...] She had made senior editor, and where did she go from there? [So-and-so] stood between editorial and upper management; [so-and-so] was publisher and she sure as hell didn't want *his* job; and then there was [the founding father]. Can't be him, obviously. I noted that 2008 was a bad year for manga too, which certainly didn't help, and she agreed.

After losing her senior editor position in the manga industry, she professed no immediate desire to return, even though she was offered positions at other publishers. She was, quite simply, burnt out. Manga had consumed her life and left no time or room for anything else. "Theoretically, I'd like to get married and have kids at some point," she said. (When I asked her how far along she was to achieving those particular ambitions, she replied, "I said 'theoretically.' Joining Match.com is one of my unemployment projects.") It would, in my view, hardly be an exaggeration to say that the US manga publishing field depends upon the youth, energy, and total commitment of its many laborers. Without the nearly superhuman effort they put into the transnational production of culture, it would not exist.

In any case, the combination of feminization and insecurity in the industry seems certain to accelerate these selfsame trends. The casualization of cultural labor is not confined to manga or, for that matter, contemporary trade book publishing. However, it is only compounded by the influx of women into the industry. Women constitute a significant majority of part-time workers in the United States (Kalleberg 2000), and as manga as a category of books became synonymous with comics for women in this country (Brienza 2011), the importance of female employees to the largely male management increased dramatically. For example, shoujo manga publishing in Japan is highly feminized because, the assumption goes, women, and young ones in particular, will know best "what girls like" (Prough 2011, 4). And sure enough, one freelancer hired by a man to be editor for the relaunch edition of a bestselling multivolume shoujo manga series told me that she was recruited specifically because she was a young woman. Not coincidentally, due to her relative inexperience in the industry, and, I suspect, because she was not canny enough to try to negotiate higher pay, her publisher offered her only $400 per volume. (This compares rather poorly to a per page rate for freelance editors offered by a competitor which averages $1,000 per volume.) At another publisher, which retains a bevy of in-house editors, one of its numbers told me that she saw significance in the ways work was allocated and their office space was arranged. The editors are all stationed at a pair of long desks partitioned into a number of semiprivate workstations, each outfitted with a desktop computer. One desk has only female editors; the other has only men. The office has an open floor plan, and these two desks form the two sides of an aisle. Because everyone sits with their back to the aisle, the men and women sit with their backs to each other. Moreover, editors get, in her words, "typecast" by their gender; the male editors are in charge of the shounen manga, while the women are in charge of the shoujo. Since shoujo does not make as much money as a whole category as shounen does, this editor felt that she and her female colleagues were accorded less status in the company. Now granted, that specific spatial arrangement was not an immutable state of affairs, but it is how the office looked in mid-2011 when I was conducting my fieldwork. Nevertheless, my informant was convinced that it was symbolically significant, and as someone who is a part of that arrangement, day in, day out, her observation is likely a valid one. Translators also, according to this same editor, get "typecast." In any case, the erosion of wages and prestige caused by the feminization of a profession is well documented (Stallard, Ehrenreich, and Sklar 1983).

The labor of domestication

To produce an English-language edition of a volume of manga, publishers first need access to the original content which they intend to transform. As discussed in the introduction, manga is no simple material commodity to be physically imported or exported. And because manga in Japan is first and foremost a medium of disposable entertainment, there is no one systematic method throughout the industry for archiving published materials. Therefore, American companies must acquire these materials, called "assets," in a variety of ways. Photo negatives of the finished pages which publishers then had to develop in-house were common in the beginning of the twenty-first century, but increasingly now high-quality digital reproductions are the order of the day. However, acquiring the rights to these assets represents a significant additional cost for licensees. One editor explains the conundrum:

> When it comes to higher production values and getting access to the film that they would use in Japan, it was perfectly doable. It was not cost-effective. When I worked at [a small manga publisher], one of the things I was fighting for was, let's do it right. We got the film; we got a professional scanner to do it, working from the original negatives. The production quality definitely showed. But it's expensive—it's really expensive compared to scanning the books. I don't remember the specific numbers, but it's something like ten times as expensive to do it that way. And the reality is with 90 percent of titles the market does not justify the cost. So while I find it very frustrating, I don't blame American publishers, and if I had to make that decision as an American publisher now, I would say that it's not worth it to take a stand on production quality. If the Japanese are not going to foot the bill or make it much more feasible, that's something they'd have to live with—inferior production. As a creator, I wouldn't want to stand for that. I would say that if you want to license my book in English, it's gotta have better quality, and it's the responsibility of the original publisher and creator to make that available at a price that's realistic.

Clearly, the adversarial relationship between licensor and licensee described in detail in the last chapter plays out here as well. American editors perceive the Japanese as willfully obstructing the free movement of manga content while merely paying lip service to artistic integrity at all costs.

The only alternative to buying rights to the original assets directly from the licensor is, as the editor quoted above mentions, "scanning the books." By this he means acquiring a copy of the original Japanese edition of a licensed property and using those pages as the basis for one's work. The main challenge is, then, to get those ¥400 paperbacks into a usable form. Therefore, for many manga titles, the life of an English-translated edition begins in front of a microwave. The manga is placed in the microwave and heated for about thirty seconds to loosen the glue so that the pages may be separated with a minimum amount of damage to the art. Employees at one company told me that they kept a microwave in-house—complete with a sign warning away the innocent not to use it for food—dedicated entirely to melting bindings. The pages are then put into a high-quality digital scanner (ideally but not always without any tiny hairs or eyelashes clinging them); interns are hired expressly to work the night scanning shift. The resulting bitmap files become the basis for all of the subsequent work to be done on that particular title.

This work is divided into a series of stages, which I termed the "domestication chain" in Chapter 2. Of course, the precise number, and their order, varies from company to company and on occasion even title to title. Financial pressures have, furthermore, led to significant compression— or outright elimination—of some of these stages, and individuals who were once responsible for only one part of the process increasingly have begun to take on others. This is the case for both salaried employees and freelancers. I interviewed one freelance translator who reported, for example, that she had been asked if she could also letter. Certainly, many editors make their corrections directly to the page proofs themselves. Editors also report doing uncredited adaptations of script translations for the books they handle. Some even do lettering and graphic design for selected titles. For clarity's sake, though, I have divided the labor of domestication into four stages for the purposes of this chapter: (1) translation and adaptation, (2) editing, (3) graphic design, lettering, and retouch, and (4) sales, marketing, and promotions. I will discuss what each entails in turn.

Translation and adaptation

Unless the manga is entirely wordless, the first step in the production of an English-language edition of any manga is the translation (Figure 5.2).

FIGURE 5.2 *A side-by-side comparison, to scale, of the front and back covers of the original Kodansha edition of* Sayonara Zetsubou-sensei *Vol. 1 (left) and the Del Rey Manga edition of the same book (right). The decision not to translate the title has been supported by a subtitle, "The Power of Negative Thinking," and an English translation, "Goodbye, Mr. Despair" on the back cover.*

Translators are, virtually without exception, freelance contractors.[4] In the early days of manga publishing, jobs were informally arranged and did not involve an actual signed contract. This has now changed, and official contracts between publishers and translators have become standard in the industry with typical clauses about date of delivery, the timing of payments, nondisclosure agreements, and so on. However, the mere existence of contracts does not necessarily mean that they are adhered to—by either party. One executive of a small company told me (and this was independently confirmed by translators who had worked for them) that they were not paying their translators on time, so for one important project he had had the translator, one of the most experienced in the business, draw up her own contract. Even that, he admitted, had not mattered: they had *still* been late with her fee. In any case, after an agreement between the translator and the publisher is reached, the translator receives a copy of the original manga in Japanese. This is typically a copy of the Japanese edition, but in other cases it may be a digital file. In those few instances where the translator is working on a series which is being released in English shortly after the original Japanese, the books may not even exist yet, and the translator may be obliged to work from photocopies of pages from the Japanese manga periodical anthologies. Because these pages can differ from what is eventually published in book form, the series editor may have to work further with the translator to ensure that the correct version of the script is being implemented in the English-language edition. They may also receive instructions about how to format their translations or a style sheet from the publisher about how to render characters' names in English and so forth. This is particularly common when a translator is picking up a series mid-run. Alternatively, they may receive next to no direction at all.

Each translator has his or her own precise method of translating. Most read through the title once to get a sense of the work before beginning; others who work more slowly may begin work on translating the text immediately. Regardless, manga is almost always translated into American English. Companies which have been forced through licensing agreements to publish books in, say, British English, have been subject to complaints and can be heard at fan conventions swearing up and down that it will never happen again. Even in rare cases where a title is actually set in another English-speaking country and the editors decide to use that region's version of English, the dialogue is usually caricatured and inauthentic. It need only be

---

[4]The only company publishing manga in English to hire translators as salaried staff was ADV, for the publication of the English edition of the magazine *Newtype USA* (2002–2008). Most of their work for the magazine was translating articles, but the magazines always also included a chapter of a manga title in each issue. These titles included *Angel/Dust* by Aoi Nanase and the exclusively for America *Lagoon Engine Einsatz* by Yukiru Sugisaki.

notionally exotic to American ears. There was also consensus among all of the translators I interviewed that it is very important to get the "voices" of the characters right. A hip teenager must sound like a hip teenager, for example. Opinions differed significantly, however, about how to deal with the many regional accents and dialects of Japanese. The accent/dialect of Osaka and the greater Kansai region, for example, is very popular in all Japanese media and for the purposes of manga translation has, when not eliminated from the prose altogether (e.g., *Love*Com*), been variously transformed into a New York accent (e.g., ADV Manga's edition of *Azumanga Daioh*) or a US southern accent (e.g., *X/1999*).[5] One of the most striking adaptations published recently was Fumi Yoshinaga's *Ōoku: The Inner Chambers* by translator/adaptor Akemi Wegmüller. This highly adapted script of a story set in a fictionalized medieval Japan featured, among other things, the use of both Japanese and Western honorifics, Elizabethan English affectations such as "nay" and "twas," as well as the American English spelling of "honor." Translators may also consult the "wisdom" of the Internet, particularly if they are working on a fan-favorite: "Because this interview is anonymous I can tell you that sometimes I will look at a fan translation to see where the fans have gone with something," admitted one translator. As to this translator's process, it was to "to read and translate the book as I go, and if I'm lucky I have time to give it a quick 'n dirty copyedit before I send it off." Some translators work in teams. One two-person team explained that they sit side-by-side when working: "She'll hold the book, and she will read a line to me, and I'll type up a translation on the computer. And then sometimes we'll argue about it, and she'll say, 'Actually, it's more like this,' and I'll say, 'No, it's more like this.'" "We don't usually argue that much," interjected her partner.

Whether or not—and how—to translate the many Japanese onomatopoeia found in manga, typically called "sound effects," sometimes abbreviated "SFX," in the comics context, varies from company to company and even, in some cases, from title to title published by the same company. After 2002, for example, Tokyopop did not as rule translate sound effects, but some titles subsequently published such as *Saiyuki* included appendices with translations to all of the sound effects appearing in the books. Other companies redraw sound effects directly into the pages; still others subtitle the Japanese characters within the panels. Precisely *how* to translate them can be tricky, as Japanese uses far more onomatopoeia than English does. Some simply render the Japanese spelling in Roman characters with a possible translation

---

[5] A professional translator of Japanese to English from Britain has told me that, in her view, the Osaka accent/dialect is closest to a Welsh accent in English. Unsurprisingly, since the English-language market these books seek is actually primarily that of the United States, there has never, to my knowledge, been a character from Osaka speaking with a Welsh accent in any domesticated manga.

in parentheses, either an approximate English-language onomatopoeia, such as "thump" for ボカン [bokan], or simply a description of what the sound effect denotes. Good examples of the latter are ジー [jii], the sound of someone staring, and シーン [shin], the (paradoxical) sound of total silence.

Some manga publishers also put endnotes (or far more rarely footnotes) in their books to explain hard-to-translate cultural references, jokes and puns, or other related trivia and historical notes. Del Rey Manga and Kodansha USA, as a rule, have endnotes in all of their books and were the first to popularize this practice in the United States. Other companies such as Viz, Dark Horse, and Yen Press now also use endnotes in some of their titles. There are occasional decisions *not* to translate words which have straightforward English equivalents. The first volume of the Viz edition of *Nura: Rise of the Yokai Clan*, for example, left the word "sakura" [cherry] untranslated. Needless to say, these sorts of practices are controversial in some segments of the industry, and some have moral objections because they make the translation more "visible," even when this is not strictly necessary. One informant felt that Del Rey Manga was insulting other companies in their explanation of their editorial policy, published at the beginning of all of their books; they seemed to be implying, he told me, that any translation which did not include endnotes was of inferior quality, whereas this informant believed that not conveying all levels of meaning within the text of the translation itself amounted to little more than sheer professional laziness. In any case, writing endnotes when required is the translator's responsibility, although on occasion editors will write additional ones as they see fit. Certainly, no translator I spoke with had difficulty producing plenty of content for endnotes. One translator, reflecting upon this practice, said,

> Some of it is [lazy translation]. What we're trying to do is making it so it's readable, so you can read it though the first time without any trouble for the most part, and for more information you can go to the back. For example, in the second [volume of a particular manga title], they take their class trip to Kyoto so there's a lot of historical Japanese stuff in there. You don't really need to know what all of it is to enjoy the story, but if you want to know what it is, it's there in the back so you can get a little idea.

Despite the various disagreements about endnotes and how to deal with sound effects, literal translations, scripts which translate prose word-for-word, are never acceptable in the industry. This means that the distinction between "translation" and "adaptation" is not standardized, and what they aim to accomplish instead is likewise completely unstandardized—and largely unsupervised. "A good, literal translation is actually going to be more adapted. If you think about the way the manga reads in Japanese, that's going to sound normal to a Japanese person. If you translate it straight word for word, it's not going to sound natural to an English-speaking person, and they're not going to have the same experience that a Japanese person would have had," opined an experienced translator who had worked for four different publishers. Whether or not a separate adaptor, also sometimes called a "rewriter," is hired, or if the adaptation is produced through a combination of the labor of the translator and the editor, depends again upon the company and the specific title. Because there is so little methodological consistency, these different combinations do not, in and of themselves, lead to consistently different creative outcomes. In practice, all that having a separate translator and adaptor means is that at minimum two people were paid to work on the script. Some translators are actually contractually paid for both a translation and an adaptation, but even when they are not it can be hard not to do this work on some level anyway. "Because I'm a writer as well as a translator," said an informant, "I can't just do a bad translation." One member of a translation team explained what happened when a particular company asked them for "literal" scripts:

One time they decided to change their [guidelines for translators], and it was completely ridiculous. And their style guide to tell us how to do it—do they actually understand what it would be like for the person who has to use this style guide to figure out how to do their job?! One of the things they said was, translate it as literal as possible, even if it sounds "cryptic," was the word they used. "Cryptic" is not the word here—the word is unnatural, or awkward. And that's what they wanted us to do because they had rewriters on everything, and they were sure that the rewriters could fix anything. We sent in a sample and said, "This is what your format is asking us to do." And they were, like, "Just keep doing it the way you've been doing it."

Interestingly, because it is an adaptation's job to make the prose of a manga less literal, I found significant variance of opinion about the degree to which it was permissible to change a text. On one end of the spectrum were adaptors who took broadly the same view as translators—that their role was to make the script read as naturally as possible and to attempt to create an identical reading experience in English as in Japanese. "I don't believe in changing the message of the mangaka," asserted one adaptor. Others were far more liberal in what they were willing to change and saw their mandate not as the unaltered transmission of a message and reading experience but rather as one of improvement. In conversation with one adaptor about the exemplary work of another for the same company, I had the following exchange:

Adaptor: He really built it, rebuilt it.

CB: So it was *better* than the original.

> Adaptor: Exactly. And that is what I'd call the ultimate goal. [...] You want something where people can say, "It's better than the original." Or people who really liked the original can say, "This improved."
>
> CB: Or that there's something new here?
>
> Adaptor: Yeah.

This adaptor's view summarizes the liberal view and does, in fact, make perfect sense purely from a business perspective. If the goal is to sell, why not try to make a book more appealing whenever it makes a debut in a new market? Why, for example, should any publisher be obliged to faithfully reproduce what it deems to be an original manga's shoddy editorial decisions (even though some companies have been known to do so)? Why not change it?

The changes liberal adaptors are willing to make range broadly across many different textual categories. Some just involve relieving the repetitiveness of the dialogue so that, for example, every other speech balloon in an action story does not simply have "Argh!" in it. This sort of change does seem to be primarily a decision made for the sake of business. Another is to add a dialectical flair to dialogue. However, in other cases the real reason for making changes seems to be primarily personal. One adaptor, an avowed feminist, said that she would always attempt to change "things where something is sexist. Especially if that doesn't have to be sexist—change it. Sorry, I'm not gonna put that in—particularly if it's an unthinking, internalized sexism." Other changes are true transformations which affect the entire run of a multivolume series. In CLAMP's *Wish*, for example, the gender of the decidedly flat-chested but androgynous angel Kohaku is never specified, giving the romance plot of the series a homoerotic edge, but in the Tokyopop English-language edition, the character is always "she."

Editing

As implied in the previous section, manga editors often have a hand in translating and adapting manga, and because it passes through their hands later in the domestication process, they typically have the final say. Eva Hemmungs Wirtén (1998) calls this "transediting" to distinguish it from the work of the translator, though in practice I find it difficult to categorically separate translation and adaptation work that editors do from that of formally identified translators and adaptors. In many instances, editors reported retranslating themselves material that was missing or incorrect, or doing an uncredited line-by-line rewrite of an entire translation script. And one company actually employs freelance editors in lieu of adaptors and expects them to adapt the script along with their other responsibilities: "We don't use adaptors because we have editors," said the company's executive. "If they're not adapting the translation it's because I haven't given them enough direction."

However, this is not, generally speaking, the editor's explicitly defined role. Although there are several different types of editors in the publishing field, in the manga industry editorial work is confined to what would typically be known as production editing and copyediting. Editors of either type may be in-house or freelance, and the biggest companies typically employ a combination of both. Some publishers organize production centrally, with a single managing editor assigning both in-house employees and freelancers to various projects. In others, each editor is individually responsible for hiring freelancers for work on titles in their care. Editors are primarily responsible for ensuring that work is allocated and delivered on time, that the textual and visual quality of their books meets an acceptable standard, and that the finished product is ready to go out to the printer on time. They also write back cover copy and other supporting material for marketing and publicity. Copyeditors do final checks for typos, grammar and punctuation errors, and for any other minor mistakes that have escaped earlier stages in the process.

The particular procedures which editors follow vary from company to company and even from book to book. Naturally, in financially straitened times dedicated copyeditors are especially likely to be eliminated, with that responsibility going instead to series editors or perhaps unpaid interns. One publisher, explained an informant, even devised a three-tier system allocating different amounts of labor to different books:

> Knowing that there were only so many hours in each day and people can only get through so much, they actually created a tier system where certain books were given more attention. I remember our editor-and-chief gave us three levels, and they were Platinum, Gold, and Lead. Platinum levels were [...] considered the rocket titles, the A titles. [...] The Gold levels were low As, high Bs, I guess solid Bs, things we could count on selling, you know, anywhere from 7,000 to 12,000. And then the Lead was anything below that. And we were basically given restrictions with the number of fonts we could use, the number of copyedits they were given because our copyeditors were busy too. So, Platinum, they got everything—however much we needed to make them perfect. Golds, we could use three fonts, and they would get two copyedits and a final proofread. Leads, they would get one font, one copyedit, and one final proofread. [...] There were these books coming out that had just one font everywhere, same font for sound effects, same font for asides. Oh, and also on the Leads, no bolding or italicizing or anything like that.

In other words, while the so-called Platinum and Gold titles were making money for the company, Lead titles were actually dead weight dragging down revenue. The reason why they could not simply and immediately jettison them from their list was because they were prohibited from doing so by contracts signed with Japanese licensors. So the next best option, organizationally, was to minimize expenditure on them. Furthermore, Leads may have been doing terribly on the market, but they were, disproportionately, among the editors' own favorite titles. Indeed, manga publishers have been known to publish titles they know will not sell because working on them increases in-house morale…and who knows? Maybe they will sell after all…someday.

The managerial role of the editor extends beyond the material elements of a publication project and even the division and oversight of any freelance labor. Manga editors are also responsible for balancing the competing demands of the various parties involved in domestication, both locally and abroad. Points of contention most commonly involve depictions of (1) sex, (2) religion, (3) drug use (including alcohol and cigarettes), and (4) prejudice, especially racism and homophobia. These often result in changes. For instance, the protagonist's side comment about being scared of AIDS upon seeing (what appeared to be) a homosexual romance was removed from the first volume of Viz's *Please Save My Earth*. The title of Tokyopop's edition of the love story *Kimi wa Pet* [You're My Pet], which could have been interpreted as referring to sex slavery,

FIGURE 5.3 *A side-by-side comparison of the original Shueisha edition of* Bleach *Vol. 46 (left) and the Viz Media edition of the same book (right).*

was changed to *Tramps Like Us*, an allusion to the Bruce Springsteen song "Born to Run." The original Square Enix edition of *Fullmetal Alchemist* Vol. 8 depicted a character being crucified on a cross, but the Viz Media edition of the same book featured a redrawn image of the same panel with the character now strapped to a vaguely pear-shaped boulder. Figure 5.3 shows one publisher's clever solution to some potentially problematic cleavage. Depictions of smoking have been removed from *Naruto* and so forth.

Unfortunately, the way forward is not always clear. Maybe a retailer wants a book to be shrink-wrapped, but the licensor does not. And what if some disgruntled reader somewhere in the Bible Belt takes offense to something that would pass without comment on the coasts? It is, granted, unlikely, but nobody wants the negative publicity and possible lawsuit. Better, in some informants' considered conclusions, to play it safe and, wherever possible, change the ages of underage characters in sexual situations. Interestingly, though, one editor in charge of a boys' love imprint told me that they had spent so much time worrying about this, yet it was the one thing that was *never* a problem. In any case, the editor must figure out what will make everyone happy—perhaps the book can be lightly censored, or perhaps one or the other party may be persuaded to change their minds. This is never an easy task because there are so many variables to take into account; different editions may, in fact, be the products of different editorial decisions, and not all instances of sex, drug use, and prejudice are censored or altered in any way. An editorial informant gave this account of a title he had worked on several years ago:

> There's a scene where they had two guys and two girls [in mildly suggestive sexual situations], and I had to white them out so they were silhouettes at the time because of [the characters' ages]. And now we just finished those volumes for the iPad, and I didn't have to anymore because three years later *Glee* is on TV and gay high school students are fine. Originally, the translator and I went back and forth because she was really worried because she thought the scene seemed homophobic and I was worried that Walmart wouldn't take it because it was two guys and two girls together. So I'm, like, whatever it is, however anybody looks at this in America there's going to be all kinds of uproar, so we toned it down. We didn't take it away, but we toned it down. And now you don't have to.

There is absolutely no consistency of decision-making across publishers, editors, or even titles because, no matter how carefully thought-through they are, any decisions made are subjective. Anything someone deems questionable is always going to be a gamble. No one can know with absolute certainty what would have happened in different circumstances. Unsurprisingly, then, given this lack of certainty, editors must become skilled in the art of persuasion, particularly when dealing with licensors: "It's stressful but not onerous," explains one. "I feel like I had a good enough email rapport with [the Japanese editor]. [...] There's a lot of time involved, and you have to explain it very carefully. Cuz you want to be respectful. But you also have to explain very clearly—they did not grow up here and don't know best." And of course there are also many cases where editors may strongly disagree with particular demands, and they must find a balance between their own convictions about what is best for a particular manga and what others want. But ultimately, explained one informant, you must prioritize the desires of "whoever is going to kill the title."

Graphic design, lettering, and retouch

Designers, responsible for marrying a translated and adapted script with actual pages of sequential art, are domestic laborers without whom the chain of production would break entirely. Their work is divided into three broad categories: lettering, retouch, and graphic design. Sometimes all of this work is the responsibility of a single person, but lettering/retouch and graphic design are discrete tasks which can be and sometimes are disaggregated. Graphic design involves the presentation of the manga itself and includes cover layouts and design, logos, title pages, and other paratextual material. Lettering and retouch involves replacing any Japanese text in the pages of the comic proper with its American equivalent, replacing or subtitling sound effects, and retouching any art damaged by the lettering process. Sometimes art is also retouched for editorial reasons; these people are responsible for actually executing the visual censorship described in the previous section. Conversely, in the case of presses specializing in adults-only erotic content, sexually explicit material censored in the original Japanese publication may be added back in, either by the original creator or by a local in-house artist.

The processes of lettering and retouch are potentially more complicated than they sound, as the great majority of published manga, even today, are not digitally produced. Relettering and retouching pages which were originally published in Japanese thus requires first being cleaned up in Adobe Photoshop and then, for most companies, finished in Adobe InDesign. One designer explained:

[Our company] didn't want to pay the licensing fees to get the assets for all the files, so we would get assets for the designs of the books, but we wouldn't get any interiors. So, all the interiors were scanned, and then we had to erase all of the text and sound effects that needed to be replaced. Then it would go get placed into InDesign where we would do all the lettering, drop in all the sound effects, page numbers, things like that. And then it would go out to the editors to do their thing and come back to us for corrections. Then it would go out to the printer—and hopefully that would be the end of it!

Different publishers have historically used different software, but in the past few years companies have increasingly converged on InDesign because, in those instances where the pages are already digitized, they have usually been done in InDesign, and paying the licensing fee for all of the assets upfront reduces the cost and workload for designers later in the process. Digital assets with image and text in separate layers continue to be a rare occurrence, however, so retouching pages actually means redrawing any portions of images that have inadvertently been erased along with the Japanese text. Often what is erased is screentone, patterns of texture or shade originally applied to pages by the manga artist or art assistants from pre-printed sheets. Screentones can be relatively easy to retouch in Photoshop by a designer who knows the ropes; this is an explanation of one of many shortcuts: "Halftones have a bunch of little circles in them. So you just take your clone stamp and line up two different circles and it'll continuously drop that tone. If you don't line it up perfectly, though, then you start getting moiré patterns and weird funkiness going on, and it's easy to tell that it was badly retouched." Other corrections, though, must be done by hand, particularly when it involves actual line art. If the lines are straight, it is possible to clone them, but this is often not an option. Wavy, flowing locks of hair are a particular headache for designers, and because long hair is a popular trope in shoujo manga, categorically they are the most difficult to retouch.

The visual presentation of the books is one of the most frequent sources of conflict between American manga publishers and Japanese licensors. Disputes over cover art and design are common because, typically, the licensors wants the cover design of the translated edition to match the Japanese original as closely as possible. Some of the changes requested are minor—designers might be asked to move a logo a millimeter more toward the center of the frame, for example, or to adjust the intensity of the orange color of a character's costume. These sorts of changes are annoying, and designers love to complain about them, but they do not object to them in principle. Other sorts of changes, however, can become the focus of serious disputes between different parties. Designers typically prefer to produce book covers with the art above the title, whereas editors and licensors tend to prefer the exact opposite. Furthermore, sometimes an original Japanese cover may strike a designer as inappropriate for the American market, too garish, perhaps, or merely uninspired. In rare cases, a distributor or retailer might veto particular design choices outright and refuse to stock the book if it is not changed. Several informants reported an instance where Scholastic, which for many years has organized book fairs for schoolchildren, told publishers that books with yellow covers have not been doing well with middle school kids, and that if they want Scholastic to include their titles in the book fairs, yellow covers are out of the question. So if manga publishers are unfortunate enough to be publishing titles for middle school kids with uninspired designs or yellow on their covers, they must seek permission from Japan to make any changes, and more often than not, permission is not given, especially from the largest Japanese publishing houses. This hurts sales in the United States and potentially threatens livelihoods, so of course the frustration expressed in cases like these is magnitudes greater.

Given that their work can be subject to so much direct, day-to-day interference from Japan, designers were, unsurprisingly, among the most likely of my informants to read personal insult and vindictiveness in the behavior of licensors. One designer working for a US-based subsidiary of a Japanese publisher told me that their parent company had recently forced them to alter the layout of their copyright pages. They had been using their old layout for years, and some series would have to be changed mid-run, but this did not matter to the Japanese. The licensor would not budge, demanding particular fonts of particular point sizes for each and every line and specifying how much space there needed to be between various lines. This designer was convinced that the whole situation was a power play, with the licensor trying to put her and her colleagues in their rightful, lowly place. Literally. While showing me an example of this new copyright page, she pointed out that they had been made to increase the amount of space between the names of the Japanese company executives and production credits specifically for the English-language edition so that they were further down the page. "They don't want to be associated with us," she explained, only half in jest.

Though it continues to be done by full-time salaried employees for some titles at some companies, lettering and retouch have, like other links in the domestication chain, also become heavily outsourced. There are freelance letterers, usually between jobs and picking up some extra work wherever they can find it, and the occasional full-time graphic designer also working for other companies. There are also independent companies providing a large number of graphic design services to paying clients, including those needing manga work done. However, because it requires less in the way of linguistic skills, the people who do this work are not, as is nearly always the case with translators, adaptors, and editors, English-speaking Westerners. Third-party design companies can be based much further afield. One former employee for a publisher now out of business explains:

Lettering used to be done in house, back in the "Golden Age." It must have been 2006 or 7 that that they decided to outsource the lettering to India, so that they could get $1 a page. So then it stayed in India all the way until the end, basically. The very, very last month of books, they switched to a company in Russia. Those books were never even printed anyways.

Some American freelancers reported receiving up to $2,000 per book for lettering and retouch, so $1 per page for a book of less than two-hundred pages certainly saves money, particularly over time. But it can also add a new layer of potential trouble, particularly when the designers are inexperienced. One full-time designer conscripted to show the Indian newbies the ropes recounts her frustrations in detail:

> There's this big, looooooooong learning curve of them sending you things where you say, "No, that's not right; no, that's not right; no, that's not right; okay like that, but *better*." [...] A lot of it was going back and forth in the beginning. Eventually we got to the point where they knew what we wanted and they finally understood the process. [...] But it's never really right because everything is being sent by email to a source who then tells another source who then says, "Oh, we're working on it." After twenty minutes of conversation they might say, "Oh, we get it!" But they might not get it.
>
> The biggest problem is a lot of the people who do this don't realize that when we say "erase and redraw" that we actually want them to go in there and redraw anything that had text over it. So sometimes they would just erase it, and maybe they would put the tone back, but that would be the extent of it, and there was just this gap that was kinda hangin' out there.

Because of this, many manga publishers refuse to outsource this work, and those which do outsource have found it best to stick with one source that has finally figured out how to do a reasonably good job, even when competitors offering slightly lower rates come calling. They have concluded that the difference in cost does not justify the additional inconvenience of cultural and language barriers.

Sales, marketing, and promotions

Sales, marketing, and promotions involve making certain that the products being produced reach and succeed on the market. Sales refers to those interactions involving other professionals in the publishing field such as distributors and retailers. Marketing is persuasion aimed at the public, such as advertisements. Promotions are special events and contests aimed at building excitement for a particular product or brand. In large culture industry firms, these may be handled by separate individuals or even separate departments. In manga publishing, however, a clear personnel distinction between the three is rare. One department—or perhaps even a single individual—might be in charge of all three, and for virtually all publishers editors play an important role in these tasks as well, attending and participating on panels at fan conventions and trade shows, for example, or giving informational, outreach talks to librarians.

Some of these activities are evidence-based. Publishers know, for example, that buying an end cap display at Barnes & Noble sells more books than a full page ad in the *New York Times Book Review* and that designing a banner ad with the word "free" on it generates more clicks than any other alternatives. However, manga publishers—indeed book publishers in general—do relatively little market research when compared to their counterparts in other better-endowed cultural sectors such as music and television, so much of this labor is determined by personal intuition, professional norms, and external proscription. For this reason, when interviewing people working primarily in this part of the process about what value their labor adds, they often looked uncomfortable. A recently laid-off marketing director told me that if he had still been around for a former employer's promotional event held at a local bookstore, at least "there would have been an overhead projector."

Apart from the occasional events management, much of this work involves making things—catalogs, tip sheets, Powerpoint presentations, viral YouTube trailers, and freebie sampler booklets, to name just a few. However, like graphic designers, who often work closely with sales and marketing, this work is subject to overt interference from licensors. Some specific instances of interference at this level have already been described in the previous chapter. As a general rule, though, publishers are never allowed to (1) use interior artwork in their promotional material, (2) put new words in characters' mouths, and (3) mix artwork or characters from different Japanese publishing houses. Unsurprisingly, they also shared with designers a disproportionate amount of the rancor directed at Japan; feelings of *schadenfreude* and acts of subterfuge were commonly reported. Although less common than in the past, companies often find it easier and better for the bottom line to do something first without permission and ask for forgiveness (if they even ever get found out) later. The behavior can be reminiscent of a rebellious teenager; "there's definitely a child-parent company dynamic going on," remarked a marketing assistant for a US-based Japanese subsidiary after working there for only a few weeks.

On the consequences of being domestic

So there is neither consensus about what the precise goals of domestic labor ought to be nor is there autonomy in its execution. Yet, irrespective of precisely how a manga title is produced, the perceived quality of the final product can never, in the view of my interviewees, be seen as a function of the excellence of the labor alone. The quality of the proverbial wool, as the informant who referred to what I have termed domestication as "shepherding," is out of their control. It is, in short, impossible to completely conceal any faults with the original Japanese work, and they do not think they should be blamed for them. One translator explains his reactions to online reviews of titles he has worked on:

> People [online] will complain that something sounds a little stilted or "translatedly," and I don't disagree with them but I want to tell them that, man, that's because the writer is not a very good writer, and his prose is *bad*. And as a result when I translate it kind of as is in English, I'm actually rewriting it more than I bet a lot of people would actually be comfortable with. Because he's just a bad writer, and in terms of reusing words a lot or reusing the same phrases a lot, his stylistics are not good. When I go over something like [another series with a different writer] his prose is just better. And so my translation—it looks great! Because the material is better.

Of course, such problems would be tolerable provided that the worker still enjoys the manga title, despite its flaws. However, few people in the industry at any level are able to work on their personal favorites all—or even most—of the time. One freelance translator told me that the most frustrating part about working in the manga industry was that you would think that more experience would lead to better gigs but that, if anything, as time went on she was doing less and less work on titles she enjoyed. Indeed, even one of the most experienced translators in the business, whose work had become synonymous with the English-language editions of one well-known manga artist over the course of a decade, was not assigned that artist's newest ongoing work after it was licensed. She found out that the publisher had decided to go with someone else only when it announced the acquisition publicly at a fan convention. I was sitting adjacent to her in the audience at the announcement, and her bewilderment and dawning frustration was palatable. She clearly felt betrayed, and although she was a "just" a freelancer, it's hard to not conclude that her feelings were at least partially justified.

Many informants with years of experience in manga publishing said that, ultimately, their exit from the field came down to continuing to work in the industry or making a living, and some are not willing to make that sacrifice. "If I'm going to be doing it for nothing, I'd rather not do it at all," said one. Yet many more people I interviewed were, in fact, still willing to make considerable personal sacrifice. Poor living conditions, no health insurance, pay cuts, and too much time spent on "spiritually challenging" titles, to use the colorful language of one freelancer, were but a few of the troubles they would face to keep on working in manga publishing. One editor for a medium-sized, independent press reported working out of her employer's converted garage. I spoke with one young aspirant to the industry who was worried that she ought not to take an editing job for a small company that was offering a pittance when she was also freelancing for a US subsidiary of one of the Japanese Big Three publishing houses. Would it, she wondered, make her look unprofessional? Granted, this particular woman also received significant financial assistance from her family, and her professional goals would not have been feasible without that. Yet, after our discussion I heard others in the industry naming her specifically and how she was doing social networking and media-related work that, in their view, was unacceptably exploitative.

So, if the tangible rewards of working in the manga industry, as I have shown, are not primarily financial, nor are they primarily related to the specific cultural objects being domesticated, why do it? Why the passion? Why the personal sacrifice? Certainly, no one is being deceived by the true conditions of this labor, and if they ever were in the very beginning, then they are quickly awoken to the reality. It is a tricky question to answer since when asked informants will invariably talk about doing it for "love," that their work is their "baby," and so forth. During the course of my fieldwork, though, I heard this answer so often, recited so glibly, that I began to mistrust it. My mistrust proved thoroughly warranted, and the real reason why people choose to continue to work under these conditions is absolutely crucial to understanding why transnational cultural production functions in the manner that it does.

Among the most astute and prolific writers on the individualization, dislocation, casualization, and neoliberalization of cultural labor today is Angela McRobbie (1998, 2002a, 2002b, 2004). She is deeply critical of the standard account of doing it for "love," arguing that this sentiment leaves workers vulnerable to exploitation:

> Professed "pleasure in work," indeed passionate attachment to something called "my own work," where there is the possibility of the maximization of self-expressiveness, provides a compelling status justification (and also a disciplinary mechanism) for tolerating not just uncertainty and self-exploitation but also for staying (unprofitably) within the creative sector and not abandoning it altogether. (McRobbie 2004, 132)

She also wonders if these people will "ever join forces to collectively challenge the conditions which give rise in the longer term to (well-documented) assorted pains," although it is clear that she does not hold out that much hope in that regard (McRobbie 2004, 133). My informants had much in common with McRobbie's description. They too, while congregating in and around urban centers of importance to the industry, were at the same time not particularly rooted to them; three whom I interviewed moved from one part of the world to another in order to take a new job within six months of my first speaking with them, and another *twenty-three* reported doing the same for the sake of work in the manga industry at least once—and in several cases more than once—in the past. For full-time workers, who reported being underpaid by even publishing industry standards, there was the promise of having one's truest self as an unabashed manga fan unconditionally validated in the context of professional life by being surrounded at all times by likeminded colleagues: "[A manga publishing company] was the place that kids dreamed of growing up to work at one day," explained one interviewee. "It was like this big, jokey house of people who loved manga, and you would eat and breathe manga. Even if it was hard and even if it was rough—the minute you work there you have an instant group of friends." Freelancers, who may not have many strong network ties in the field, also felt a strong sense of connection, not to colleagues *per se*, but to the work itself. Doing good work made them feel virtuous and personally validated, as if by a just universe. Even the most underpaid freelancers felt deep attachment and responsibility to their work, and even the most underpaid translators have been described to me as both very qualified and profoundly, passionately committed by informants who are equally passionate, if not outright defensive about their own professional choices:

> They were pretty high level translators, but they also took this shit very seriously. And they were big fangirls as well [...], pages and pages of notes about mahjong or, like, Buddhism, these things they had done all this research on so they were representing things right. [...] And just because they weren't being paid a lot of money, where are they coming from and what were they doing? Quite frankly it's none of [their] business, and I don't think [some people] *want* to understand. The fact that because I came out of nowhere, I didn't go study it, doesn't mean that I wasn't with the fandom from the ground up and researching it on a cultural, pop level sort of thing. We thought very carefully about what we wanted to do and had very specific directives and stuff.

Indeed, though feedback of any sort from editors is rare, freelancers assume a tremendous amount of personal responsibility for the quality of their labor; one translator even said that "the buck stops with me." This is especially ironic given that an executive of a company he works for contradicted this view explicitly and told me that any textual uncertainty was *their* responsibility, and they would certainly never allow a mere freelancer to contact a licensor with questions about translation.

But the reason why they work in manga is not merely to maximize their own avenues for self-expression and feelings of professional validation; comments during interviews about the limitations original creative texts place upon the value of their own creative contribution suggest that self-expression is not sufficient reward. When I pushed informants to explain— *really* explain—their reasons for working in manga publishing, they did on occasion prove quite informative. "Fans like to feel like they're part of the [production] process," the head of a small press explained. Why? Because, as one editor explained her own motivations for seeking employment in the industry, upon seeing manga that has already been published back when they were teenagers, they think, "I can do it better." Everyone thinks they can do it better, in fact. "Translators," pointed out a translator, "always think their version is best." And if someone dares to disagree? "Well, *they're* wrong," asserted an experienced full-time editor whose series had been widely criticized both within the industry and by fans for its controversial English-language adaptation choices. In other words, what domestic laborers love is imposing their will upon the manga text.

Furthermore, they also take great pleasure in superimposing themselves upon it—at any possible stage of the domestication process. At the 2009 New York Comic Con, Del Rey Marketing Director Ali T. Kokmen told everyone conspiratorially as he handed out his imprint's latest free sampler book that it had a secret message in it. "I don't see any secret message," I heard his assistant grumble to herself at one point. Later, though, upon inspection of the book, I noticed that the first letter of each paragraph of its two introductory messages spelled out, "DEL REY ROCKS AK." Kokmen had signed his initials to an object that would otherwise have been produced anonymously. And there are numerous other, perhaps more subtle, cases of self-insertion as well. For example, the most liberal adaptor I interviewed in the course of my fieldwork explained how she, in collaboration with her editor, devised a way of "improving" a manga about an exorcist and his many demon friends:

> It was kind of incoherent and weird, and the tone was all over the place. So I couldn't figure out how I was going to make it sound pretty consistent. I wanted [the protagonist] to be basically like a New England academic, and all the monsters would be essentially like West Coast people. So they're all on the same page in terms of their ideas about progression and inclusion and diversity and everything, but they came to those conclusions from very different routes ... [F]or the West Coast demons it was because they felt in their hearts that it was the right thing to do, whereas for [the protagonist] it was because "I researched it, and it doesn't work the other way." This is something [my editor] and I had actually discussed, you know, her being from New England and [living] on the West Coast ...

This adaptor went on to explain to me that she too had grown up in New England and believed that people on the East and West coasts of the United States have a proclivity for arriving at their identical conclusions about politics and society in very different ways. By rewriting this manga series in such a way, both she and the editor were able to represent an important piece of themselves in the text. It was quite likely, in the adaptor's view, that few readers would notice what she had done; the real reason for doing it was twofold: it made her feel closer to her editor and to the manga series itself. Luckiest of all then, arguably, is the industry insider who lands an appearance in a manga series even earlier in the process. Hiro Mashima, the creator of *Fairy Tail*, puts cartoon versions of people he has met in new installments of the series; former Associate Publisher of Del Rey Manga, now Director of Random House Publishing Services, Dallas Middaugh makes a cameo appearance in volume thirteen—which he never fails to point out gleefully during public appearances at fan conventions.

In fact, feeling like one has become a part of the final product itself is such a powerful reward, so craved and sought after, that some laborers will accept that in lieu of any upfront economic reward whatsoever. The Digital Manga Guild, for example, has recruited teams of translators, editors, and graphic designers. These teams are modeled on scanlation groups and include many scanlators and have agreed to do the work of domestication for no payment upfront. They will not begin to make money until their books begin to sell. However, DMG soon realized that the promise of a pittance later was not sufficient even to digital pirates who would have otherwise done this work illegally and anonymously. For legitimately licensed manga, these people wanted credit—the names of their group and quite possibly the names of each member, published prominently along with the book. Now DMG sends out regular email newsletters with subject lines such as "Shameless Self-Promotion (A How-To Guide)" and "Custom Ad Banners to Promote Your Titles." They also offer webinars which focus upon "Building a Brand: Using Your Good Name to Grow Long-Term Sales" and "Protecting Your Work: Piracy and Credit for Your Group." Clearly, the culture industry imperative to make consumers to buy more and ever more products has become inextricably intertwined with the integrity of one's sense of identity. It is, in short, the neoliberal ethos at its finest—the organization's capitalist ambitions made personal.

Amazingly, one's identifying mark stamped onto a manga during the domestication process can be both an act of self-assertion in a professional, as well as a far more profoundly personal, sense. Most telling of all, one woman in the industry, after much urging, admitted to me that she felt like a "white knight" saving manga from those others who would, in her view, mistreat it. This comment, when unpacked, strikes right to the heart of matters. The work has assumed a level in her mind of the personal quest, or conquest, motivated by deeply personal, spiritual imperatives. Yet obviously, the historical medieval knight was not actually in the business of saving much of anything for anybody besides the powerful, so it's difficult not to conclude that there is a fundamental misrecognition of her own actions here. Furthermore, for a white woman to talk about whiteness in the context of an East Asian medium is telling; she may be underpaid, casualized, and subordinate to the whims of licensors in Japan, but she is still part of a racial majority, and that, along with the status of her nationality, gives her a different sort of authority. Thus, in the broadest sense, the passion for this work is in fact a love for being in control.

Of course, the reality of freelance work in manga publishing is always a complex calculus between obligation and desire, between the real needs of the body and the proverbial needs of the soul. One former freelance editor told me in no uncertain terms that he was "not wed to manga" but readily admitted believing that others like him stay solely "for love." I, however, did not interview any of those spiritually pure people, so perhaps they are just a myth. Among my informants, there was *always* some level of concern that the current job may be one's last—this is, after all, the great unknown in the insecure worker's professional life—and that refusing a job, even a low-paid one, might mean never working again. Even full-time salaried employees reported being afraid of being laid off; some were freelancing for rival houses on the side as a hedge, with varying degrees of openness about their intent. In fact, the most radical pay cuts in 2010–2011 were coming from the large companies, and again, contra John Thompson (2010), freelancers were much more likely to report swallowing a 40 percent cut than they were to report entertaining a small-press "supplicant." After all, between the two, which is more likely to be left standing to offer you work, however meagerly paid, in the future?

The editor quoted in the previous paragraph, for example, while insisting that he ultimately refused to sit idly by while his income dropped and dropped and dropped indefinitely as the years went by, admitted that he absolutely loved what he did back when he was doing it. "I got to read comic books all day!" he crowed. Precise calculations of what was acceptable and what was not differed in their specifics from individual to individual and cannot be neatly mapped onto some generalized cognitive psychological model of motivation, such as a hierarchy of needs (Maslow 1943). One freelancer adamantly reported refusing to go without health insurance; another, who had worked on many of the same titles for the same publishing house, had never had health insurance ever in her entire adult working life, assuring me that she was "young and healthy" and didn't need it. In fact, I am more persuaded by the classic argument made by Ulrich Beck (1992) about the risk society; nobody, including these freelancers, is currently able to fully recognize and evaluate all of the sources of risk they face out in the world.

Nevertheless, there is perceived to be a clear reward to be had in the precarious labor of manga publishing which is not monetary in nature. It is not the realization of their creative impulses, nor even is it the apparent moral superiority they feel when granting some publishers boons, though certainly there may be elements of both at certain times. Given that these people labor in the production of a medium of human communication and expression, it should come as no surprise that the impulse is relational. However, this impulse is not, I would argue, about any of the needs anywhere on Maslow's pyramid. It is, rather a yearning for the feeling of authority, of power over another, so in contrast to the feeling of powerlessness in the face of one's employers—and even in the face of risky fate itself—accompanying a life of precarious labor.

Therefore, the domestic laborers of the manga industry must be understood as motivated not by any perfect transmission of the text's message but rather by their desire for power over the text—achieved by controlling the conditions of its production and putting one's name, personality, and/or other mark upon it. In this light, their allegiance to the founding fathers of the industry, along with their willingness to further the aims of these men on the one hand, and their frustration and on occasion outright hostility toward the restrictions placed upon them by Japanese licensors on the other, makes perfect sense. Although the pinnacle of professional achievement is symbolic self-annihilation, the so-called invisibility of the translator, following Lawrence Venuti (1995), this is not why they are motivated to become manga publishing professionals. Were that the case, there would never be any complaints about the terms of their work or, say, the number of spaces between their names and those of the Japanese executives on the copyright page. But in reality, they are engaged in a daily struggle for control over the Japanese *text* with the Japanese *people*, and this desire for control has been effectively harnessed by the American manga industry to produce manga which suits the market cheaply.

Indeed, I would argue, domestication on this scale would simply not be possible without these sorts of people—period. Their youth, precarious employment, and femininity are no mere side effects of late modernity, neoliberalism, or unregulated capitalism; they are, rather, absolutely necessary for the process to continue effectively. Making them feel like they are a part of something bigger than themselves, standing shoulder to shoulder with fellow travelers, is important but not in itself sufficient. Their subordination to capital, and the lack of self-determination they have over the day-to-day conditions of their own lives, only magnifies their yearning to have control over *something*. This is especially true for women who continue to face subtle inequality and discrimination in all aspects of their lives and have become identified with low prestige but fast-selling shoujo manga titles in the office. They thus take particular pleasure in pushing such works onto the market; an editor in her forties may have just been priced out of her one-bedroom apartment and now needs to downsize into a studio, but dammit that new teen vampire manga is going to be the way *she* wants it! These women become entangled in the pedagogical imperatives of transnational cultural production, while their femininity in turn becomes conflated with the industry as a whole, feminizing it. The opportunities afforded to women in manga cannot be understated, and on some level their work produces both collective and individual emancipation. Yet they are still enmeshed in a web of power relations wherein they are exploited while exploiting others. And as a consequence, in the end, everyone, female *and* male, feels subordinated; even founding fathers crave "revenge," as I have already shown. The white knight's conquest of the text—along with the steady supply of fans who will take up the sword of the fallen—is a precondition for the sustainability and the longevity of this field.

To conclude, then, the invisibility of the translator does in fact afflict the entirety of the American manga industry because all of its many workers at each stage of production, like the translator, labor to simultaneously transform the manga object and to conceal the magnitude of the symbolic transformation that is required. Furthermore, it becomes tangled up with all of the problems which afflict working conditions in the culture industries, such as long hours, low pay, and casualization. From this perspective, then, it is no coincidence that domestication is feminized work and has become ideologically connected to women and other significations of the female and the feminine. This work, after all, often literally happens in the private, concealed spaces of the home. Moreover, its purpose is pedagogical, the creation and maintenance of practices associated with media consumption, so transnational cultural production is inextricably tied to assumptions about domesticity and the role of women as primary agent of socialization. It once more proves that my use of the term "domestication" is appropriate; global flows of culture are not merely uneven, restricted by rights negotiations across national boundaries— they are also highly feminized.

In the next chapter, I will explore these struggles for control over the text and the conditions of its production in the context of the rapidly changing publishing landscape. What does a digital future hold for the domestication of manga?

6

Off the Page: New Manga Publishing Models for a Digital Future

If you wanna change somebody, you have to change yourself first. (Interview 2011)

In the country of his birth, the famed manga artist Osamu Tezuka is remembered primarily for the comics he created for children, such as *Tetsuwan Atom*, a.k.a. *Astro Boy*. He was, however, a fabulously prolific creator, and during his long career he penned well-respected titles in virtually every manga genre. His seinen manga, which with the exception of *Black Jack* are not generally well known in Japan, have become particularly popular among critics and indie comics fans in the West due to their publication in English translation by presses such as Vertical and Digital Manga Publishing. Yet, despite their visibility in the critical sphere, manga like *Ode to Kirihito*, *MW*, *Swallowing the Earth*, and *Ayako* are not runaway commercial success stories; seinen manga do not sell well as a rule in a market where the consumer base is made up primarily of teenagers and women.

Nevertheless, books like these are not entirely bad bets. Although they do not make much money, they elevate their publisher's status in the field, and working on these books is often seen as being especially rewarding for the press's own employees, whom it might find difficult to retain with the meager salaries on offer alone. In the long run, though, these sorts of symbolic and emotional rewards do not put food on the table; "at a certain point," one publishing executive with a particular personal passion for seinen titles told me, "you have to start giving the fans what they want." You don't like the sappy-sweet romance of shoujo and boys' love? Well, that's just tough. Something's gotta pay the bills! Yet on the other hand, presses such as DMP, which are very good at making money on trashy romance manga, want to generate other sorts of capital from their business. Wouldn't it be nice if the one roadblock—the financial risk—could be removed?

At the beginning of 2012, DMP unveiled its solution. High off of their successful attempt to use Kickstarter to fund a reprint run of Tezuka's *Swallowing the Earth*, they decided, with the consent of the licensor, to "fan-fund" their new Tezuka manga publishing project, *Barbara*. Using the website Kickstarter, they solicited cash pledges from fans who would, essentially, be paying for all the upfront costs of domestication, from licensing to graphic design, even paying for printing, and provided that they pledged $25 or above, they would also effectively be preordering the 430+ page paperback. To sweeten the deal, DMP offered numerous exclusives, including "a PDF copy of the *DMP Platinum Digital Companion to Barbara*, with bonus art and commentary on the manga" for a $35 pledge or more and "an original Tezuka tribute T-shirt made and designed in the USA and printed exclusively for Digital Manga" for a $60 pledge or more. They also offered copies from a selection of backlist titles and a digital subscription to *Astro Boy Magazine*. Of course, anyone geographically located outside of the United States would be expected to pledge between $9 and $60 extra to cover the cost of shipping. But perhaps most appealing of all to the fans were not the tangible goodies. "Fans like to feel like they're a part of the process," observed the founder of another indie press, and now DMP was offering fans the opportunity to become a "Producer" of *Barbara*, giving them "a chance to weigh in on the logo and cover art" and to have one's name listed on the DMP Platinum website and even, with a large enough pledge, in the published book itself.

The project reached its $6,500 target in under just forty-eight hours, and by the time the funding window had officially closed on February 13, DMP had raised a total of $17,032 from 353 backers. A resounding success for the company, this meant that it would accrue respect in the field for publishing seinen manga by Tezuka without having to invest even a penny upfront. Surely, they had hit upon the perfect solution to niche publishing in a fast-changing digital landscape? Some commentators were nonetheless skeptical: For starters, they argued, the bonus merchandise was not really that exciting, and the selection of backlist titles on offer had many in the industry thinking that DMP was also using its Kickstarter project to clear poorly performing, unsold stock out of the warehouse. Furthermore, some observers even thought that using Kickstarter reeked of outright exploitation of the fans. After all, in a traditional publishing model the costs of licensing, translating, lettering, and printing would be borne directly by the publisher, and any customer who preorders or purchases a book would normally be entitled to return it for a refund if unsatisfied. This model leaves no room for buyer—or rather investor—remorse. Precisely how DMP would use the funding they generated was not entirely spelled out, either. Kickstarter does not promise that donations will not be misused, relying instead upon informal networks of trust within particular fields. It is easy to imagine how the system may be abused, particularly by an Opportunist founding father. One fan, echoing the anxieties of Angela McRobbie (2004), summarized her views to me on Twitter a few hours before DMP met its goal for *Barbara*: "[T]here's so much love in manga that there's always that someone [who] abuses this love."

There is indeed so much love and other sentiment in the American manga industry that, as I have shown in the two previous chapters, the power struggle between licensor and licensee and the casualization and feminization of employees in the manga industry, taken together, have produced a workforce keen to sustain the field. The exploitation of labor is endemic in the culture industries, a side effect of neoliberalism, and in this the transnational cultural production of manga is typical, not unique. But it is no mere ornamental feature (or hairy wart, depending upon your view). Without the desire of those without much power to themselves control something or someone, I would argue, there would be no domestication at all—it is, in other words, a necessary condition. If there were no love in manga, there would be no one to use—let alone abuse—it.

In this chapter, then, I will explore the ways in which this dynamic affects manga publishing models in the context of a rapidly changing digital landscape. The changes that have already been effected in the past few years cannot be understood apart from enduring cleavages across national, racial, and gendered lines and the battles fought across them. First I will discuss the ways in which publishing has changed since 2007. I will then explore the ways in which professional imperatives within trade book publishing, as well as the conditions unique to the manga medium and its mode of production, have driven experimentation with a variety of new manga publishing models. Finally, I will discuss the likely sociological implications of these new models.

The changing landscape for books, 2007–present

Although the intermediate stages of the publishing workflow have been digital for many years (Thompson 2005), the final product that reached customers was still a printed book, unchanged significantly for decades. It is for this reason that manga publishers were able build an industry atop an ocean of illegal digital piracy through the first decade of the mid-2000s. However, by 2007, even before the manga boom had slowed to a halt, changes to the trade book publishing field were to have dramatic effects upon the manga industry's business model. In this section, I discuss three of these interconnected changes.

E-Books, tablets, and apps

The first change to the field of contemporary trade book publishing has been the sudden emergence of a viable market for e-books since the Amazon Kindle debuted in November 2007. Barnes & Noble introduced the competing NOOK in 2009 and has been promoting it heavily in its physical stores. Apple's iPad, though not specifically designed for books, is a popular platform for media consumption generally since its debut in April 2010 and, along with competing tablets and smartphones, another possible e-reading device. Retailers such as Amazon, Barnes & Noble, and Google, as well as a range of publishing houses large and small have all also developed a range of apps to sell and display e-books on these devices. By April 2011, sales for e-books were exceeding sales of books in any other single format (Flood 2011).

So, why is this happening now? Why had the United States not gone "e-" earlier? The ability to produce and render text digitally was one of modern computing's earliest breakthroughs, yet the recent rise of the market for e-books post-dates the market for digital music and even video. Publishing houses invested heavily in books on CD-ROM in the 1990s, and again in digital books in the early 2000s, yet they never caught on (Thompson 2005). One might argue that the eyestrain caused by ordinary backlit screens provides an inferior reading experience to paper, a concern with which the proliferation of E Ink technology has dispensed. Yet, all of the major e-reader and tablet players, including Apple, Barnes & Noble, and Amazon, have color screens as well, and they also provide apps which are broadly compatible with personal computers and cell phones, which typically have backlit screens.

The reason for the digital delay, in my view, is quite simple: Yes, e-books have the potential to benefit some retailers, particularly those with a strong online presence, and this is why Amazon has invested so heavily in the Kindle. But other links in the book production chain, the authors and the publishing companies, had concluded based upon recent bad experience that the world did not want or need e-books. Having been burned on multiple occasions, there was little confidence in the immediate prospects of e-books through 2007. Furthermore, fears of piracy facilitated by digitization aside, they were extremely wary of ceding Amazon the de facto authority to make the rules for them, as the music industry did Apple with its iTunes store. Amazon's aggressive discounting could then devalue books and thereby drain value—along with good employment opportunities—away from publishing itself. There was also concern that if Amazon became the first place the majority of consumers go to shop for books that Amazon could compete directly with publishers by producing its own material and giving it top billing. (This particular anxiety may well be justified, as Amazon has started its own publishing division.) And finally, as ardent lovers of "real books" themselves, few in publishing wished to hasten the advent of a world where print is dead. As with so much else in the field lately, the chain superstore was a key factor; only with the economic downturn in 2008 and the long foreseen but now soon to be realized demise of Borders, one of American book publishing's most important retail venues, was there sufficient motivation to take e-books seriously, purely as a matter of professional survival. After all, there will be no jobs in publishing if there is no way to keep on selling the books they are producing.

Publishing and bookselling after Borders

Of course, it is easy for the layperson to assume that the reason why Borders finally went out of business on September 18, 2011 was because of e-books. This is not strictly the case. Yes, it was indeed punished by investors for not having a coherent digital strategy, for not competing in the online space with Amazon as effectively as Barnes & Noble does. This, though, was as much about selling ordinary printed books online as it was about e-books. Borders was also overinvested in leases on real estate for its physical stores, as well as in CD and DVD sales, and overall the chain was too deeply in debt. With the economic crisis in 2008, it became clear to everyone in the industry that Borders would not survive, and new ways of selling books would become absolutely imperative—sooner rather than later. At that point, the publishing industry put its lingering reservations about the Kindle and its ilk aside and truly began putting its collective weight behind e-books.

And sure enough, e-books have taken off in the market like a rocket. However, publishers having all jumped onto the e-book bandwagon is only a part of the reason for this phenomenon. Another significant factor is that, with the demise of Borders, a significant proportion of the American populace no longer has a local bookstore. The way in which the superstore chains drove independent bookstores out of business in the late twentieth century meant that, once one of the chains was gone, there was no alternative brick and mortar store to patronize instead. This was the case not only in far-flung rural and suburban areas but also in urban centers. Cities as big, highly educated, and affluent as Nashville, Tennessee had no general, nonspecialty bookstore at all in their central commercial districts. My fieldwork informants, many of them urban, were reliable sources of similar complaints; shopping for books and manga in the nonvirtual world had become suddenly inconvenient, something requiring a lengthy, preplanned journey as opposed to a quick hop outside on a whim or a break from the office. Although it seems likely that in the long run new businesses will emerge to exploit this newly vacated market, in the short- to medium-term the only real recourse left for people in these areas was to buy books online, where Amazon was incentivizing e-book purchases with loss-making discounts. If Barnes & Noble and/or Books-a-Million, which together represent nearly a thousand stores, also start to go under, this problem will only increase.

Naturally, the experience of buying books online differs fundamentally from buying books in an ordinary retail store. Although sites like Amazon have developed complex algorithms to make recommendations based upon one's own and others' purchasing histories, search engines are, as a rule, actually better for searching than for browsing. There is, therefore, far less pure serendipity involved in online shopping; as a consequence, publishers can no longer rely upon the same level of onsite promotion of particular titles with mass appeal. This means that publishers are less willing to publish books that do not make at least a modest amount of money. The big corporate publisher model whereby as many as 90 percent of all books released never make money for their publishers is starting to look less sustainable, while alternative publishing programs which emphasize the cultivation of smaller lists of books, which will all, hopefully, generate profits, are attracting attention throughout the industry. And in a similar vein, the advances to authors they are willing to offer have shrunk correspondingly. "$10,000 is the new $50,000," opines an agent on her blog (Hellmann 2011).

The logical endpoint of these trends—and the worst-case scenario for traditional book publishers and literary agencies—is that the field of contemporary trade publishing as it is now organized will in effect be made completely redundant. Among the most important services publishers have offered their authors is the advance, as well as good distribution to retail venues and the publicity of prominent placement on the most-trafficked bookstores' shelves. If getting substantial advances becomes too difficult, if Amazon maintains its large share of e-book sales, and if e-books become the most popular reading format, then authors may deem it preferable to cut the middleman out altogether. After all, one can always hire an editor and a copyeditor by oneself, and different authors will value the prestige of a big publisher's imprimatur differently. It may thus strike certain authors as far more straightforward to self-publish a book and list it on Amazon. That way, they retain a share of profits that would otherwise have gone to the publisher and the agent.

At this point, though, it is crucial to recall one of the greatest insights of the sociologists of culture like Howard Becker (1982): change the social arrangements within which an artistic work is produced, and the content of that artistic work will also change. Though I remain deeply skeptical, should this future I have described above come to pass, it is important not to forget that the books that might have otherwise been published in hardback by Random House, HarperCollins, or Hachette will *not* instead be e-books self-published on Amazon. Instead, those books which would otherwise have been produced by the big publishing houses simply will not exist. To give just one example, the creative affordance of the advance will no longer be as common, so it will become far more difficult for authors to make a living off of their writing. Writers will have less space purely to hone their craft and their reputation; authors will instead be people with full-time jobs or people with other independent means, who are, essentially, writing only in their spare time. There will, in short, be books, but these will not be the same books that would have been produced under different conditions.

Digital deterritorialization?

Nonetheless, I am not wholly convinced that the scenario I have described above will actually become the new state of affairs—at least for books published in English. Although troubles in the built retail environment have thrown the proverbial wrench into book publishers' promotional machines, there are surely other ways to publicize new books. Furthermore, the American publishing industry has a head start; it is the biggest in the world, and it produces content in the de facto global language. Even now, books that have been translated from English into other languages represent the vast majority of translations published (Heilbron 1999; Sapiro 2008), and the global popularity of American media, even in an environment of increased competition from non-Western sources of production, is undeniable. However, the circulation of books has been limited by the cost of moving these heavy objects about. Thus, titles are traditionally published for specific regions—the UK Bloomsbury editions of the *Harry Potter* books are not, for example, supposed to be sold in the United States, where Scholastic holds the relevant copyrights. But online retailing has naturally gone a long way toward making such rules unenforceable. Only the cost to consumers of having books shipped halfway around the world to their doorstep has kept this movement in check. But if the book exchanges its materiality for a wholly digital existence, bits of data stored in a mainframe warehoused in some remote part of the desert of New Mexico, say, and distributed worldwide to readers via "cloud" computing, then a book's audience could become truly global. Instead of just targeting people who patronize bookstores, they might instead target anybody who is online.

In this light, then, the publishing house does not look quite so obsolete. The values which they add to a publishing project—editorial guidance and intervention, marketing and publicity, prestige—become even *more* important in a global marketplace with its ever-expanding and changing range of media choices. It is no coincidence that many of the most popular news media websites are the digital extensions of so-called "legacy media" companies like the BBC, CNN, and the *New York Times*. Of course, the very real troubles confronting ad-supported media such as newspapers in the digital age must not be downplayed, yet book publishers which do not depend upon producing content in order to sell advertising seem well positioned to reap the benefits of a digital deterritorialization of the global marketplace. They may be able to trade the Borders retail space for the far vaster, online one.

Naturally, obstacles blocking the realization of such a deterritorialized future remain. The digitization of media content has, for the music, film, and television industries, led to increases in digital piracy. These wealthy industries have been fighting piracy for years with only limited success, and their recent attempts to lobby the US government for a new legal framework that would allow them to more effectively police unauthorized dissemination of their products have not thus far been successful in eliminating piracy. Publishing houses have fewer resources still for these battles; they simply do not have enough labor power or hours in the day to send everyone pirating their content takedown notices, let alone enforce them.

Furthermore, despite corporate concentration, there remains a tremendous amount of regionalism in publishing. Different publishing houses operate in different countries; even when producing content that will be distributed internationally, their employees tend to know their home territory well while remaining largely ignorant of others. I encountered this many times firsthand in my fieldwork. For example, when Random House was publishing manga under their Del Rey Manga imprint in North America, they were also releasing these books in the United Kingdom. But because the Del Rey imprint was not as an established name abroad, the Random House UK imprint for manga was called Tanoshimi. With the exception of the different logo and a quick find-and-replace job that switched any paratextual references to "Del Rey Manga" with "Tanoshimi," the books, complete with their American English vernacular, were virtual facsimiles. Yet during one press conference, when a British journalist asked the head of Del Rey Manga questions about Tanoshimi's choice of printer for their titles, he professed to know nothing. Also, there is a gentlemanly concern that globally publishing manga in English can have deleterious effects upon manga industry counterparts working in different languages—or even in other English language speaking territories. Particularly for manga titles with modest prospects, the easy availability of an English-language edition makes publishing translations in many other European languages (with the exception of French) less financially appealing. Some informants in Japan were worried that worldwide digital publication in English of manga might drive many non-English language presses straight out of business.

This was not a view, though, which I heard expressed all that much by American manga publishers. If anything, they felt that the horse had already left the gate with pirated digital editions of manga, which are, according to

Hye-Kyung Lee (2009), produced primarily by Americans for a global audience anyway. As such, they have been experimenting with a whole host of new publishing models.

New manga publishing models

Digitization in the field since 2007 has, in some cases, affected manga in unique ways. The demise of Borders ("everyone's biggest account," in the words of one executive) and corresponding rise of the e-book are likely to have a profoundly transformative effect upon manga publishing. Manga in the United States, which exists as it does because of Borders, has not been annihilated by its closure, but in the short- to medium-term, there is nothing to replace it as a retail outlet. The viability of the current available menu of alternatives lags behind that for prose. Independent bookstores, for example, have been far more conservative overall when it comes to stocking manga. Online sales of manga have likewise been much less important than chain retail sales historically, representing about 10 percent or less for most publishers. Why this is the case industry insiders can only speculate, but I suspect that it is because sales at Amazon and other online retailers require a credit card for the advantage of their convenience to be fully realized, and children and teenagers, who are manga's most important demographic, do not usually have credit cards. After all, it's much easier to buy a volume of manga at a chain store with leftover lunch money, no questions asked, than convincing parents to trust their child with a credit card number so that the child may buy a book of unknown literary value. The underrepresentation of online sales as a proportion of total manga revenue also makes the transition from the online sales of printed books to the online sales of e-books, successfully pioneered by Amazon, all the more difficult for manga.

Being networked with the field of contemporary trade publishing, of course the manga industry is under intense pressure to climb onto the e-book bandwagon. However, manga does not display well on the E-Ink screens used by the most popular device the Kindle, and some presses, such as Yen Press, flatly refuse to sell Kindle e-books out of concern that these would be subpar products. Besides, many were wary of marrying their fortunes to Amazon's. Also, manga has had the unique (mis)fortune of being the first new category of books in the twenty-first century, and as a medium it expanded on top of an unplumbed ocean of illegal translation and digital publication called scanlation. How much digital piracy helped or hurt the manga industry during its expansion is impossible to know for certain, but what *is* certain is that at the beginning of the manga boom books whose scanlations were readily available to anyone with an Internet connection became print bestsellers anyway.

Rurouni Kenshin is one of the most prominent examples of this, and as an early test case it eased publishers' anxiety from the start of its serialized publication in 2003 through the mid-2000s. Indeed, one head of a company admitted that the dirty secret of the manga industry is that, in his experience, the books which have been scanlated sell better. Another pointed out that some of the manga titles they had licensed were not scanlated until *after* they began publishing them. Now, though, the proliferation of so-called "aggregator sites" such as One Manga and Manga Fox, which collect scanlations produced by numerous groups and aggregate them onto an easy-to-navigate web platform, are seen as an enormous threat to the industry, both because their growth may be mapped directly onto the drop in manga sales since 2008 and because scanlations are seen as competing directly with the digital reading experience of e-books.

Still, if scanlations are a global phenomenon, why can't e-book editions of translated manga be likewise? Although American manga publishers have been pressuring Japanese licensors for digital rights for years, it is only late in the first decade of the 2000s that they would even begin to consider it. The reasons for this were primarily cultural. The most popular digital platform for manga in Japan has been the mobile phone, and the market for these keitai manga peaked in 2007. However, the sorts of devices widely sold in Japan are not popular elsewhere, and until the US debut of the iPhone in 2007, mobile phones with screens large enough to display sequential art images were not common outside Japan. Web-based and tablet reading platforms were, in contrast, virtually unheard of in Japan and therefore easy to mistrust. Japanese rights holders are far more open-minded about digital publishing now, but years of dragging their feet have resulted in many instances of confusion. So, in many cases, the company which has the rights to a print edition might not be the same company now holding the digital rights. For example, a Japanese printer, fearing for the future of its core business printing paper books, has been buying up world digital publishing rights for many manga titles. In other instances, Japanese companies have concluded that they in fact own the digital distribution rights to books already published in English. Square Enix has posted e-book editions of Viz's *Fullmetal Alchemist*, Yen Press's *Black Butler*, and other titles it had originally published in Japanese to its own English-language website, infuriating American publishers who quickly realized that someone was selling carelessly scanned copies of books they had worked hard on and that there was nothing they could do about it. In the case of *Black Butler*, for example, the website in mid-2011 provided little indication of the book's provenance other than the person credited for lettering the manga, Tania Biswas, who is Yen Press's editorial assistant and occasional in-house letterer. In the worst case scenario, there may be one version of a manga made available in print from one publisher and an entirely different version available digitally from another. Furthermore, Japanese rights holders are increasingly asking for minimum guarantees on e-books as part of initial licensing deals, potentially exposing licensees to even greater levels of risk than ever before.

In sum, then, the publishing landscape has changed with lightning speed, and although there have certainly been many in the industry who were correctly reading the proverbial tea leaves in years prior, the manga industry is still trying to figure out what sorts of modes of production offer the best chance of survival—and, ideally, prosperity. In the space of less than two years, five new publishing models have emerged: (1) publisher as retailer, (2) direct-to-digital publishing collectives, (3) fan-funded publishing, (4) simultaneous laydowns, and (5) original global manga. I will discuss each of these models, along with their attendant pitfalls, in turn.

Publisher as retailer

In the seventeenth century, it would not have been unheard of for a publisher to be its own printer *and* retailer, with a printing press and a storefront all housed within the same building (Howard 2005). This is now the exception rather than the rule. Traditionally, publishers contract with a printer and a distributor, and their books are sold through to consumers by yet other retail entities, potentially with a wholesaler in-between too. The manga industry in its maturity has historically been no exception. Viz, for example, which had its own warehouse and mail-order business in the 1990s, no longer ships books directly and relies instead upon a distribution deal with Simon & Schuster. Dark Horse, as described in Chapter 3, uses Diamond Book Distributors. Until its closure in 2011, Tokyopop was distributed by HarperCollins and had even co-published selected titles with them. US anime companies with manga publishing arms were, due to incomplete professionalization into the trade publishing field, more likely to maintain substantial stock to sell directly to fans at conventions, but these presses were vulnerable and have either gone inactive or been formally shuttered for good. In 2012, only DMP takes selling books at conventions seriously, and they do so only at one, the locally sited Anime Expo. DMP also has its own online storefront for printed books, Akadot Retail.

But with brick and mortar stores on the decline, manga publishers have increasingly come to the conclusion that, at least for the near term, only they can save themselves. Although the Kindle, for reasons described previously, is not an optimal platform, the iPad, which debuted in April 2010, seemed to have more promise, and with Apple's global cachet, it would hopefully be easier to persuade Japanese licensors that iPad manga were worth pursuing. One informant described how her company's founding father was running around the office waving a new iPad excitedly; meanwhile, in-house designers had already begun experimenting with the devices to see what they might be made to do. Dark Horse had an app for iPad as early as March 2010, but it was focused upon selling single issues of American comics, not manga. Yen Press was otherwise the first to go public with its iPad ambitions, announcing its own proprietary app at their industry panel at the New York Comic Con on October 2010. The imprint's own original graphic novel publications, such as the manga spinoffs of the *Maximum Ride* and *Gossip Girl* properties, as well as Svetlana Chmakova's *Nightschool*, would be sold for reading on the iPad at a price of $8.99 per volume. So, while the app did not actually offer any of Yen Press's translated Japanese manga or Korean manhwa for sale when it went live at the beginning of 2011, the digital architecture would already be in place so that the company would be able to act quickly to implement any new licensing deals they were able to make with Japanese rights holders.

As of this writing in early 2012, Yen Press has not been particularly successful in securing digital rights to its manga backlist. Other publishers, however, have had more luck. Viz Media announced its own iPad Viz Manga app in November 2010, less than a month after Yen Press. Some backlist volumes of the most popular properties from their Shonen Jump imprint, such as *Naruto, Bleach, Death Note*, and *One Piece*, would be made available at $4.99 per volume, and new titles would be added at a regular rate. In successive months, the company would add a web-based storefront and another app for iPhone and iPod Touch, along with cross-platform functionality which allows a customer who has purchased a copy once from the Viz Manga store to download and read it on any compatible platform. DMP also launched an iPad app for its own manga in November and has committed itself to making its titles available on every digital platform—mobile, tablet, *and* Internet. Their books are available on both the Amazon Kindle and the Barnes & Noble NOOK, for example, and in this they are the exception rather than the rule. Kodansha Comics announced an iPad app developed by Random House in October 2011.

The rollouts of content for the iPad and other platforms, all within the space of less than a year, may have seemed quite organized from the outside. Within the industry, however, there was remarkably little coordination or even agreement about what sort of business model the iPad, and by extension e-books, ought to be in the context of manga. Financial viability—or lack thereof—was on everyone's mind. Speculation was rampant: What if e-book sales start to cannibalize print sales? The total cost associated with a book's materiality, that is, its manufacturing, shipping, and warehousing, is no more than 20 percent of a book's list price, yet readers tend to place a far higher valuation on print than it actually costs publishers. This has arguably been exacerbated by Amazon's pricing schemes for e-books. Publishers who have priced their digital editions nearly the same as their print editions, such as

Yen Press, are clearly concerned that the move to digital will extract so much value from the entire domestication chain and that producing new content will become impossible. Moreover, they also fear of getting locked into a race to the bottom with other publishers.

There are more immediate financial problems as well. Software programming and app development is not free. A proliferation of possible platforms only increases those upfront costs for publishers, and at the moment there are almost certainly too many competing devices, digital storefronts, and files standards to choose from. The landscape is confusing to consumers and risky for publishers, who would rather not invest in a format or device which will be obsolete and forgotten in a few years. This is why some companies are expanding their digital range very cautiously. Furthermore, digital publishing is not free either, and it costs publishers money simply to make their old books available on these new platforms. Granted, individual costs per volume are modest, but if sales are also modest, problems quickly arise, as evidenced by this conversation with an industry informant:

CB: How much does it cost to digitize and put [e-book editions] up? Is that a big money sink?

Informant: [Digital reissue of previously published titles] costs a few hundred dollars per book, and we're doing, you know, five-hundred books. That's, like, a lot of money. I think we calculated that we have to sell, like, twenty copies to break even, but the problem is . . .

CB: The problem is that you're not selling even twenty copies for most books?

Informant: Probably. Or we wouldn't for a long time. The bestsellers [in print] are selling a few hundred [in digital format].

CB: That's not exactly bestseller territory.

Informant: Yeah, I know.

The utopian vision of digital distribution of media content is the unlimited, instantaneous availability of the sum total of human knowledge and creative production, and it has in recent years become trendy to argue that the culture industries can benefit from this if they are able to sell a very large number of products in small numbers (Anderson 2006). For manga publishers, though, this "long tail" model has yet to be realized. A company like Viz with a quarter-century of publishing under its belt might theoretically reissue in digital format books first published in the 1980s and now long out of print, but this is precisely the sort of digital publishing that does not pay off.

Instead, the most popular properties are the first to go digital, yet even they have difficulty improving—or even maintaining—their visibility in this new space. The reason for this is simple: Most readers do not have the slightest clue who publishes what. Unlike in Japan, where manga is organized by genre and then by publisher in bookstores, manga is usually shelved in a single section, all genres and publishers mixed together, and alphabetized by title. Thus, informants regularly reported being approached at conventions and trade shows about books they do not publish; fans would arrive at the Tokyopop booth asking for *Naruto*, for example, or to the Yen Press booth asking for *Vampire Knight*. Viz, in turn, might get asked about their plans for *Sailor Moon*. Unsurprisingly, manga publishers have recently stepped up initiatives to burnish the reputation of their respective publisher brands, with Viz in particular, not a company in the past with much presence in book exhibits, making appearances and hosting evening industry receptions as never before in its history.

Direct-to-digital publishing collectives

Nevertheless, it will certainly be an uphill battle for companies trying to build their respective brands—generally speaking, people know "manga," not "Viz Manga," "Kodansha Comics," or "Yen Press." Furthermore, all American publishers are, to a greater or lesser degree, caught in a complex web of historical alliances and rivalries. For example, the only imprint that does, arguably, already have brand recognition on a global scale is Shonen Jump, yet Viz, which is co-owned by two Japanese publishing houses, cannot exclusively promote Shueisha titles and expect Shogakukan to be the least bit happy about it. Perhaps, then, it would be more efficacious for someone to produce the digital equivalent of the "Manga" section in Barnes & Noble, a one-stop storefront which would sell manga from every publisher. Several new players have stepped in to do just that.

The market for digital manga content distributed via mobile phone networks exploded in Japan during the mid-2000s and, like the print manga boom in the United States, peaked in 2007. Facing stagnation at home, these mobile manga vendors started to look abroad for new market share, and with infrastructure and experience in the digital space already in place, they have been among the first to initiate direct-to-digital English-language publishing collectives. These are to be distinguished from the digital storefronts maintained by publishers described above in that they are not selling e-book reissues of print titles produced by a single local publisher but rather titles licensed directly from many different Japanese publishers and domesticated exclusively for the digital platform. Currently there are four companies following this model, and three of them are Japanese.

The three Japanese companies are NTT Solmare, NEC Biglobe, and the Toppan Printing company. All have previously developed a successful mobile manga presence in Japan, and all went public with their English-language initiatives in 2011. NTT Solmare now offers iPad and iPhone apps under the ZQ Books name; NEC Biglobe offers an Android app as Sugoi Books. Both offer a relatively small range of vintage manga titles (including some overlap) in specially formatted panel-by-panel mobile displays. Sugoi Books also sells e-editions of American comics published by IDW. The last of these initiatives, JManga.com, a website run by Toppan in partnership with the Digital Comics Association, a coalition of thirty-nine Japanese publishing houses, went live in August 2011. JManga aspires to be both a directory indexing information about all of the titles published by its partners, presumably to compete with the scanlation-friendly Baka Updates, as well as a storefront selling English-translated e-books. Some of these titles have never been published in English before, and their domestication has been newly commissioned by JManga. Other titles have been published in the past in print editions by US presses such as Aurora Publishing, Broccoli, CMX, Tokyopop, and Media Blasters; these may be facsimiles of the now out-of-print books, their licenses having reverted back to the original rights holder, while others have new translations. This depends upon whether the American company owned its own translation or not.

These companies face numerous troubles as they try to break into the American market. The first is simply a problem of visibility—distinguishing oneself in a sea of apps and online sites is hard enough for experienced publishers and exponentially more difficult for new players trying to build reputations from scratch. Other sites, many of them trading in scanlations, tend to dominate Google search hits for manga titles and artists—and these must be unseated. This is especially difficult, given that these new apps and sites are proposing to sell what scanlators already offer free of charge. The second is funding—they do not have the resources to build up the volume of content that is necessary to make their spaces attractive to readers as one-stop shopping: sales are low, and ad revenue is, at least at the present time, out of the question. So, precisely how they expect to turn a profit is unclear. Yet another problem is the logistics involved in managing the egos of multiple companies. Getting everybody's books in one place sounds like a good idea in principle, but whose books, say, get the prime real estate on the top of the front page? Selling that space may garner the ire of those smaller presses less able to pay. Publishers may then decide to pull out of agreements with these companies if they do not feel that they are being given enough attention, and loss of even a few minor players means damage to a whole that has the potential to be more than the sum of its parts. A fourth problem is the absence of global availability. The one great advantage of e-books is their portability; a single reader's entire library need only weigh a few ounces. Yet these online storefronts cannot be accessed everywhere; Sugoi Books are available exclusively in North America, while ZQ Books is only available on iPad/iPhone in North America and selected European countries. Global digital distribution is not impossible (as shall be shown below), but it requires a transformation of licensing practices which are segmented by territory and built upon a system of advances and fees. And last but not least, there are a whole host of problems related to the formats themselves. All three companies have been criticized for the low quality of their domestic labor; translations are unreadable, as if they have been done by Google Translate or Babel Fish, and the choice of fonts is ugly, the naysayers contend. This is especially problematic given the high prices currently being charged, and complicated point systems, popular in Japan but rare in the United States, make it even more difficult for consumers to figure out precisely what they are paying. Sugoi Books does not even price its points in US dollars but rather charges everything in Japanese Yen! JManga's points are worth one cent each, but to buy e-books on the site one must first buy either a $10 or $25 per month subscription. The $10 plan provides an equivalent value of 1,000 points, a one-time 500 point bonus, and an ongoing 50 point bonus per month. Additional points can be purchased only in $5, $10, or $25 bundles, and since books tend to be priced at 899 points, it is difficult to spend precisely what one has already paid. Moreover, reading manga on cell phones or computer screens, particularly at prices virtually identical to the cost of a print book, may not be appealing to most readers. Less than a year after their debut, some informants placed elsewhere in the manga industry were already writing these companies' obituaries.

The fourth and final of these direct-to-digital publishing collectives is eManga.com, the California-based Digital Manga's website. Begun in August 2008 as a digital rental site, eManga is significantly older than any of the other Japan-based digital collectives, and because the company has become known for its boys' love manga, the site has had an advantage distinguishing itself on the market. Indeed, most of the books available on the site are boys' love or Harlequin manga, two genres with a niche yet loyal readership of women. eManga went live with iPad and Android versions of their store in November 2011. The stores are not, at least at the moment, compatible across platforms, and the same books are priced differently depending upon the platform. However, Digital Manga publishes manga originating from quite a large number of Japanese presses, including Shinshokan, Taiyo Tosho, Oakla Shuppan, and Libre, and with the addition of Digital Manga Guild titles to their eManga store, they have become, for all intents and purposes, a direct-to-digital publishing collective. Eventually, they hope to build mini-storefronts on their eManga site for all of their Japanese publishing partners.

Fan-funded publishing

The only press which has both become its own retailer *and* formed a direct-to-digital publishing collective is Digital Manga. It should come as no surprise, then, that the company has also been experimenting with other innovations as well. Among the most important—and controversial—of these is the mobilization of fans in direct investment and revenue-sharing schemes. I call this model "fan-funded publishing" because both of its variations require fans to fund projects themselves.

The first type of fan-funded publishing has been described at the beginning of this chapter. Using the Kickstarter website as a third-party collection agency, DMP is able to solicit upfront injections of cash for publishing projects with a potentially highbrow, and presumably moneyed, readership, but with limited mass appeal. The title even being published in the first place is contingent upon it being funded on Kickstarter, so DMP can satisfy the Japanese rights holder that wants its licensing fee without having to pay itself. It does not even need to pay for printing or shipping the finished product. The first test of this model was a Kickstarter project to reprint Osamu Tezuka's *Swallowing the Earth*. In their project description, they wrote (all formatting as originally published):

> Two years ago, we published an incredible piece of sequential art by "god of manga" **Osamu Tezuka** (the creator of Astro Boy, Kimba the White Lion, Blackjack and many others) called **Swallowing the Earth**. It was the first book he meant strictly for adults and it had never been published in English before. Unfortunately we printed too few copies, and the book is no longer available anywhere (except on eBay for exorbitant prices). **Fans are constantly asking us to print more of the book, but simply put, we're a small company, this is an expensive book and we can't afford to put up the cash for another print run**. Because we love this book so much and we want Tezuka to be around in English for everyone to enjoy, we are hoping to raise funds for another printing of this important book through Kickstarter instead. All of the licensing and production work is already done, and printing and delivery should take just 30–60 days (our delivery estimate listed on our rewards is as conservative as we can possibly be).

Their project goal was $3,950, and they made their target in just under a month. If they ended up with more money than that, they would print and ship more books. By the time it closed, DMP had received a total of $8,806 from 194 backers. DMP also promised at that time that, if this initial experiment with Kickstarter proved successful, they would use it in the future for all-new publishing projects. The English-language publication of *Barbara*, described at the beginning of this chapter, immediately followed the success of *Swallowing the Earth*, and as a Kickstarter project it proved even more popular than its predecessor.

An even more radical version of fan funding is the Digital Manga Guild, or DMG. Launched in 2010, DMG seeks to monetize the practices of scanlation groups through a revenue-sharing scheme whereby no one—not licensor, licensee, or domestic laborer—gets paid until actual copies of the books start to sell. For licensor and domestic laborers, who would ordinarily receive the bulk, if not all, of their money prior to actual publication, this represents considerable sacrifice. But for the licensee, who would normally be bearing the lion's share of the burden of financial risk, having been the one to pay upfront, it is a vast improvement. Furthermore, instead of making the majority of one's annual profits on the sale of just one or two bestsellers, the publisher would be able to profit through modest sales of a very large number of books. Having that large number is crucial; otherwise, it has wasted money upon the construction of a digital infrastructure which houses little content.

Therefore, DMG requires, on the one hand, publishers to commit a huge number of titles to this initiative and, on the other, a huge number of people who are willing and able to do this work for no money upfront. Taiyo Tosho was the first Japanese press to grant DMG access to their backlist under these terms, and others have since joined, providing hundreds of titles for the company to publish in English-language e-book format. As for the domestic laborers, at the 2011 Anime Expo in Los Angeles, Digital Manga's founder Hikaru Sasahara reported that DMG had over 1300 "localizers" registered to the site, although not all had been vetted. These localizers are required to self-organize into named teams able to perform three tasks on the domestication chain: translation/adaptation, editing, and lettering/graphic design. In theory, each team is a trio, consisting of one person in each role. But other groupings are possible, as Sasahara explained:

> If you could localize, say, five titles a month, which is kind of tough, but...you could do it. And you could potentially form a company and you become the president, whatever. And you hire localizers under your wing. Or even a single person could do all three roles, translating, editing, typesetting, if one person can do them all, you can get the full percentage. You don't have to share with the others. You're gonna be rich. But you're going to have to localize a lot of titles to make a decent amount of money. Don't count on just one single title to keep you in pizzas, Cokes, stuff like that. You have to localize as many titles as you can, but you can still enjoy doing so. Cuz we're gonna bring in all these titles you've never seen before.

Clearly, this seems to be a promotion of a spirit of entrepreneurialism, but in fact DMG's teams do not stand to make much money under this model. At present, only 12 percent of the sales of a particular title goes to its "localization team"; the rest of the revenue is split between Digital Manga and the licensor. When these books are sold through eManga.com, there is no retailer cut, but any DMG books available through Kindle, iPad, Android, and so on will be priced higher to accommodate the retailer's cut. In any case, the low numbers speak for themselves. Take a book that is priced at $4.99. Twelve percent of that is approximately $0.60. If that is to be split three ways, the book would need to sell 3,000+ copies before each translator, editor, and graphic designer would earn anything approximating the rates they would have received as ordinary freelancers. That is simply not going to happen, and as the number of titles starts to grow exponentially, each team stands to earn progressively less and less for each book they work on. Perhaps some books will sell better than others. That is possible, but the beneficiaries of any unexpected hits will be entirely random because DMG does not allow teams to pick the titles they will work on; instead, the company bundles a few titles together and allocates these bundles to teams with a word of "Congratulations!" on Twitter. Were this truly a revenue-sharing scheme, the teams would be given some opportunity to take bets on titles themselves. When I suggested this to DMG, however, company representatives were adamant that this not be allowed, out of concern that certain titles would never be completed. It gives lie, quite frankly, to the entrepreneurial spirit that these teams are supposedly embodying. These women—and they are virtually all women because the books are all boys' love, and boys' love fans are mostly women—are, in fact, modern-day sharecroppers working someone else's land. At best, the fans will be allowed to sign and promote their own names on the pages of that which they adore.

There are several potential problems with the fan-funding model. First, making the release of a book contingent upon fan-funding requires cutting a deal with the original rights holder, and thus far only Tezuka's estate has gotten onboard publicly with the use of Kickstarter and only smaller publishers of niche genres have partnered with DMG. There is also concern that DMP is exploiting fan affect for financial gain; the company runs the risk of losing face among both fans and other manga industry players. Indeed, I encountered deep skepticism from interviewees from other presses about how much influence DMP ever stands to wield in the field. The third and final potential problem with fan-funding is a longer-term, existential one. Kickstarter may be a "crowdfunding" site, but the people funding these projects are not some faceless crowd; they are the American manga industry's most committed consumers—the hardcore fans—and their tastes are not representative of the mainstream readership that makes traditional bestsellers. If your primary audience, your most devoted readers, become investors and indeed outright producers of all publishing projects, then the field as a whole is likely to become increasingly myopic and inward-looking over time. It is a model in which "I am in it for me," and the world outside of oneself need not enter into consideration. How will manga titles find new audiences if the majority of a print run has already been purchased before the labor of domestication has begun? An ever-shrinking readership is not, as the American comics field has long known, a recipe for long-term publishing success.

Simultaneous laydowns

Both the new direct-to-digital and fan-funded publishing models deliberately appropriate the practices—and often the labor as well—of scanlators. They are, in other words, trying to beat scanlation sites at their own game. Even the most optimistic will admit that they face an uphill battle because the one thing they are *not* doing is fundamentally changing the rules, and this puts them at a distinct disadvantage. Scanlators do not need to enter into licensing negotiations with Japanese rights holders, while publishers are constrained by international copyright laws. Thus, in a race to domesticate the latest manga title, the scanlation sites will always be first. To combat this problem, a fourth new publishing model has emerged: simultaneous laydowns. The simultaneous laydown is what it sounds like—the release of a new book at the same time everywhere.

Publishing has traditionally been constrained by nation and territory, each defined not just by its own laws but also by its own publishing players, geographic limitations, and temporal realities. Only recently have book publishers begun to coordinate their efforts transnationally to combat the growing threat of digital piracy to their frontlist titles. The most well-known case of this is the simultaneous laydown of the later *Harry Potter* novels (Gunelius 2008; Striphas 2009). Starting with the fourth book in the series, UK publisher Bloomsbury coordinated with the US Scholastic to release their two editions on the same day. Retailers were asked not to open shipments of the book until July 8, 2000. These requests were largely ignored, and for subsequent installments retailers were required to sign an indemnity form in order to receive cases of the new books, making them liable for any books that might become public ahead of the official release date.

Of course, with the growing prominence of the publisher as retailer model, the risk of occasional leaks by unruly retailers troubling Rowling's publishers diminishes, and direct-to-digital publishing eliminates some temporal and geographic constraints. Additionally, the ephemeral qualities of digital publishing map neatly onto the Japanese practice of periodical serialization of manga. A collected print and/or e-book publication at a later date may, in theory, also be simultaneous, since much of the labor of domestication will have already been completed. New opportunities for the simultaneous (or very nearly simultaneous) laydown of new manga in multiple languages have thus emerged, and manga publishers have, increasingly, exploited them. I will discuss three instances of this new manga publishing model in detail: (1) *RIN-NE*, (2) *Weekly Shonen Jump Alpha*, and (3) *Soul Eater NOT!*.

Viz has published the manga of Rumiko Takahashi for many years, and its release of her *Ranma ½* is regarded as among its early success stories. So when her first new manga series since the long-running *Inuyasha* was in the planning stages, Viz saw an opportunity and pounced on it, announcing their first ever simultaneous release with Japan. *Kyoukai no Rinne*, or *RIN-NE* as it is called in its English-language release, would be serialized in the venerable *Weekly Shonen Sunday* magazine in Japan and in digital, web-viewing format online in English. As the Japanese magazine hits newsstands each Wednesday, Viz's digital chapters would also be scheduled to go live online each Wednesday. Simultaneous releases began in April 2009 and continued for nearly two years before being quietly discontinued with the March 17, 2011 release of Chapter 89.

As *RIN-NE* is still going strong in Japan, and collected editions of the title have appeared on the *New York Times* bestselling manga lists in the United States, Viz had clearly run into problems with the logistics of simultaneous laydown. Nevertheless, the company was not entirely deterred from this publishing model, and in October 2011 at the New York Comic Con, Viz and Shueisha announced the joint launch of *Weekly Shonen Jump Alpha*, a digital-only English-language edition of the *Weekly Shonen Jump* magazine starting in January 2012. Viz's own monthly print edition of *Shonen Jump* would be discontinued. Access to the magazine on the web and across multiple devices was set at $25.99 for a year, and single issues could also be rented for 99 cents for four weeks. New issues would be available each week, with selected manga series from the Japanese magazine made available in English two weeks after their first publication. All of the imprint's most popular titles in the United States still ongoing in Japan, such as *Naruto*, *Bleach*, *Bakuman*, and *One Piece*, would be included. Viz also announced that it would offer advance e-book versions of any collected volumes of these series not yet published in print format through their Viz Manga store so that readers would be able to "catch up." However, *Weekly Shonen Jump Alpha* would only be offered in the United States and Canada.

Not to be outdone, Yen Press also announced its own simultaneous laydown at the same New York Comic Con. The company's *Yen+* magazine would be going digital-only, and for $2.99 per issue, subscribers would be able to read new chapters of Atsushi Okubo's manga series *Soul Eater NOT!* on the same day that they are published in print in Square Enix's *Monthly Shonen Gangan* magazine in Japan. Unlike *Weekly Shonen Jump Alpha*, however, access to the magazine would be offered globally, and its other serials include a mixture of licensed Korean comics called manhwa and all-original English-language sequential art adaptations of various novel series published by Hachette. At the announcement, Yen Press founder and head Kurt Hassler pleaded with an audience of fellow industry insiders, journalists, and manga fans to support this venture, hinting that future simultaneous laydowns would be contingent upon the success of this first experiment. They need to show Japanese licensors that they can outcompete scanlation sites.

Although this model is, in principle, a good way to outcompete scanlators, it too has limitations. First of all, the amount of global coordination required to simultaneously publish a book in multiple languages and territories is tremendous, and complications at any stage of this complex process can grind production to a halt. New manga pages may only be complete a week before they go to press, and therefore the entire process of domestication would have to proceed at lightning speed to achieve simultaneity with Japan. The resources required for this are substantial. Also especially problematic is the way in which everyone must cede some amount of creative control. What will happen if, as has been the case in the past, a US publisher decides that the latest chapter's content contains something that must be censored? If, let's say, Yen Press cannot get Square Enix to approve its domestication of the latest chapter of *Soul Eater NOT!*, the chapter will not debut on time, and that narrow window of opportunity for simultaneity will be irrevocably lost, as might consumer confidence in Yen Press's promises. To eliminate these problems, either the US publisher will have to domesticate the text precisely as the Japanese rights holder requires, the Japanese rights holder will have to trust the US publisher to reproduce the text as necessary without onerous approval processes, or—perhaps the best of both worlds—there is transnational cooperation right from the initial moment of creation, with editors on both sides of the Pacific supervising the artist's production. Given that there seems to be little incentive for Western presses to bother with the extra effort simultaneous laydown demands without concessions from Japan, such creative interference would appear to be inevitable should this model become standard practice.

Nevertheless, none of these possibilities seem ideal, and the transnational coordination required, the loss of control for one or more parties, and last but not least the speed-up of the process of domestication together make simultaneous laydown appealing to publishers both in Japan and abroad primarily for potential short-cycle frontlist titles. When I wished an editor working for a press planning a simultaneous laydown the best of luck with this new endeavor, her face twisted into a tight-lipped grimace as she said,

"We're still only [so many] people; we're gonna need it." This editor's pained expression spoke to a simple truth: This model requires a lot of extra work, and finances constrain the amount to which any publisher is able to dedicate new resources to it. Her company actually has fewer personnel now than when it was first founded. Furthermore, historical frontlist manga titles such as *Rurouni Kenshin* and *Naruto* may have benefited from the lengthy periods prior to their US license and English-language release, during which their brands had built up grassroots buzz, which in turn lent a big boost to those books when they did finally appear in every chain bookstore in the nation. Even if Borders were still around, simultaneous releases do not stand to benefit in this way because they will be new to everyone at the same time, untested. Besides, it's actually the midlist that is hurt the most by piracy, not the frontlist, because there are far smaller sales numbers between profit and loss, and it is precisely that vast sea of midlist titles which, due to the extra labor expenditure required, will *not* get the day-and-date treatment.

While the problems described above reside behind the scenes, the hidden troubles of the invisible domestic laborer, there are equally, if not more, immediate problems in Goffman's front stage: These new publisher websites must somehow gain reader recognition and visibility for their releases in the digital space. They must make themselves the default destination for existing manga readers and, in the future, attract new ones. This, unfortunately, is easier said than done without the free publicity of the big box bookstore shelf. One month after *Yen+*'s *Soul Eater NOT!* debut, Yen Press's website was ninth on a Google search for "soul eater not." The other nine hits on the first page of search results were illegal scanlation sites; the top hit, to an aggregator site called Manga Fox, offered free scanlations of the series in one simple click. Viz, too, has faced controversy, with fans responding to the takedown of *Shonen Jump* titles from a scanlation site called Mangastream by informing Viz in no uncertain terms on fan forums that they preferred Mangastream. It may well be that the proverbial horse has already left the gate, and reader practices have already shifted to a default digital consumption of scanlations. Perhaps true simultaneity for a price will not trump near-simultaneity for free.

Original global manga

If that is the case, if even simultaneous laydowns are not going to save the manga industry, then one last option remains—to abandon Japanese manga altogether and make their own instead. Not all collective responses to new opportunities and risks in the digital age need be, in and of themselves, natively digital. The ways in which manga in the United States has been standardized as a paratextual format readily identifiable by its trim size and basic price point merely facilitates this move (Brienza 2009b). Moreover, as I have shown in Chapter 3, one consequence of the manga boom was the socialization of people working in manga into the norms of the field of contemporary trade book publishing. One of these norms is the practice of commissioning original work for publication; translation, at the heart of the American manga industry, is in fact a practice very much on the periphery of a field where only a tiny proportion of the books published every year are translations. Thus, as publishing professionals enter manga from other categories, and as longtime manga veterans are disciplined in the outlooks and practices of trade publishing, original manga publishing becomes an obvious strategy.

Of course, there have been "manga-influenced" American comics for as long—and perhaps even longer—than there have been Japanese manga published in the United States. *Elfquest* artist Wendy Pini and *A Distant Soil* creator Colleen Doran are but two veteran comics creators who have cited manga among their influences. Antarctic Press, specializing in manga-influenced content, was founded in 1984. CPM's first comic in the 1990s was actually an original, US-produced adaptation of the Japanese anime *Dirty Pair*. Fred Gallagher's webcomic *Megatokyo*, which debuted in 2000, is also manga-influenced and has been collected in print by several different publishers, including Studio Ironcat, CMX, Dark Horse, and even, in Japanese translation, Kodansha. As manga burst onto the scene in the 2000s, several new small presses focused on publishing niche manga-like titles. These included Yaoi Press (boys' love), SelfMadeHero (adaptations of Shakespeare plays), and Seven Seas (various genres). Several trade presses, such as St. Martin's Press, Penguin, and Thomas Nelson, which do not otherwise publish Japanese titles or much in the way of comics content, period, also got into the game at the height of the manga boom, experimenting with their own "manga" (Brienza 2009b, 2011).

For my purposes here, though, I will focus upon manga publishers and imprints whose reputation has been built on Japanese titles in English translation and who have since branched out into commissioning and publishing original content. Therefore, this does *not* include American comics publishers with a manga side business such as DC Comics and Dark Horse. Nor does it include Seven Seas, the only press expressly founded to publish original content that now also publishes selected licensed Japanese and Korean titles. I focus instead upon presses such as Viz, Digital Manga, and, despite having plans to publish original content from its inception, Yen Press. Del Rey Manga also commissioned original manga. The now defunct Tokyopop was famously the first to systematically adopt this new publishing model in response to an increasingly competitive licensing environment as early as 2002 with regular "Rising Stars of Manga" contests and ambitious quotas for numbers of new titles released annually. As such, the model technically predates 2007, but it has become *de rigueur* post-2007. In fact, by the end of 2011, with the exception of Vertical and the new Kodansha Comics, *all* manga publishers still active had added original global manga to their lists.

It is important to note that while I have chosen to call these books "original global manga," there is little agreement within the industry itself about what the official label is. Terms bandied about over the years include "OEL (Original English Language) Manga," "OGM (Original Global Manga)," and "GloBL (a portmanteau of 'global' and 'BL' for boys love titles)." Others simply call it "manga" or "graphic novels." Yen Press's first original fare was an adaptation of James Patterson's *Maximum Ride* series of young adult novels, and it is billed on the back cover of the first volume as a "manga rendering." Conversely, the original titles commissioned for Viz's VizKids line are all called "graphic novels" on the publisher's website.

There are several reasons for this absence of industry consensus. "Manga's just a trim size," asserted the head of the manga imprint of one of the large US publishing houses, rehearsing what has quickly become the common wisdom in trade publishing. Yet other American manga industry insiders prefer to think of manga as being from Japan and are wary of anything that could become stigmatized as, "fake manga," as one informant called it. Their concerns are partly self-serving, that is, "What will the fans think?", but also ethical. After all, festooning oneself in another's ethnic characteristics has a long and inglorious history in America's culture industries, from nineteenth century blackface minstrelsy to persistent "yellowface" impersonation in Hollywood film (Lott 1995; Ono and Pham 2009). Obviously, they want no part of that.[1] The alphabet soup of acronyms was therefore an act of distinction—and, for Tokyopop, which pioneered the use of both OEL and OGM—of branding as well. Furthermore, some informants were also hesitant to use the word manga because they were concerned about maintaining good relations with their Japanese counterparts. Although for most Japanese people "manga" is merely a word for comics irrespective of country of origin, some have succumbed to recent appeals to national pride and now view manga as "uniquely Japanese," a concept with its own long and inglorious history (Dale 1986).

Other reasons are legal. Beginning in the mid-2000s when "Manga" became an official category in the retail chains, literary agents sighted a new opportunity. Manga and graphic novels, they contended, are different media, and therefore rights to one does not equal rights to the other. As manga

---

[1] In fact, the problem of "yellowface" was fresh on my informants' minds circa 2010–2011. In 2009, a live-action film based upon Akira Toriyama's *Dragon Ball* was released by Twentieth-Century Fox. Viz, which publishes *Dragon Ball* in English, was involved in brokering the deal which ultimately culminated in *Dragonball Evolution*. The film was neither a commercial nor critical success, and some reviewers decried the use of a white actor to play what, in their view, really ought to have been an Asian protagonist (Duralde 2009; Thompson 2009). "Viz is pretending that movie never happened," one informant told me sarcastically.

began to pull all forms of sequential art into the trade publishing field, some of the large trade houses began demanding ancillary rights to the "graphic novel" adaptation of all the novels they commissioned. Agents complained at industry events that this had become nonnegotiable. Thus, selling "manga" adaptation rights to a new third party was a way for agents to work around preexisting contracts, secure some extra money for authors, and actually get a comic version of a popular property out there into the world (since rights that are optioned are often not being exploited and realized). Of course, publishers can easily close this loophole in new contracts and, if desired, ask for both, but the legacy of these old deals will surely continue working their way through the system for years to come.

Nevertheless, irrespective of what they do or do not call it, there are obvious benefits. With original global manga, the American publisher does not have to cede control to a Japanese rights holder over the way in which the text is produced and marketed; there is far more room to exercise personal judgment about what is or is not suitable for US audiences. It is also compatible with other new publishing models, publisher as retailer and direct-to-digital. They also do not need to worry about competing with scanlators who can get a finished product out before they can (or have better online search visibility than they do even when they are not faster)—because there *is* nothing to scanlate. Finally, and perhaps most compellingly of all from the current business perspective, there is the transmedia potential of original global manga.

Popular properties originating in other media such as novels, film, animation, and video games can be made into manga, and the big publishers with manga imprints have the capacity to produce transmedia content themselves in-house. There is no need to rely entirely upon Hollywood anymore to give book sales a boost, and proliferation of a single franchise across multiple media platforms assists with visibility at a time when bookstores are thin on the ground. The best example of this is Hachette with its Yen Press imprint, which has published numerous original global manga based upon novels already published by Hachette. The first volume of *Twilight: The Graphic Novel* (Figure 6.1), for example, boasted a 350,000 first print run, the biggest for any manga or graphic novel to date in the North American market (Memmott 2010). Its Korean artist Young Kim relies heavily upon the visual conventions of Japanese manga, and it has become the imprint's bestselling graphic novel series. Indeed, it's only a small step further to begin deliberately commissioning novels with original global manga potential, and that's likely to already be happening. A blurb credited to Danielle Trussoni printed on the US hardcover edition of Julianna Baggott's *Pure*, published by Hachette in February 2012, says, "Pressia Belze is one part manga heroine and one part post-apocalyptic Alice..." Furthermore, some novelists, such as Sherrilyn

FIGURE 6.1 Twilight: The Graphic Novel *Vol. 1. A Walmart price tag offering a considerable discount off of the $19.99 suggested retail price is visible in the upper right-hand corner.*

Kenyon, are themselves manga fans and would be pleased to see their work turned into manga. Giving them what they want is one possible way for a publisher to dissuade a frontlist author from defecting to a competitor.

There is really only one problem with original global manga—one of perception. Publishers worry about (1) what Japanese partners, investors, and parent companies will think and (2) what fans will think. The latter concern is more easily dispelled; although it is true that most original global manga do not sell well, most books do not sell well period, and some publishers have had successful titles. Svetlana Chmakova's *Dramacon*,[2] for example, did very well for Tokyopop—it was one of ICv2's "Top Manga Properties" of 2007 and the first original title to crack BookScan's top ten bestselling graphic novel list (Anon. 2006)—as did some of their other original global manga. Then there is Yen Press's *Twilight*, mentioned above. The solution would be to devote a larger share of resources to a smaller number of titles, to make original global

---

[2] *Global Manga: "Japanese" Comics without Japan?* (Brienza 2015) explores the worldwide output of original global manga and also provides a history of so-called "OEL manga" and the works of creator Svetlana Chmakova.

manga "big books," in other words. This is a politically nettlesome prospect, particularly for those companies which are subsidiaries of, or part-owned by, Japanese publishing houses because there is ongoing confusion and tension with regards to what their purpose actually is from Japan's perspective. "Is the idea to distribute Japanese content in the West or to make money?" I asked again and again. "Nobody knows," was the consensus. "And if these are mutually exclusive propositions?" Nervous laughter. Even a founding father who confided that he had received permission from Japan to lose money if it meant building cultural bridges told me he was desperate not to out of fear that it would increase creative and organizational interference from Japan. Profits help to secure his company's autonomy; "I would *lick your ass* to publish [the next] *Naruto*," he emphasized with characteristic vulgarity. It therefore stands to reason that, given the opportunity, he would also happily publish the next *Twilight* graphic novel. Moreover, some Japanese publishers are anxious about original global manga being presented alongside their manga. Viz, for example, publishes under Shueisha and Shogakukan-branded imprints like Shonen Jump and Shonen Sunday. Sure, publishing a serial of an original title alongside the *Shonen Jump Alpha* serializations of *Naruto* and *Bakuman* might be a fabulous way to publicize it from Viz's perspective. But will it be up to Japanese Shonen Jump standards? And will it be a hit? Inasmuch as any US manga press is not trusted to deliver on such issues, the full potential of original global manga as a new publishing model may remain unexplored.

But is it still "Japanese"?

Taken together, the endgame of these five new models may be summarized as follows: a gradual but progressively accelerating minimization of Japanese content in the space of the visible. Publisher as retailer and fan-funded publishing are aimed at already knowledgeable, dedicated readers who are willing to proactively seek out new content. They are profoundly unsuited to attracting new audiences. That, in turn, is a recipe for marginalization and year-on-year declines of sales figures as readers lose interest and are not replaced. Direct-to-digital collectives might work in an ideal world, but at the moment there are too many sites, legitimate or otherwise, in competition with each other, and the scanlation sites have had several years' head start. Publishers would, in my view, benefit the most from this model if they were able to join forces and co-opt one or two of the most prominent sites (as Google has done with YouTube, say), but this, informants assure me, will not happen...or will only happen with their profoundest reluctance. As culture industry professionals, they have moral objections to associating publicly or colluding with intellectual property thieves. This was true even among informants who were themselves former scanlators! In fact, only two models, original global manga and simultaneous laydowns, are particularly suited to the most profitable forms of frontlist publishing. The latter greatly increases the likelihood of Western influence upon the initial creation, and not just the *post hoc* domestication, of a manga text; the former, meanwhile, does not strictly require the participation of anyone Japanese whatsoever.

Yet that emphatically does not mean that the Japanese will not be involved, albeit in new ways. Numerous informants suggest to me that, for the first time ever, Japanese publishers are showing interest in publishing content and creators of non-Japanese origin in Japan. Year on year declines have left everyone looking for someone to blame, and some have decided to blame themselves. Japan just does not produce great manga anymore, they have concluded. While of course it is always necessary to be suspicious of claims that manga artists were more exciting and original (or people more hardworking, children more respectful of their elders, etc.) in the past, the conviction, not the objective reality, is what matters here, and there are many industry professionals on both sides of the Pacific who believe the Japanese manga publishing field is creatively tapped out. This then means that some US publishers are less enthusiastic than ever about new licenses and that Japanese publishers are looking overseas for possible new talent. Japanese cooperation with US counterparts becomes one obvious solution. Precisely how serious they become about such possibilities remains to be seen, but at minimum there is now an entire generation of young people outside Japan for whom manga translated into English has become a part of the everyday media landscape. A handful of these may become artists themselves. Combined with a bevy of professionalized editors in the American manga industry who have learned how to develop and manage original content—and newfound will throughout the field of contemporary trade book publishing to do so—the West may become a source of content and creators for Japan.

There are early signs of precisely that. Manga artist Felipe Smith[3] got his break in the industry with the publication of *MBQ*, a three-volume original global manga series for Tokyopop, and these books in turn attracted the interest of an editor at Kodansha. In 2008, Smith became the first ever American citizen to write and illustrate his own multi-chapter work for Japanese publication. This manga, serialized in the magazine *Morning Two*, was called *Peepo Choo*, and it was collected into three volumes which were, in turn, published in English by Vertical with a script provided by Smith himself (see Figure 6.2).

Is *Peepo Choo* a "Japanese manga"? The answer, naturally, depends upon how one defines "Japanese," but irrespective of this, clearly something,

---

[3]For more information about Felipe Smith and his global manga, see Brienza (2013).

FIGURE 6.2 Peepo Choo *Vol. 2.*

qualitatively, is changing radically. Indeed, I would argue that to conceive of such content as it emerges and gains prominence in the future solely in terms of a unitary national origin is wholly insufficient. And since it is likely to be the production of frontlist manga in the United States that is most affected by these transnational transformations, the way that the word "manga" is understood in the public space will likewise be disproportionately affected. Manga publishers know this, as the interviewee quoted at the beginning of this chapter acknowledges. These new models are an act of self-transformation aimed at influencing the transformation of others, a restructuring of the entire manga publishing value chain, as well as the expectations and practices of consumers. When I asked the informant if in fact at the end of the day all this is really about is trying to change how people consume media, she replied, "Yes. I think it goes for many media, but particularly for manga that needs to happen in order to survive. Really. You gotta think about business model, business structure—how people interact within this whole system needs to be redesigned entirely." She, working in America for a US-based press, meant this in a transnational sense; everyone, American companies as well as Japanese, needs to change themselves in order to succeed commercially in the United States, and the pressure to do so will emanate from America.

It is especially interesting to note that Smith, who emigrated from the United States to Japan in order to produce *Peepo Choo*, exists as a living, breathing example of what journalist Douglas McGray (2002) really intended for the future of the Japanese cultural economy when he developed the concept of "Japan's Gross National Cool." The idea was *not* that foreigners from beyond the shores of the Japanese archipelago would merely consume their favorite Japanese popular cultural goods, such as manga, in their own countries; the article was actually suggesting that these foreigners' attraction to Japanese popular culture would draw them into Japan proper. They would bolster Japan's economy, not primarily by buying manga, say, but by studying, working, and otherwise contributing to the reinvigoration of Japan's economy *while living there*. As card-carrying members of Richard Florida's "creative class" (2002), these mobile artistic and intellectual entrepreneurs would add their energy to Japan's own—and help to ameliorate the nation's all-too-impending demographic disaster. Needless to say, given Japan's restrictive immigration policies, which show little sign at the moment of budging to accommodate large numbers of individuals who want to join and become productive members of Japanese society simply because, in the first instance, they loved manga, this is all too often conveniently forgotten in the debates, discourses, and governmental policies related to "Cool Japan." And it would probably be more realistic to conclude, in the absence of a radical policy shift, that it is more realistically American publishers such as Simon & Schuster than Japanese publishers such as Shueisha which stand to benefit from the long-term consequences of the transnational cultural production of the American manga industry. Still, even the glimmer of a suggestion that new transnational social arrangements in the culture industries might someday result in the transnational movement of actual people is no small thing by any means. And taken to the logical extreme, then, *this* ultimately is what may be meant by the successful, large-scale domestication of manga.

7

Conclusion: Making Manga American

By the end of 2011, as I was beginning to writing up the research for the manuscript which would eventually become the book you are now holding in your hands, a brand new story about manga in America had begun to be told. Manga was not actually, according to these self-appointed truth tellers, about "air" or "export," let alone cultural "conquest," "invasion," or "revolution." It was, in fact, about failure, and Japan's Gross National Cool was at best a flash in the pan and at worst a tall tale cooked up by state and corporate interests to make the Japanese feel good about themselves. Now the party is over, the boom has gone bust, and there is nothing left but to pick up the pieces and move on. An interview with Japanese artist Takashi Murakami (of "superflat" fame) published in the *Asahi Shimbun* in March 2012 is representative of the most extreme position:

Q: Japanese animation and manga are being praised abroad now under the theme of "Cool Japan." How do you feel about your role as standard bearer for that trend?

A: No one overseas talks about "Cool Japan." That is a lie and rumor.

It was intentionally created to satisfy the pride of the Japanese and is nothing more than ad copy to allow public funds to go to advertising companies.

While Japan's manga and animation are slowly being understood abroad, even if the cultural background and context may be difficult to comprehend, it is only being accepted by a small group of fanatics. It is nowhere near a level of becoming a business, so there is nothing to be especially excited about. (Ikeda 2012)

Does this position have any merit in the context of the United States? Certainly, there is some justification for his claims; my graph of annual US manga sales from 2002 to 2011 (Figure 3.3) charts a rapid rise and decline that looks an awful lot like a bubble which began to deflate in 2008. Yet, a closer look at the data suggests a more nuanced picture. Even in 2010 sales at $120 million are still fully twice as large as they were in 2002, the year the manga market began its dramatic expansion. Meanwhile, attendance at Anime Expo, the largest Japanese popular culture convention in the United States, rose from approximately 15,000 registered attendees in 2002 to 40,000 in 2007 (Anon. 2002, 2007), and there has been no drop off in line with the decline of manga sales. The convention, in fact, has been posting modest but steady increases in attendance since 2007, with nearly 50,000 people registered in 2012 (Anon. 2012a).

Whether or not any of these numbers count as "small" is, ultimately, a matter of opinion, but more telling still are the mere 3,826 attendees registered at Anime Expo in 1997 (Anon. 1997), back when the sales of manga in the United States were not worth measuring.1997, as described in Chapter 4, is the year that Mixx Entertainment, later Tokyopop, debuted the first US edition of the Naoko Takeuchi's *Sailor Moon* manga and kicked off what would eventually culminate in the manga boom. So, was *Sailor Moon* just a one-time fad, "nowhere near a level of becoming a business"? The answer to that question is a resounding no. The Kodansha Comics reissue of *Sailor Moon* (titled *Pretty Guardian Sailor Moon* in full for this edition) has, since the publication of its first volume in September 2011, been a bestselling series. The first volume sat at the top of BookScan's monthly bestseller list in September 2011 (Anon. 2011a), and its seventh volume (out of a total of twelve) was at the top of that same list exactly a year later in September 2012, the month of its release (Middaugh 2012). To make it to the top of these lists, *Sailor Moon* needed to outsell world famous American comics properties such as *Batman*, *The Avengers*, and *The Walking Dead* in mainstream book stores such as Barnes & Noble, and this may well mean selling at a rate of over 1,000 copies per week (see Appendix). Moreover, approximately half of the rest of these top twenty throughout 2011 and 2012 have been manga, such as the latest volumes of *Naruto* and *Bleach* (Anon. 2012b).

At minimum, this does not suggest popularity at levels insufficient to maintain publishing manga at the level of a sustainable business. Nor does it suggest a fad, infectiously popular for a short period of time and then forgotten a few years later. Otherwise, *Sailor Moon* would not have become a hit twice with over a decade in-between releases. Manga series, such as *Naruto* and *Bleach*, continuous stories told over tens of thousands of pages, would not still be bestsellers at volumes 58 and 47, respectively (Middaugh 2012). The facts speak instead to continuity, to enduring popularity, in the present—and to genuine and rapid social change in the immediate past. If there was ever any fad here, it was a fad for telling manga's story. Manga such as *Sailor*

Moon have gone from something no one had ever seen before in the 1990s to just another part of the American publishing landscape in the 2010s. The extraordinary became ordinary, and the very fact that commentators can, with a straight face, pronounce "Cool Japan" a failure is actually proof of success. Like Lawrence Venuti's translator, the American manga industry's instantiation as a mature transnational field has, for a fourth and final time, made them invisible.

The movement of culture does not happen on its own. Back in Chapter 1, I set myself the task of telling a story of Japanese manga in America that takes into account the people whose labor and cooperation is required to make it happen. These people are highly motivated, driven professionals operating in a transnational field of cultural production which I term "the American manga industry," whose core activities, which I term "domestication," are organized along a directionally oriented domestication value chain. I show how, in the construction of this chain, linking the Japanese publishing field with the American trade book publishing field to generate a transnational field, they became professionalized, themselves oriented toward trade book publishing. I describe in detail how none of the links of the domestication chain, from licensing to translation to graphic design, are as straightforward or standardized as the presentation of the manga object itself on the bookstore shelf, all of them subject to continuous cross-national cooperation, negotiation, and struggle. This work, though often undercompensated financially, is rewarded through individual involvement in—and being given a measure of control over—the process of domestication. And finally, I discuss how global financial crisis and the pressures of digitization in American trade publishing are beginning to change precisely what it means to domesticate manga in the first place.

What, then, can truly be said about manga as an example of the transnational production of culture? I have already dispensed with the assertion by the likes of Murakami that nothing worthy of note has ever happened, so what about the three standard stories discussed in the introduction? Let's begin with the first of these stories: Is there anything to be redeemed about manga as odorless air? Well, the idea that culture crosses national boundaries at random like currents of air particles was clearly wrongheaded right from the start. Tremendous effort and coordinated action is required to publish manga in America. And now I have proven that there is no persuasive evidence, furthermore, of a coherent effort to conceal manga's Japanese origins; there is no consistent way in which words are translated or not translated, images altered or left unaltered. So the first story can be safely dismissed once and for all.

What about the notion of manga as a commodity export which will help revive Japan's ailing economy? Well, that is just as misleading; save for occasional shipments of Japanese editions to overseas branches of specialty bookstores such as Kinokuniya, manga are not just exports. Moreover, there are "manga" for sale in the United States that did not originate from Japan in any form, either as material or as matter of intellectual property law, and all US manga publishers, increasingly, are looking to make original global manga serious frontlist contenders. What has been exported—or rather appropriated—I would argue, is not so much the object at all but rather the signs and social practices around the production and consumption of comic books like manga. Comics used to be a far smaller part of the media landscape. Such practices simply did not exist prior to the manga boom in the way they do now. And while they are not precisely identical to those in Japan, they are analogous. Transnational fields, in short, operate through their production of new practices.

Indeed, it may be worth reflecting one final time upon ICv2's data for North American manga sales first presented in Chapter 3. These numbers are, in my view, useful for identifying broad trends, as they survey both the trade stores and indie comics shops. But they must be taken with a grain of salt, particularly post-2007 with the start of the economic downturn, since they do not include sales data for some of the key titles which I would categorize as original global manga. These books, though often classified in the trade publishing industry as "graphic novels," not "manga," absolutely cannot be understood in isolation from domesticated manga from Japan and are an integral—and increasingly substantial—part of the transnational industry's political economy. So, inasmuch as original titles have become important frontlist bestsellers for manga publishers, any extrapolated decline of the industry to be interpreted solely from this data is likely to be overstated.

This brings me to the final story, the idea that manga conquered, invaded, and/or revolutionized the United States, proving the soft power of Cool Japan. Certainly, I would readily concede, there is genuine and rapid transformation here. But to imply that something or someone Japanese was effecting this transformation would be entirely inaccurate and ahistorical. Time and time again throughout this text I have shown how non-Japanese actors and structural logics were responsible for key moments in the formation and evolution of the field. The particular realities of Japan and the Japanese manga publishing field certainly mattered, but they reacted to and, in some cases, got swept up in that change; they were not its primary instigators, nor, in the long run, do they stand well positioned to be its primary beneficiaries. Bestselling American "manga-influenced" comics such as the *Scott Pilgrim* series prove that greater transnational integration and exchange in the symbolic dimension does not automatically generate economic value back in Japan. It was, in other words, not the Japanese at all but rather Americans who were most instrumental in making manga American. This is why US manga publishers have found it so easy to eliminate Japan from the publishing value chain altogether. There was never any real invasion, and if there ever was any conquest or revolution at all, it was self-induced. Manga publishers had indeed changed themselves.

In line with my three-part model of a transnational field that is both separate from and embedded in two national fields, there are three ways in which this change is happening. The first is to expand the remit of the transnational field, appropriating links of the value chain which had heretofore been left to the US national field, such as distribution and retail, and taking new responsibility for those functions. The second way in which change is being effected is the way in which actors in the Japanese publishing field are being persuaded to become transnational players, both in terms of assuming greater degrees of upfront financial stake in the international success or failure of a property and in terms of transforming their own publishing workflows to accommodate simultaneous laydowns in multiple languages. The third and final way the meaning of domestication—and indeed that of "manga" itself—has been changing is the devolution of the transnational field into the purely national as manga publishers choose increasingly not to bother licensing content from Japan but rather to develop it locally themselves.

This all adds up to an increase in the intensity and complexity of the network ties between the Japanese and American national publishing fields. What it does *not* imply, however, is a substantive realignment or rebalancing of the power between national publishing fields. Why? Because the American manga industry upgraded to functions higher up on the value chain and no longer needs to rely solely upon Japanese intellectual property in order to make money, so the Japanese must in turn increase their transnational activity further down the domestication chain merely to maintain the flow of revenue that used to come in with hardly any effort on their part at all. In financially straitened times, Japanese manga publishers may come to depend upon the health of the transnational field more than American manga publishers. This, in turn, as elsewhere noted, means the presence of Japanese subsidiary companies in the United States as well as adjustments to the workflow back in Japan to make manga easier to domesticate at a later date. And it can, moreover, have an effect upon manga before it even exists. Informants confidentially named particular manga titles which are only still being serialized in Japan because they are selling well in America. Some manga in print in Japan today, therefore, can be understood as products of the American manga industry. Put differently, the US market is interfering with Japan's internal affairs, while the Japanese can but play by America's rules if they wish to do business in it. The processes of domestication, in sum, simultaneously re-inscribe and rearticulate the very same imbalances of national power that might otherwise seem to have been transformed by them.

FIGURE 7.1 *Manga section in Waterstones on Sidney Street, Cambridge, UK (February 2012).*

Furthermore, links to the American national publishing field have opened up access to markets for manga outside of Japan. Other English-language markets are a given; rights to print editions (but not digital . . . yet), at least, are being streamlined so that one company has world English-language rights and the same manga purchased in the United States can be purchased in, say, the United Kingdom. There are sections for manga in Waterstones that look virtually identical to those in Barnes & Noble—and upon closer inspection all the books prove to be identical as well (see Figure 7.1). However, as discussed previously, these are emphatically *American* books, targeted to an imagined, idealized reader in Middle America, not the United Kingdom, Australia, or even Canada. Increasingly, though, the US manga industry is structuring the way in which manga is seen outside of the English-speaking world as well. The European publishing activities of two of the Big Three Japanese houses is called Viz Media Europe, not Shueisha Europe or Shogakukan Europe, or some other entirely different, locally relevant name, and the German branch of Tokyopop is still an important player there, even after its US enterprise went bust. These sorts of asymmetrical relations are to be expected given that the world reads American books in translation in far higher proportions than America reads books originally written in languages other than English

(Sapiro 2010). Hye-Kyung Lee (2009) states, moreover, that English is the global language by default for pirated digital manga. American companies are quite aware of that, according to informants, and those who aspire to publish their titles in both paper and e-editions know that to succeed in the long run is to work to suppress and ideally fully supplant illegal global circulation. All this has led to a basic conclusion about the current global state of affairs that can be summarized by a PowerPoint slide prepared for the Sugoi Books industry panel at the 2011 Anime Expo. The slide says, "We Distribute Manga from Japan to Worldwide!" This, however, is visualized with a map of the world and a sweeping yellow arrow crossing the Pacific and pointing directly from Japan to the United States. The United States *is* the world in this formulation or, rather, playing in its national publishing field—since the service was only available in the United States when launched—gives the Japanese access to it. Iwabuchi's "Americanization of Japanization" still has hold in a digital future (2002, 38).

Sugoi Books was discontinued in August 2012, barely a year after it was first launched. JManga soon followed, leaving a thin trail of angry customers who had not expected to lose access to the titles they had purchased. Their brief lives have somewhat chilled the enthusiasm in the field for new digital ventures. And certainly, they are stark reminders that it was never the Japanese, historically, who most desired to make manga succeed in America. The commitment to building transnational networks and to doing the underpaid (or free) intensive labor required to make that happen came from Americans themselves. Their desires have always structured this story, so it stands to reason, therefore, that knowing the future of the American manga industry is to know what the Americans actors in the field want to see happen. I asked all of my interviewees about the future, but the majority were perhaps too anxious about their careers in 2010 and 2011 to entertain serious thoughts about the proverbial bigger picture. Most simply hoped to be able to press on with their current role in the industry, and it stands to reason that this transnational field would be difficult to dismantle now that there are so many entrenched collective and individual interests with a stake in it.

This could suggest continuity with what has come before, incremental change to adjust to the digitization of print, or, most pessimistically, an unstoppable, albeit gradual, decline of interest in licensing new manga titles from Japan. All of these possibilities would be supported by my research findings. And yet, there was little ambition or enthusiasm to realize any of these changes for their own sakes. Any effort in those directions was fueled by anxiety, the necessities of survival, and a desire only to save what remains. The extent to which these sentiments were purely a snapshot of the particular time in which I conducted my fieldwork would be impossible to ascertain without extensive follow-up research; the Great Recession had opened some deep wounds, and the manga industry was still very much in the process of healing. It can be hard to think about the future when one is so focused simply on recovery. Nonetheless, these are people who proactively changed themselves, often at considerable personal cost, in order to change others. And recall that the transnational field of cultural production, which is the American manga industry, began as a dream "to build a bridge between Japan and America," which by Levy's own admission was a success. Might there be any new dreams waiting to be realized in the wings?

In pursuit of a potential answer to that question, one particular incident toward the end of my fieldwork year stands out. An editor, whom I will call Eve, regarded by her peers in the American manga industry as among the best in the business, had allowed me into her home. Like everyone else whom I had met thus far, she had an ample collection of books. Hers, though, were neatly arranged (albeit shelved two layers deep) and appropriate for a bit of show and tell. I stood next to Eve in front of a bookcase. Pulling a slim volume off the shelf and handing it over for my inspection (and, presumably, approbation), she said, "This was one of my proudest moments." The volume in question was the Japanese edition of an original American title, one of the first original global manga that this woman, the series' editor, had ever worked on in her career. Though already several years old, her copy's dust jacket had not yet lost that distinctive, hot-off-the-press shine; this book had only rarely been exposed to the open air, and it was clearly very precious. Yet until that moment, I had not known that this original global manga first commissioned and published in the United States had also been released in Japan and that this book I was holding in my hands even existed in the first place.

That brief moment, flipping reverently through a comic book taken down from its place of pride in Eve's apartment, was telling. Many of the Japanese titles she had edited had been bestsellers in the United States for her company. The original title in question had, in fact, been a bestseller too—important evidence to all in the field that "manga" which had not come from Japan had the potential to be profitable. Indeed, this editor's work had been instrumental in supporting her company's entire publishing program, and her professional reputation in the field had been built upon this record of success. Yet that was not the part of her career she wished to highlight. Instead, Eve wanted to show me physical evidence of the directionality of the transnational field being put in reverse, an instance where the American was made to become Japanese.

In short, Eve was not proudest of changing herself or the American publishing field anymore. She most reveled, instead, in the possibility of effecting change within the publishing field in Japan. Of course, it is still far too early to tell whether or not American-made original global manga will have a significant impact on Japanese manga publishing or what, precisely, that impact may be. Certainly books like the Japanese edition of *Twilight: The Graphic Novel* or the *Peepo Choo* manga series would not exist without the transnational field which was precondition for their production. Likewise, the pessimism I encountered everywhere throughout my fieldwork about the future creative potential within Japan suggests that the Japanese themselves might become interested as they never have before in publishing content and talent from non-Japanese sources. Of course, should any of this happen it would not be the first time American interests have forced Japanese markets open and ended the country's self-imposed isolation. So, perhaps the future for the domestication of manga is to make manga *in Japan* more American too.

Appendix

House Calls: Notes on Research Methodology

At first glance it may seem all well and good to define transnational cultural production, as I do in this book, in terms of collective social action. However, for the ethnographer, this theoretical understanding presents an immediate and pressing methodological problem: *Where*, precisely, is the actual, on the ground location of this action? After all, if the role of the American manga industry is so defined by its domestication of manga for the United States, it need not actually be geographically situated in America to accomplish this end.

And indeed, it is not. Although several important US manga companies, along with many full-time and freelance laborers, are based in urban centers, including the iconic global cities, for example, New York and Tokyo, of urban sociologist Saskia Sassen (2001), others are quite far off the beaten path. Important companies can be headquartered in Oregon or Texas, and industry professionals can be found living everywhere from suburban New Jersey to inland central Japan to rural Cambridgeshire in the United Kingdom. Other organizational and individual actors in the field may be even more far-flung; printing operations can be practically next door to publishers or as far away as Canada or China. Graphic design may be outsourced to India or Russia. One of the most important independent US manga retailers on the web, Right Stuf, is headquartered in Iowa. In fact, whether individual or organization, one can in principle move either across the neighborhood or halfway around the world and still maintain one's industry position.

Therefore, to locate the US manga industry in any one particular place, or even a finite set of geographically noncontiguous places, is impossible in practice. Yes, the industry is, at the moment, concentrated in New York, San Francisco, and Tokyo. Yet the fact remains that it is not strictly bound to any of those metropolises. To tackle this methodological conundrum I therefore rely upon Bourdieu's conception of the field, which he defines not in geographic but in relational terms: It is, in his own words, a "network or configuration of objective relations between positions" (Bourdieu 1993, 97). As an ethnographer, then, my field site is not a village, a city, or even a handful of global cities; it is, rather, the sum total of ongoing collective social action, a constantly moving, ever changing web of interactions taking place in many different parts of the world but constitutively tied down to none.

So, to call this research a multi-sited ethnography would, in my view, be misleading. I study a single field—a Bourdieuian field of transnational cultural production. Nevertheless, since one cannot pay visits to "objective relations between positions," for the sake of practicality, I divided my fieldwork year, beginning in September 2010 and ending in October 2011, between the New York and San Francisco metropolitan areas, with shorter visits to Los Angeles, Tokyo, Toronto, and surrounding environs. Again for expediency's sake, I traveled from East to West, starting in New York in the autumn and ending in Tokyo a year later before stopping again in New York for some final fieldwork on the way back to England. As noted above, the US manga industry is concentrated in particular places, both because key companies are headquartered there but also because cultural laborers in the field also tend to congregate nearby, either because they have moved there from elsewhere in pursuit of a career in manga or simply because they have prior geographic ties or constraints (finances or family obligations, for example) and have been locally sourced by nearby organizations. Even in an age where digital communication has weakened the territorial constraints of the past, a significant number of industry insiders get their proverbial break through face-to-face networking, and this is far more likely to happen when a hiring manager and prospective employee live near enough to each other to meet at, say, a book launch.

But because "to think of the field is to think relationally" (Bourdieu 1993, 92), it is not enough to step off a plane that has landed at Newark International Airport and conclude that I have arrived at the site of my research. The field is a networked group of people, not the expanse of (tarmacked) ground under my feet, and I am not automatically one of them. To actually enter the field, I have to become a part of their network—and to become embedded in one's field site is always to risk altering the very dynamic in which one seeks to study. In fact, the great challenge to an ethnographer entering a field is to maintain a sufficient amount of critical distance while not being so far away as to be unable to get any real sense of the field at all.

For this reason, while I toyed with the idea of trying to find temporary work in the US manga industry, I ultimately rejected it. To become an active participant in the labor of domestication before fully comprehending how it all works and why seemed too much of a risk; I could not guarantee to myself that I would not have an unintentional, undue influence upon the web of social relations constituting the field, thereby, through my mere presence, changing the results of the research. Besides, I subsequently learned from informants that they found their day-to-day labor conditions rather frustrating, lonely, and isolating, long hours spent communing with a computer screen. One interviewee working full-time reported being so overworked that the only time she and her colleagues got a break was when their company's overloaded servers crashed (an inevitable, daily occurrence) and needed to be rebooted. (They called this "beach-balling," an ironic reference both to the Mac operating system's spinning wait cursor indicating a nonresponsive system and a metaphor for the brief window of downtime it permitted.) Freelancers, in contrast, usually characterized the rhythm of their professional lives as alternately waiting around at home for weeks for work to arrive and then occasional bursts of working frantically for a few days straight to meet tight deadlines. In short, an optimal, well-situated perspective on the field was uncommon even for veterans, and although industry insiders were often acquainted with many others, they did not interact with the fullest extent of their personal network with much regularity. Electronic communication with distant others was standard, sometimes even within a single company (such as the one publisher on noncontiguous floors of an office building); face-to-face encounters may happen only a few times a year at industry and fan conventions. Clearly, participation in this field by becoming a low-level worker within it would have produced rich, but profoundly myopic, ethnographic data ill-suited to answering my research question.

Moreover, it could be argued that I was always already within, albeit marginally, this relational network of publishing, so it is worth explicating my own background in some detail. I was, to start with, raised in the New York City metropolitan area, one of the book publishing capitals of the world, and my mother worked for a legal publishing firm. However, I had no particular interest in book publishing growing up or any aspirations to a career in it. About the most I could claim about myself and my relationship to the field at that time is that I was an avid reader as a child and that I occasionally read American superhero comic books. Because I patronized independent comic book stores and browsed their shelves as a teenager, I had known vaguely that Japanese comics existed and that some had been translated into English, but I only began reading manga in earnest as a college undergraduate double-majoring in English literature and East Asian studies, the latter of these involving intensive Japanese language study. I became conscious of their growing popularity in the United States, particularly among my peers, during that period but did not consider reading manga—let alone trying to understand its social context—to be more than way of enriching my language skills while keeping myself entertained. Early in 2005, however, about a year and a half after graduating, I was recruited by the editor of the monthly magazine *Anime Insider* to write the Manga Department, a standard section set aside in every issue covering American manga publishing news and new title releases. At its peak, this magazine's circulation was 100,000, and it could be purchased at the newsstands of chain bookstores, grocery stores, and other retail chains such as Walmart and Target. My literary background, writing skills, and cultural competencies made me ideal for the role. The *Anime Insider* gig gave me entry into the world of freelance writing on the periphery of the manga industry, and in subsequent years I wrote news pieces, feature articles, columns, and reviews for a number of well-known niche media outlets, such as *Otaku USA* and Anime News Network. It was during this period that I first took seriously the idea that there was something sociologically important and interesting about the manga boom.

Unfortunately, my dual literary and East Asian area studies background provided little to help me interpret what I was seeing on the ground, and pursuit of better theoretical frameworks is eventually what brought me back into the academy and graduate study. I commenced a terminal MA program in Media, Culture, and Communication at New York University in the fall of 2007 and completed my degree at the end of 2008. It was there that I began researching the American manga publishing field in earnest, both upping my workload as a freelance writer and beginning to experiment with actual fieldwork. That preliminary work culminated into coursework papers and a master's thesis which would subsequently be published as three journal articles (see Brienza 2009a, 2009b, 2011). By mid-2009, however, as a consequence of the 2008 financial crisis, freelance work had begun to dry up, and my first and oldest gig ended abruptly when *Anime Insider* was discontinued. I was at the time entertaining multiple funded offers for PhD study and took it as a sign that I ought to be focusing on my academic career. These two things led to the de facto end of my career in manga journalism.

Upon commencing PhD study at the University of Cambridge in October 2009, geographic realities and the absence of freelance work made separation all the easier. And I had furthermore by that point consciously resolved to put some distance between myself and the manga publishing field, the better to cultivate a critical perspective. Following theoretical interventions from postmodern ethnographers (e.g., Clifford and Marcus 1986), I do not presume that perfect impartiality is possible. Nevertheless, I am sympathetic to Georgina Born (2004, 15), when she writes, as an advocate of ethnographic fieldwork:

> One of the marks of social power is how in enables those who hold it to determine the very framework of what can be said or even thought in a given social space. To understand any organization, it is therefore imperative

to uncover not only what is insistently present, but the characteristic absences and rigidities—what cannot be thought, or what is systematically "outside."

In other words, actors fully embedded within a given field might not even be able to articulate the workings of power in their own lives. (This strikes to the heart of why I do not readily accept the word "localization," for example, to describe what these people do.) Too much proximity seemed to risk the possibility that I too would be unable to think certain things, and I wanted very much to avoid that. This cooling off period proved effective and put me, in fact, in a position I had not anticipated but which nonetheless turned out to be particularly efficacious.

Even so, although I would never be able to draw a direct line between the geographic location and circumstances of my upbringing and education to my eventual involvement around, and research interest in, the publishing industry, I would also be hesitant to state with absolute certitude that there is no connection whatsoever. Early in my fieldwork, for example, I learned that a key executive player in the American manga industry had first become familiar with the publishing field working as a manager at one particular branch of a national chain bookstore. This in itself is not exceptional; five informants had experience in book retail. What *is* exceptional is that the store in question that he had managed was one which I had frequented extensively while growing up during his tenure. How could I, with total certainty, assert that I have not been formatively influenced by any personal worldview he was communicating through that built space? To ask such a thing is to ask the impossible.

In any case, after deliberation I concluded that, since one cannot simply hover invisibly over one's field, the best position for the ethnographer in this particular field is that of the semioutsider—and that I was very well situated to take such a position. By "semioutsider," I mean that I strove to present myself as someone who was familiar to my informants but not so similar that the answer to any question I might pose would be, "Well, *you* know." Familiarity was accomplished in two basic ways: The first and most straightforward was through a shared biography. In terms of age, interests, and educational attainment, I was similar to many of my informants, and that in a slightly different universe I could have been them or they me was not lost on any of us. The second was through actual shared history. As a freelance writer, I had become personally acquainted with a handful of key industry players, and my name may have rung a familiar chord to several more. This also helped me reenter the field from new directions, although I was careful not to lean too much on friends for favors. In fact, it was common for interviewees who were complete strangers to me to assume that the one who had passed me onto them was a close, personal acquaintance. Some had experience being interviewed by journalists before, but the journalistic interview is usually superficial and interested in the latest scoop, not the long-term social processes. Thus, the vast majority had never encountered a researcher so avidly mapping out and moving through their professional networks; it comes as no surprise that some could only imagine, prior to meeting me and drilling me with questions about myself and my research till they were satisfied that I must be a friend of a friend. Although I could never be certain precisely how—or whether—my semioutsider positioning was working for any particular individual, in the aggregate this vague sense of familiarity neither positioned me centrally in the field nor left me entirely outside of it. Instead, I was so far to its periphery that I could not, in layperson's terms, be considered a part of the manga industry...yet I was something ever so slightly more to them than a mere stranger.

The centerpiece of this research, therefore, is a snowballed sample of seventy in-depth, semistructured interviews, mostly conducted in-person and one-on-one. In total, I conducted formal interviews with seventy informants ($n_1 = 70$), though as can be seen from the breakdown on Tables A.1 and A.2, many informants have occupied multiple roles for multiple employers. Two interviews out of the total were follow-up meetings with previously interviewed informants, and another two interviews were with pairs of informants who wished to be interviewed together. Sixty-eight were conducted in-person in the greater metropolitan areas of New York, Toronto, San Francisco, Los Angeles, and Tokyo; only two were, out of necessity, completed over Skype webcam. Interviews averaged ninety minutes in length, as that was the length of time I requested of informants, and on occasion lasted in excess of three hours. Because all interviewees were fluent in English, this is the language in which interviews were conducted.

TABLES A.1 Interviewees by role[a]

Management/Leadership	11
Licensing	6
Translation/Adaptation	15
Editorial	29
Graphic Design/Lettering	4
Sales/Marketing	12
Distribution (incl. international and digital)	4
Retail	5
Libraries	4
Interns (unpaid)	6
Other (e.g., support staff)	6

[a] $n >$ seventy because many interviewees occupy (or have occupied) more than one role

TABLES A.2 Interviewees by employer affiliation[a]

Salaried	
Subsidiaries (large)	21
Subsidiaries (small)	2
Trade publishers, incl. imprints (all)	3
Comics publishers, incl. imprints (all)	1
Manga imprints of anime companies	4
Independents (all)	23
Retailer	6
Other (e.g., distributor, library, agency, Japanese publisher)	9
Unsalaried	
Subsidiaries (large)	11
Subsidiaries (small)	1
Trade publishers, incl. imprints (all)	7
Comics publishers, incl. imprints (all)	1
Manga imprints of anime companies	2
Independents (all)	12

[a] n > seventy because many interviewees work (or have worked) for more than one employer

My aim was to include people from as many manga publishers as possible. I started by focusing upon companies and imprints which had successfully licensed and released ten or more properties—and were still in business—as of the beginning of my fieldwork in the autumn of 2010. Companies and imprints fitting this profile included Viz Media, Tokyopop, Yen Press, Dark Horse, Seven Seas, Bandai, Fanfare, Vertical, and Digital Manga. However, given that even large manga publishers may have less than five full-time staff, I continued tracing out the contours of the field by reaching out to people working for publishers which did not fit my initial parameters yet had been active on or after 2005, the year the manga industry had reached maturity. They may have recently become inactive, gone out of business, or been reorganized out of existence. Examples of these include Del Rey Manga, CMX, Media Blasters, Aurora Publishing, Go! Comi, ADV Manga, and DramaQueen. Alternatively, they may still be active but so small in the scale of their operations that they had not yet published more than ten titles. These include ALC Publishing, Picture Box, Fantagraphics, and Kodansha Comics, the last of which did not seriously kick off its publishing operations until 2011. By prioritizing in this manner whom I contacted, I sought to avoid getting inadvertently bogged down in out-of-date perspectives or the experiences of people who had published manga in English but had not been socialized into the practices of the American manga industry proper.

I succeeded in securing interviews with people with experience working for sixteen manga publishing companies and imprints. Types of publishers covered in this research included the subsidiaries of Japanese companies, imprints of trade book and comics publishing houses, publishing arms of animation companies, and independently owned presses. Their respective levels of publishing activity ranged from large (80+ new books per year), to medium (approximately fifty books per year), to small (less than ten new books per year). As can be seen in Table A.2, different types of publishers are unevenly represented. These numbers do, in large part, reflect the actual numbers of people working for different types of employers. Viz, a large subsidiary, and Tokyopop, an independent, in particular have had large staff numbers for much of their recent history. Imprints of comics publishers and the publishing arms of animation companies are not as well represented as a consequence of my method—they, more so than any other type of company, have abandoned the field post-2008. This comes as no surprise given manga's increasing incorporation into trade book publishing (Brienza 2009a).

Interviewees include both salaried full- and part-time employees as well as freelancers, and range in rank from founders of presses and company executives at the top to unpaid summer interns at the very bottom of the corporate hierarchy (see Tables A.1 and A.2). In terms of experience in the industry, the vast majority had ten years or fewer; only five of my interviewees reported having worked in manga for more than a decade consecutively. Again, there are no surprises here, given the rapid expansion of the industry in the 2000s and its contraction post-2008. Further added to this are a selection of interviews with people in a range of other roles helping to constitute the field but who do not participate in the core functions of the domestication chain *per se*, such as book and comics retail, distribution, libraries, and events planning, who were suggested to me by informants.

As mentioned above, I did not depend upon prior contacts to help me get the proverbial ball rolling initially. This is because many of them, early in their careers when I first met them as a freelancer circa 2005, are now quite highly placed within their respective organizational contexts. As much as possible, I wanted to work my way up the chain of command, not down, and since people I interviewed were most likely to refer me to others like themselves, to start with them would have been to do the opposite. Instead, I reached out to suitable people whose contact information was publicly available online or whom I had met only briefly at events. This, with my "semioutsider" status and a promise of the strictest confidentiality, proved sufficient to start snowballing the names of subsequent contacts. I also continued reaching out to promising interview subjects without prior introduction as their names surfaced or as I happened to run into them at events throughout the fieldwork year. These two strategies together allowed me to work more systematically through the corporate hierarchy.

At this point, the delicate issue of maintaining the confidentiality of everyone who granted me interviews must be discussed. All email requests for interviews included the following disclaimer: "Please note that this would not be the same as a journalistic interview. For the purposes of this research, your identity, and the identity of your employer(s) past or present, will be kept strictly confidential." The level of concern I encountered about secrecy varied widely from individual to individual; some told me blithely that they did not care whether or not I put their name next to anything they said to me, while others kept nervously looking over their shoulders to make certain that no colleagues materialized behind them throughout the interview.

Irrespective of how any one particular individual felt about being identified or identifiable in this text, however, this stipulation makes systematically coding interviewees and other informants, or the companies they have worked for, profoundly problematic. This is a *very* small world. I am confident that no one can be reliably recognized by any one particular type of role, as can be seen from Table A.1. Moreover, as noted above, many interviewees have had more than one role—in fact, nearly half of the total ($n_2 = 30$) have worked in two or more roles, for two or more companies, or both. So, while any number of people may have occupied roles x, y, or z, the person who began a career in manga in role x, went on to work for several celebrated years in role y, and is now making do in role z is, in my view, too recognizable.

It's a similar story if I were to code interviewees by their various employers. A few career trajectories are reasonably common; several former Tokyopop employees have gone on to work for Viz Media, for example, and this can be seen from the names credited in the two press's books. Other transitions, however, are more unusual and would be, especially in the context of attributed quotes and the like, too easy to identify with a bit of Internet keyword searching. Even identifying people by a single role and a type of employer, for example, to say "does role x at company a," where "company a" is the manga imprint of a trade house, break confidentiality if only, say, Del Rey Manga but not Yen Press ever had someone doing x. Numerous cases like this emerged during the course of my fieldwork. As a matter of fact, there are several industry players who can be identified solely by naming a town or city in which they have at any point called home!

Likewise, individually coding all sixteen employers by their various characteristics such as size, type, and location is unworkable if company names too are to remain confidential. Publishers are, except at the most superficial levels, often too dissimilar, and the rapid shifts in the publishing landscape mean that, during certain time periods, even two basic, key features are enough to single out a company. For instance, the only large independent in 2010 was

Tokyopop; the only large subsidiary active prior to autumn 2011, meanwhile, is Viz. Table A.2 reflects the greatest amount of detail I can comfortably disclose without any one category becoming equivalent to a single publisher.

For the sake of consistency, then, and to uphold the principle of confidentiality as rigorously as possible, I have provided throughout this text only the minimum amount of biographical information necessary to make any particular quote or reference intelligible—and no more. If, for example, I quote an editor who has gone on to become a vice-president at her firm about editorial work, I refer to her as an editor, not a VP. If the reader does not need to know where I interviewed a particular person, I do not divulge it. If to write "large subsidiary" would identify the company in question, but "large" or "subsidiary" would not, I choose one of the latter. Every attribution has therefore been judged individually to best ensure both the maximum possible reader comprehension while preventing any informant or employer from being identified, either directly or through a text-wide process of elimination. If I err too far on the side of caution, so be it. Some of these people worried that they might have been risking their jobs by speaking to me, and not to treat their contribution with the greatest of respect would be nothing short of unethical. And it would, furthermore, jeopardize the reputations and prospects of any other researchers who might wish to explore this field in the future.

The content of all interviews were organized around the interviewee's own personal narrative and trajectory through time. This was intended to reflect the actor-centered properties of a field of cultural production, where each individual's actions are simultaneously structured and structuring. In other words, mapping out the collective life courses of my informants would in turn help me to map out the dynamic—and ongoing—transformations in the American manga industry. As such, I began by asking them how they "got into manga, or into the industry, whichever came first." At first, this was intended primarily as an icebreaker question which would then suggest further areas of inquiry. Over the course of the first six interviews, though, I soon came to realize that the specifics of the answer were often less important than the expression of feeling accompanying it. In fact, with only a few exceptions, particularly among the most experienced, these people *wanted* to work in manga, often quite desperately, and this desire has had, as I have discussed elsewhere, enormous influence. With that in mind, my final planned question was always, "Where do you think it's going to go in the future?" Deliberately vague in its wording, this question seemed to invite interviewees to reflect philosophically and to make predictions about their field in the manner they considered most pertinent. In actuality, it was meant to capture the expectations for the future of those in a position to help make it happen without putting them in the potentially uncomfortable position of acknowledging the extent of their own social power. All other questions were specific to each individual, based either upon information gleaned from other sources (see below) or asked on the spur-of-the-moment as the discussion unfolded.

Interviews were audio recorded with permission after reestablishing the principle of confidentiality, though permission was not always given. At my own discretion I occasionally decided not to record particular informants, particularly if I had been personally acquainted with them prior to this research and felt that they might get nervous or attempt to perform in front of the mic, as it were. Fifty-one interview participants were recorded in total. I produced and privately stored all transcripts of recorded interviews in Google Docs, a free, cloud-based word processing program which I was able to access from any device with an Internet connection. The transcriptions were typed up piecemeal in a personal shorthand throughout the course of ongoing research, as time permitted, and have been annotated with field notes throughout. This process allowed me to reflect upon patterns as they began to emerge and to highlight themes, questions, or confusions which I might raise with future interviewees. Time and time again, informants would express frustration—as well as outright ignorance—that could, when mentioned to subsequent informants with different perspectives on the field, be understood in an entirely new light. Events planners, for example, could not understand why US manga publishers were often so unenthusiastic about participating in programming or co-sponsoring Japanese guests. In some cases, furthermore, informants would misattribute the motivations of others. During one memorable exchange, an interviewee complained to me about the head of a particular company: "He doesn't care about manga; he doesn't care if he's selling manga or . . . lamps!" When later I interviewed that company head, I asked him outright whether it mattered that he was selling manga and not lamps, and he was, needless to say, scandalized: "Who said that?!" he exclaimed. (I did not tell him.) He then showed me a tote bag with a popular manga series on it that he has been using daily since the 1990s, before the American manga industry even existed as such. In this manner, I was able to put people who otherwise had only a nodding acquaintance, despite being in the same field, in dialogue with each other. The rare places where they disagreed or came into professional and ideological conflict were often more revealing than the many instances in which there was broad agreement.

This interview data was supplemented by extensive participant observation. Annual industry and fan events provided opportunities for countless informal chats with people in the field, particularly during after-hours parties and get-togethers. During my fieldwork year, I was able to attend New York Comic Con in both 2010 and 2011, along with Anime Expo and the Toronto Comic Arts Festival in 2011. I also attended a book launch, a publisher launch, and an author signing. There were even unexpected occasions where my field site intersected with my scholarly pursuits; at the book exhibit of an academic conference I engaged a marketing representative from one of the large trade houses staffing a booth about her views on her company's manga imprint. She told me that the force of the personalities working for that imprint could be felt throughout the publishing house, influencing company policy at the highest levels and, from her own more humble standpoint, adding manga to the menu of categories of books she must become conversant in to do her job.

I was also, on occasion, invited to the offices, favorite lunch and after-hours hangouts, and even living spaces of my informants. One editor I interviewed read particular significance into the way that her office space had been organized, and it was, therefore, useful to have seen what she was talking about for myself. Moreover, for many American manga industry laborers, their home *is* their office, the arrangement of the space invariably an instantiation of the interpenetration of the personal with the professional. Colorful figurines jostled for shelf space with well-tended books; bookshelves jostled for space with sofas, tables, and chairs; and informants folded themselves into these oft-cluttered spaces in creative and novel ways. Needless to say, people who work in manga are among the most avid consumers of manga, their everyday lives blurring the ordinarily fixed boundaries between producer and audience, subject and object. I certainly had plenty of time to contemplate the material peculiarities and symbolic significations of their homes; in several instances my informants actually put me up for several days as I traveled to their respective parts of the world to conduct research.

Last but certainly not least, I used online and social media such as Twitter, Facebook, and Gmail Chat throughout my time in the field. This was useful, first, to keep up with the latest developments. I was able to follow collective reactions to breaking news, such as the demise of Tokyopop or Digital Manga's first use of Kickstarter, in real time. The field is, after all, constituted by a large number of people networked to each other but geographically separated across great distances. Using social media, then, is an elegant solution for professionals who spend much of their working life in front of a computer screen anyway to express their views, trade gossip, and promote themselves. Not everyone is active on it, but many throughout the field are, in either professional or personal capacities (sometimes both). The Twitter feed thus became a kind of semipublic chat room where even people who watch what they say may still say more than they necessarily intend. There were, for example, several instances where, had it not been for their microblogging, I would have assumed certain people were more informed about events than they revealed themselves as being. These cleavages between my semioutsider presumptions and reality led to interesting, productive discussions in subsequent interviews. However, being in roughly the same time zone proved absolutely critical for this sort of online participant observation; if I am copresent from a temporal standpoint, then I can intervene selectively in the conversation, asking questions or checking my impressions against those of others. If, on the other hand, everything happens while I am sleeping, going back over the feed is no better than reading a historical archive.

Social media was also useful in keeping up with the lives and daily habits of some of my informants. A handful of informants are heavy social media users, tweeting or posting status updates not just about the state of their field but also several times each day about everything from their morning commutes to their holiday pursuits. Through these media, I learned what sorts of things made them happy (e.g., the latest manga) and what kept them awake at night (e.g., the rent). Some even wrote—or complained—candidly about work. For instance, one woman in the industry vented her professional frustrations to her Twitter account one day: "Clearly, I should just sleep at the office and never leave. Quick, bring on the chains." Her status update on a different social media platform during the same day said, "[S]hould just set up a regular meeting for getting reamed out, clearly." Vulgar language of this type was quite common, colorfully articulated in terms of constraint or outright violation upon the body. Coupled with a parallel discourse about loving one's work, which I probed deeply during interviews, these sentiments came to inform a central part of the argument of this book.

For consistency's sake, I have decided to protect the confidentiality of the names of online informants and their companies in the same way that I have my face-to-face informants. Even in cases where they blog and tweet publicly under their own names, some do not like having their writing archived and attributed. While it would be fair to argue that any reasonably well-educated, digitally literate adult ought to know that such online traces, even if written at the spur of the moment and later regretted, might be permanent, in practice I have seen people time and time again forget it. Furthermore, as I have interacted with many people both online and in person, to reference their names and views in the online context may compromise their confidentiality in the offline one.

I wish to conclude with a brief discussion about access. As discussed in Chapter 2, both Sharon Kinsella (2000) and Jennifer Prough (2011) have written about their fieldwork in the Japanese manga publishing industry, characterizing it as a "secretive" world, only reluctantly "providing interviews and information about internal affairs" (Kinsella 2000, 15). Prough (2011, 14) in particular notes that "economic hard times" restricted the amount of access she was able to attain. As such, I was aware that similar troubles might await me and went into the field deeply concerned. As it turned out, however, my experiences with American manga publishing proved rather different; access never became a serious problem for my research. Even when particular individuals were unreceptive, many others were not, and by utilizing alternative routes I was never systematically shut out from any company.

How do I account for this success? While the cover of confidentiality may have given some interviewees the assurances they needed to talk to me, this was not universal. Some told me I was welcome to attribute anything they said, while others were clearly surprised when I told them the interview would be confidential—they had not even read my email request all the way through before agreeing to meet with me! Upon reflection, I believe that some of my good fortune may be in part because, unlike the media moguls of film and television, manga industry insiders do not truly have groupies. Though they may have hundreds, even thousands, of followers on Twitter, manga fans do not make pilgrimages to stand outside the doors of Viz Media waiting for the editors of their favorite *Shonen Jump* titles to clock out—even though the company is currently headquartered in an architectural landmark, the historic Northpoint Theatre, just a few blocks away from a major San Francisco tourist attraction, Pier 39 (see Figure A.1). They do not mob the editors of Yen Press outside their office across from New York City's Grand Central Station on their cigarette breaks. So, while, yes, people can be reluctant to talk about

FIGURE A.1 *Viz Media, headquartered at the historic Northpoint Theatre in San Francisco.*

certain topics, those topics tended to be the sort of fodder for journalists which interested me least, such as their latest unannounced license. Some seemed flattered by the attention; others were confused, not quite able to understand why I was interested in the first place. But at minimum chatting with a sociologist was, if nothing else, a change of pace. Even several of the most prominent players in the field volunteered to me that they had never been approached by a researcher before, good indication that I was truly breaking new ground. Furthermore, while economic uncertainty did cause a few informants to clam up, more often still I encountered people who felt that they had less than ever before to lose by truth-telling. For example, one recently laid off editor answered my email requesting an interview with the following salutation: "Are you kidding? It's not very often that I'm given a truly legitimate reason to spend an hour and a half dishing on manga and [my ex-employer]." Of course, it's important to take an individual's bitterness with a grain of salt, but the willingness, eagerness even, to talk was not confined to the newly unemployed; those left standing after mass layoffs and the gutting of opportunities for freelance work had, it seems, become less personally invested in protecting their employer. The most comprehensive access was achieved, in fact, where I had been warned elsewhere in the field that I would find nothing but closed doors and sealed lips. If their own professional futures are suddenly revealed to be so precarious, irrespective of past loyalty, why bother?

So, at least for me, an excellent level of access was attainable, and I have no reason to believe that my particular experience in the field was extraordinary. It is in fact possible that the publishing field will, at least for the near- to medium-term, make itself more accessible to readers as their traditional retail venues wither and they are forced to "hand sell" their books themselves without the benefit of the usual intermediaries. Publishing houses have been experimenting as never before with social networking, assiduously curating Facebook pages, Twitter accounts, and nascent communities on their own company websites, as well as making in-person appearances and glad-handing at live events. Inasmuch as these outlets become important, companies will not be content to leave the job of responding to readers on, say, Facebook to the least experienced, unpaid interns, and the veteran "invisibles" of the field may become quite visible. Even if this new openness proves itself to be superficial, for the ethnographer it could well be an invaluable source of new opportunities to get a foot through the door.

Yet, many researchers, including those who acknowledge the importance of the sociological study of the production of culture, still seem afraid to take even that first step. The following comment about accessing informants in the US manga industry was sent on November 1, 2011 to a discussion forum for researchers of Japanese popular culture called the Anime Manga Research Circle mailing list:

> As far as I know, there has also been no research on manga licensing (if there has been, please tell me!). [...] Speaking of editors, I also have the feeling, that research on manga publishing/ the editors themselves is underdeveloped. Maybe it's because of the difficulty of access (or us supposing that it might be difficult knowing about how secretive companies can be when it comes to their strategies)...

In reply, the list moderator wrote the same day:

> Regarding the difficulty of access issue that you bring up, I agree—calling an editor out of the blue for an interview is probably not going to get you very far no matter what your intentions or credentials are. But if you know how and where to look, there's quite a lot of content out there to build an article from. Other articles in the mainstream and specialist press (the major newspapers, *Publisher's Weekly*, magazines aimed at the library community, that kind of stuff) will occasionally have things you won't see anywhere else, and, hey, a manga editor will generally be much more open talking to a reporter from the *New York Times* or *USA Today* or *Wired* than they would be talking to a grad student. [...] [S]omeone who wants to write on manga publishing (and anime distribution) should probably know that things like podcasts on fan sites will be where much of their background information is going to have to come from...

In short, these researchers assume without really trying it for themselves that making industry contacts as a researcher are too difficult—and then they provide justifications for why they are absolutely right to think so. If they are to do work on this topic at all, they believe they will need to rely entirely upon secondary sources. The great irony is that this conversation took place a mere two weeks after I had completed the very fieldwork standing in utter contradiction to their conclusions. Perhaps the biggest barrier to access is, in fact, the researcher's own inhibition. The takeaway lesson, I maintain, is that one must at least try, for any success leads to important knowledge about an extremely understudied field.

Glossary

Anime (Japanese)—Short for "animation." Japanese animation

Boys' love/BL (Japanese)—Genre of manga focusing on male/male homoerotic romance for women

Circle (Japanese)—Doujinshi publishing group, which may consist of one, two, or more individuals

Cosplay (Japanese)—Short for "costume play." Fan practice of dressing up as and role-playing favorite characters

Doujinshi (Japanese)—Literally "same-person-publication." Self-published materials, often comics

Fansub (English)—Pirated episodes of anime subtitled by fans

Fujoshi (Japanese)—Literally "rotten girl." A fangirl, particularly focused on BL and yaoi

Gekiga (Japanese)—Literally "dramatic pictures." Japanese comics for adult men, published primarily in the 1950s to 1970s. Coined by Yoshihiro Tatsumi

Josei (Japanese)—Genre of manga for women

Keitai Manga (Japanese)—Literally "cell phone manga." A sequential art medium optimized for display on a cell phone, usually frame-by-frame and with limited animation and other effects

Kodomo (Japanese)—Genre of manga for young children

Ladies (Japanese)—Genre of manga for women, often assumed to be more focused on sexualized romance themes than josei

Lolicon (Japanese)—Short for "Lolita Complex." A genre, usually for men, featuring underage girls in sexual situations

Mangaka (Japanese)—Manga artist

Manhua (Chinese)—Comics from China, Hong Kong

Manhwa (Korean)—Comics from Korea

Mecha (Japanese)—Short for "mechanical." A genre featuring giant robots

Moé (Japanese)—Short for "moeru [to bud; to burn]." Refers to super-cute character designs (and properties which feature them), typically intended for male otaku

Otaku (Japanese)—Literally "your household." An obsessed fan, stereotypically male and socially awkward

Scanlation (English)—Pirated digital copies of manga pages translated by fans

Seinen (Japanese)—Genre of manga for young men

Shotacon (Japanese)—Short for "Shotarou Complex." A genre, either for men or for women, featuring underage boys in sexual situations

Shoujo (Japanese)—Genre of manga for girls

Shounen (Japanese)—Genre of manga for boys

Shounen ai (Japanese)—Subgenre of shoujo manga from the 1970s featuring schoolboys in tragic, homoerotic relationships

Tankoubon (Japanese)—Collected editions of manga

Yaoi (Japanese)—Short for "yama nashi, ochi nashi, imi nashi [no peak, no denouement, no meaning]." Male/male homoerotic fiction. Typically refers to fanfiction in Japan but may be used in place of BL elsewhere

Yonkoma (Japanese)—Literally "four panels." Four-panel comic strips

Yuri (Japanese)—Literally "lily." Genre of lesbian manga, either for men or for women

References

Adorno, Theodor W., and Max Horkheimer. 1947. "The Culture Industry: Enlightenment as Mass Deception." In *Dialectic of Enlightenment*, 120–167. London: Verso.

Allison, Anne. 2000. "A Challenge to Hollywood? Japanese Character Goods Hit the US." *Japanese Studies* 20 (1): 67–88.

Allison, Anne. 2004. "Cuteness as Japan's Millennial Product." In *Pikachu's Global Adventure: The Rise and Fall of Pokémon*, ed. Joseph Tobin, 34–49. Durham, NC: Duke University Press.

Allison, Anne. 2006a. "The Japan Fad in Global Youth Culture and Millennial Capitalism." *Mechademia* 1: 11–21.

Allison, Anne. 2006b. *Millennial Monsters: Japanese Toys and the Global Imagination*. Berkeley: University of California Press.

Allison, Anne. 2008. "The Attractions of the J-wave for American Youth." In *Soft Power Superpowers: Cultural and National Assets of Japan and the United States*, eds. Yasushi Watanabe, David L. McConnell, and Joseph S. Nye, 99–110. Armonk, NY: M.E. Sharpe.

Anderson, Chris. 2006. *The Long Tail: Why the Future of Business Is Selling Less of More*. New York: Hyperion.

Andreeva, Nellie. 2010. "Marvel Entertainment Launches TV Division." *Deadline Hollywood*, June 28. http://www.deadline.com/2010/06/marvel-entertainment-launches-tv-division.

Andrejevic, Mark. 2004. *Reality TV: The Work of Being Watched*. Oxford: Rowman & Littlefield.

Anon. 1997. "Anime Expo 1997 Convention Information." *Animecons*. http://animecons.com/events/info.shtml/327.

Anon. 2000. 2000 nen Kyouiku Hakusho [2000 Education White Paper]. Tokyo: Ministry of Education, Culture, Sports, Science and Technology. http://www.mext.go.jp/b_menu/hakusho/html/hpae200001/index.html.

Anon. 2002. "Anime Expo 2002 Convention Information." *Animecons*. http://animecons.com/events/info.shtml/277/Anime_Expo_2002.

Anon. 2006. "American Comics Crack the BookScan Top Ten." *ICv2*, November 2. http://www.icv2.com/articles/news/9568.html.

Anon. 2007. "Anime Expo 2007 Convention Information." *Animecons*. http://animecons.com/events/info.shtml/1071/Anime_Expo_2007.

Anon. 2008. "ICv2 Top 50 Manga–Summer 2008." *ICv2*, September 7. http://icv2.com/articles/comics/view/13211/icv2-top-50-manga-summer-2008.

Anon. 2009. "The Disney/Marvel Deal: What It Means for Movies." *IGN*, August 31. http://uk.movies.ign.com/articles/101/1019890p1.html.

Anon. 2010a. "Establishment of the Creative Industries Promotion Office." *Ministry of Economy, Trade and Industry*, June 8. http://www.meti.go.jp/english/press/data/20100608_01.html.

Anon. 2010b. "Time to Capitalize on 'Cool Japan' Boom." *The Daily Yomiuri,* August 30. http://www.yomiuri.co.jp/dy/editorial/T100830002730.htm.

Anon. 2011a. "Sailor Moon Is #1!." *ICv2,* October 6. http://www.icv2.com/articles/news/21189.html.

Anon. 2011b. "Wall Street Journal to Debut E-Book Best-Seller Lists Provided by Nielsen." *Nielsen Company.* http://www.nielsen.com/us/en/insights/press-room/2011/wall-street-journal-to-debut-ebook-bestseller-lists-provided-by-nielsen.html.

Anon. 2012a. "Anime Expo 2012 Convention Information." *Animecons.* http://animecons.com/events/info.shtml/2792/Anime_Expo_2012.

Anon. 2012b. "BookScan Top 20 GNs Index." *ICv2,* November 11. http://www.icv2.com/articles/news/13709.html.

Azuma, Hiroki. 2009. *Otaku: Japan's Database Animals.* Minneapolis: University of Minnesota Press.

Bagdikian, Ben H. 2004. *The New Media Monopoly.* Boston: Beacon Press.

Banks, Mark, Rosalind Gill, and Stephanie Taylor, eds. 2013. *Theorizing Cultural Work: Labour, Continuity and Change in the Cultural and Creative Industries.* London: Routledge.

Baudrillard, Jean. 1988. "Consumer Society." In *Selected Writings,* 32–59. Cambridge: Polity.

Beasi, Melinda, ed. 2013. *CBLDF Presents Manga: Introduction, Challenges, and Best Practices.* Portland, OR: Dark Horse.

Beck, Ulrich. 1992. *Risk Society: Towards a New Modernity.* London: Sage.

Becker, Howard S. 1982. *Art Worlds.* Berkeley: University of California Press.

Benjamin, Walter. 1936. "The Work of Art in the Age of Mechanical Reproduction." In *Illuminations,* ed. Hannah Arendt, 217–251. New York: Harcourt.

Berker, Thomas, Maren Hartmann, Yves Punie, and Katie J Ward, eds. 2006. *Domestication of Media and Technology.* Berkshire: Open University Press.

Blanchard, David. 2015. "An American Manga Artist's Journey Down a Road Less Drawn." In *Global Manga: "Japanese" Comics without Japan?,* ed. Casey Brienza, in press. Farnham: Ashgate.

Bolter, Jay David, and Richard Grusin. 1999. *Remediation: Understanding New Media.* Cambridge, MA: MIT Press.

Born, Georgina. 2004. *Uncertain Vision: Birt, Dyke, and the Reinvention of the BBC.* London: Random House.

Bouissou, Jean-Marie. 2000. "Manga Goes Global." *Critique Internationale* 7 (7): 1–36.

Bouissou, Jean-Marie. 2006. "Japan's Growing Cultural Power: Manga in France." In *Reading Manga: Local and Global Perceptions of Japanese Comics,* eds. Jaqueline Berndt and Steffi Richter, 149–165. Leipzig: Leipziger Universitätsverlag.

Bouissou, Jean-Marie, Marco Pellitteri, and Bernd Dolle-Weinkauff. 2010. "Manga in Europe: A Short Study of Market and Fandom." In *Manga: An Anthology of Global and Cultural Perspectives,* ed. Toni Johnson-Woods, 253–266. London: Continuum.

Bourdieu, Pierre. 1977. *Outline of a Theory of Practice.* Cambridge: Cambridge University Press.

Bourdieu, Pierre. 1984. *Distinction: A Social Critique of the Judgement of Taste.* Cambridge, MA: Harvard University Press.

Bourdieu, Pierre. 1990. *The Logic of Practice.* Cambridge: Polity.

Bourdieu, Pierre. 1993. *The Field of Cultural Production: Essays on Art and Literature.* Cambridge: Polity.

Bourdieu, Pierre. 1996. *The Rules of Art: Genesis and Structure of the Literary Field.* Cambridge: Polity.

Brienza, Casey. 2009a. "Books, Not Comics: Publishing Fields, Globalization, and Japanese Manga in the United States." *Publishing Research Quarterly* 25 (2): 101–117.

Brienza, Casey. 2009b. "Paratexts in Translation: Reinterpreting 'Manga' for the United States." *The International Journal of the Book* 6 (2): 13–20.

Brienza, Casey. 2010. "Producing Comics Culture: A Sociological Approach to the Study of Comics." *Journal of Graphic Novels and Comics* 1 (2): 105–119.

Brienza, Casey. 2011. "Manga Is for Girls: American Publishing Houses and the Localization of Japanese Comic Books." *Logos: The Journal of the World Publishing Community* 22 (4): 41–53.

Brienza, Casey. 2012. "Localization." In *The Wiley-Blackwell Encyclopedia of Globalization*, ed. George Ritzer, 1304–1305. Oxford: Wiley-Blackwell.

Brienza, Casey. 2013. "Beyond B&W? The Global Manga of Felipe Smith." In *Black Comics: Politics of Race and Representation*, eds. Sheena C. Howard, and Ronald L. Jackson II, 79–94. London: Bloomsbury.

Brienza, Casey, ed. 2015. *Global Manga: "Japanese" Comics without Japan?* Farnham: Ashgate.

Carter, David, and Anne Galligan, eds. 2007. *Making Books: Contemporary Australian Publishing.* Brisbane: University of Queensland Press.

Castells, Manuel. 2009. *Communication Power.* Oxford: Oxford University Press.

Clark, Giles, and Angus Phillips. 2008. *Inside Book Publishing.* 4th edition. London: Routledge.

Clarke, M. J. 2009. "The Strict Maze of Media Tie-In Novels." *Communication, Culture & Critique* 2 (4): 434–456.

Clements, Jonathan. 2010. *Schoolgirl Milky Crisis: Adventures in the Anime and Manga Trade.* A-Net Digital.

Clifford, James, and George E. Marcus. 1986. *Writing Culture: The Poetics and Politics of Ethnography.* Berkeley: University of California Press.

Condry, Ian. 2006. *Hip-Hop Japan: Rap and the Paths of Cultural Globalization.* Durham, NC: Duke University Press.

Coser, Lewis A. 1975. "Publishers as Gatekeepers of Ideas." *Annals of the American Academy of Political and Social Science* 421: 14–22.

Coser, Lewis A., Charles Kadushin, and Walter W. Powell. 1982. *Books: The Culture and Commerce of Publishing.* New York: Basic Books.

Creighton, Millie R. 1991. "Maintaining Cultural Boundaries in Retailing: How Japanese Department Stores Domesticate 'Things Foreign'." *Modern Asian Studies* 25 (4): 675–709.

Cronin, Anne M. 2004. "Regimes of Mediation: Advertising Practitioners as Cultural Intermediaries?" *Consumption Markets & Culture* 7 (4): 349–369.

Dale, Peter N. 1986. *The Myth of Japanese Uniqueness.* New York: St. Martin's Press.

Deuze, Mark. 2007. *Media Work.* Cambridge: Polity.

Donovan, Hope. 2010. "Gift Versus Capitalist Economies: Exchanging Anime and Manga in the U.S." In *Boys' Love Manga: Essays on the Sexual Ambiguity and Cross-Cultural Fandom of the Genre*, eds. Antonia Levi, Mark McHarry, and Dru Pagliassotti, 11–22. Jefferson, NC: McFarland & Co.

Duralde, Alonso. 2009. "You'll Have a Ball at 'Dragonball Evolution'." *TODAY.com*, April 10. http://today.msnbc.msn.com/id/30157543/ns/today-entertainment/t/youll-have-ball-dragonball-evolution/.

English, James F. 2005. *The Economy of Prestige: Prizes, Awards, and the Circulation of Cultural Value*. Cambridge, MA: Harvard University Press.

Epstein, Jason. 2001. *Book Business: Publishing Past, Present, and Future*. New York: W.W. Norton.

Erik-Soussi, Magda. 2015. "The Western *Sailor Moon* Generation: North American Women and Feminine-Friendly Global Manga." In *Global Manga: "Japanese" Comics without Japan?* ed. Casey Brienza, in press. Farnham: Ashgate.

Fitzpatrick, Kathleen. 2011. *Planned Obsolescence: Publishing, Technology, and the Future of the Academy*. New York: NYU Press.

Flood, Allison. 2011. "Ebook Sales Pass Another Milestone." *The Guardian*, April 15. http://www.guardian.co.uk/books/2011/apr/15/ebook-sales-milestone.

Florida, Richard L. 2002. *The Rise of the Creative Class: And How It's Transforming Work, Leisure, Community and Everyday Life*. New York: Basic Books.

Gabilliet, Jean-Paul. 2005. *Of Comics and Men: A Cultural History of American Comic Books*. Jackson, MI: University Press of Mississippi.

Gereffi, Gary. 1994. "The Organization of Buyer-Driven Global Commodity Chains: How U.S. Retailers Shape Overseas Production Networks." In *Commodity Chains and Global Capitalism*, eds. Gary Gereffi, and Miguel Korzeniewicz, 95–122. Westport, CT: Praeger.

Gereffi, Gary, and Karina Fernandez-Stark. 2011. *Global Value Chain Analysis: A Primer*. Durham, NC: Center on Globalization, Governance & Competitiveness.

Gereffi, Gary, John Humphrey, and Timothy Sturgeon. 2005. "The Governance of Global Value Chains." *Review of International Political Economy* 12 (1): 78–104.

Giddens, Anthony. 1984. *The Constitution of Society: Outline of the Theory of Structuration*. Cambridge: Polity.

Giddens, Anthony. 1990. *The Consequences of Modernity*. Cambridge: Polity.

Giddens, Anthony. 1991. *Modernity and Self-Identity: Self and Society in the Late Modern Age*. Cambridge: Polity.

Goldberg, Wendy. 2010. "The Manga Phenomenon in America." In *Manga: An Anthology of Global and Cultural Perspectives*, ed. Toni Johnson-Woods, 281–296. London: Continuum.

Gravett, Paul. 2004. *Manga: Sixty Years of Japanese Comics*. New York: HarperCollins Design.

Greco, Albert N. 1997. *The Book Publishing Industry*. London: Allyn & Bacon.

Greco, Albert N. 2009. *The State of Scholarly Publishing: Challenges and Opportunities*. New Brunswick, NJ: Transaction Publishers.

Greco, Albert N., Clara E. Rodríguez, and Robert M. Wharton. 2007. *The Culture and Commerce of Publishing in the 21st Century*. Stanford: Stanford University Press.

Grigsby, Mary. 1998. "Sailormoon: Manga (Comics) and Anime (Cartoon) Superheroine Meets Barbie: Global Entertainment Commodity Comes to the United States." *The Journal of Popular Culture* 32 (1): 59–80.

Gunelius, Susan. 2008. *Harry Potter: The Story of a Global Business Phenomenon*. New York: Palgrave Macmillan.

Hayley, Emily. 2010. "Manga Shakespeare." In *Manga: An Anthology of Global and Cultural Perspectives*, ed. Toni Johnson-Woods, 267–280. London: Continuum.

Heilbron, Johan. 1999. "Towards a Sociology of Translation." *European Journal of Social Theory* 2 (4): 429–444.

Heilbron, Johan, and Gisèle Sapiro. 2007. "Outline for a Sociology of Translation: Current Issues and Future Prospects." In *Constructing a Sociology of Translation*, eds. Michaela Wolf and Alexandra Fukari, 93–107. Amsterdam: John Benjamins Publishing.

Hellmann, Libby Fischer. 2011. "To E or Not to E: An Update." *Say the Word*, October 22. http://www.libbyhellmann.com/wp/?p=133.

Hemmungs Wirtén, Eva. 1998. Global Infatuation: Explorations in Transnational Publishing and Texts: The Case of Harlequin Enterprises and Sweden. Doctoral Dissertation, Uppsala: Uppsala University.

Hennion, Antoine. 1989. "An Intermediary between Production and Consumption: The Producer of Popular Music." *Science, Technology & Human Values* 14 (4): 400–424.

Hesmondhalgh, David. 2010. "User-generated Content, Free Labour and the Cultural Industries." *Ephemera* 10 (3–4): 267–284.

Hesmondhalgh, David, and Sarah Baker. 2011. *Creative Labour: Media Work in Three Cultural Industries*. London: Routledge.

Howard, Nicole. 2005. *The Book: The Life Story of a Technology*. Westport, CT: Greenwood Press.

Humphrey, John, and Hubert Schmitz. 2002. "How Does Insertion in Global Value Chains Affect Upgrading in Industrial Clusters?" *Regional Studies* 36 (9): 1017–1027.

Ikeda, Yoichiro. 2012. Takashi Murakami: "3/11 Brings Japan's Subculture into Perspective." *Asahi Shimbun*, March 10. http://ajw.asahi.com/article/cool_japan/culture/AJ201203100024.

Ito, Kinko. 2011. *A Sociology of Japanese Ladies' Comics: Images of the Life, Loves, and Sexual Fantasies of Adult Japanese Women*. Lewiston, NY: Edwin Mellen Press.

Iwabuchi, Koichi. 2002. *Recentering Globalization: Popular Culture and Japanese Transnationalism*. Durham, NC: Duke University Press.

Iwabuchi, Koichi. 2004. "How 'Japanese' Is Pokémon?" In *Pikachu's Global Adventure: The Rise and Fall of Pokémon*, ed. Joseph Tobin, 53–79. Durham, NC: Duke University Press.

Iwabuchi, Koichi. 2010. "Undoing Inter-National Fandom in the Age of Brand Nationalism." *Mechademia* 5: 87–96.

Johnson, Rich. n.d. "Rich Johnson | LinkedIn." *LinkedIn*. http://www.linkedin.com/in/rjhnzn.

Johnson, Rich. 2011. "Tokyopop to Close at End of May." *Bleeding Cool*, April 15. http://www.bleedingcool.com/2011/04/15/tokyopop-to-close-at-end-of-may/

Kalleberg, Arne L. 2000. "Nonstandard Employment Relations: Part-time, Temporary and Contract Work." *Annual Review of Sociology* 26: 341–365.

Kelts, Roland. 2006. *Japanamerica: How Japanese Pop Culture Has Invaded the U.S.* New York: Palgrave Macmillan.

Khagram, Sanjeev, and Peggy Levitt. 2008. "Constructing Transnational Studies."
In *Rethinking Transnationalism: The Meso-Link of Organisations*, ed. Ludger
Pries, 21–39. London: Routledge.

Kimbell, Keith. 2011. "Comic Book Movies: Marvel vs. DC vs. Indie Publishers."
Metacritic, July 26. http://www.metacritic.com/feature/comic-book-movies-by-
publisher.

Kinsella, Sharon. 2000. *Adult Manga: Culture and Power in Contemporary
Japanese Society*. Honolulu: University of Hawai'i Press.

Last, Jonathan V. 2011. "The Crash of 1993." *The Weekly Standard*, June 13.
http://www.weeklystandard.com/articles/crash-1993_573252.html?nopager=1.

Latour, Bruno. 2005. *Reassembling the Social: An Introduction to Actor-Network-
Theory*. Oxford: Oxford University Press.

Lee, Hye-Kyung. 2009. "Between Fan Culture and Copyright Infringement:
Manga Scanlation." *Media, Culture & Society* 31 (6): 1011–1022.

Lopes, Paul. 2009. *Demanding Respect: The Evolution of the American Comic
Book*. Philadelphia, PA: Temple University Press.

Lott, Eric. 1995. *Love and Theft: Blackface Minstrelsy and the American Working
Class*. Oxford: Oxford University Press.

Luey, Beth. 2009. "The Organization of the Book Publishing Industry." In *The
Enduring Book: Print Culture in Postwar America*, eds. David Paul Nord,
Joan Shelley Rubin, and X. Schudson, 29–54. Chapel Hill: University of North
Carolina Press.

Malone, Paul M. 2010a. "The Manga Publishing Scene in Europe." In *Manga:
An Anthology of Global and Cultural Perspectives*, ed. Toni Johnson-Woods,
315–331. London: Continuum.

Malone, Paul M. 2010b. "From BRAVO to Animexx.de to Export: Capitalizing on
German Boys' Love Fandom, Culturally, Socially and Economically." In *Boys'
Love Manga: Essays on the Sexual Ambiguity and Cross-Cultural Fandom
of the Genre*, eds. Antonia Levi, Mark McHarry, and Dru Pagliassotti, 23–43.
Jefferson, NC: McFarland & Co.

"manga, n.2." *OED Online*. June 2012. Oxford University Press. http://www.oed.
com/view/Entry/244747?rskey=ulvX1Y&result=2&isAdvanced=false.

Maslow, Abraham H. 1943. "A Theory of Human Motivation." *Psychological
Review* 50 (4): 370–396.

Matsui, Takeshi. 2009. The Diffusion of Foreign Cultural Products: The Case
Analysis of Japanese Comics (Manga) Market in the US. Working Paper.
Princeton: Center for Arts and Cultural Policy Studies, Princeton University.

Mazur, Dan, and Alexander Danner. 2014. *Comics: A Global History, 1968 to the
Present*. London: Thames & Hudson.

McAlprin, Gordon. 2006. "An Interview with Bryan Lee O'Malley." *Gordon
McAlprin*. http://www.gordonmcalpin.com/writing/interview-bryanomalley.html.

McCarthy, Helen. 2009. *The Art of Osamu Tezuka: God of Manga*. New York:
Abrams ComicArts.

McChesney, Robert W. 1999. *Rich Media, Poor Democracy: Communication
Politics in Dubious Times*. Urbana: University of Illinois Press.

McChesney, Robert W. 2004. *The Problem of the Media: U.S. Communication
Politics in the Twenty-First Century*. New York: Monthly Review Press.

McCurry, Justin. 2009. "Japan Looks to Manga Comics to Rescue Ailing
Economy." *The Guardian*, April 10. http://www.guardian.co.uk/world/2009/
apr/10/japan-manga-anime-recession.

McGray, Douglas. 2002. "Japan's Gross National Cool." *Foreign Policy* 130 (May/June): 44–54.

McRobbie, Angela. 1998. *British Fashion Design: Rag Trade or Image Industry?* London: Routledge.

McRobbie, Angela. 2002a. "From Holloway to Hollywood: Happiness at Work in the New Cultural Economy?" In *Cultural Economy: Cultural Analysis and Commercial Life*, eds. Paul Du Gay, and Michael Pryke, 97–114. London: Sage.

McRobbie, Angela. 2002b. "Clubs to Companies: Notes on the Decline of Political Culture in Speeded Up Creative Worlds." *Cultural Studies* 16 (4): 516–531.

McRobbie, Angela. 2004. "Making a Living in London's Small-Scale Creative Sector." In *Cultural Industries and the Production of Culture*, eds. Dominic Power, and Allen J. Scott, 130–143. London: Psychology Press.

McRobbie, Angela. 2014. *Be Creative: Making a Living in the New Culture Industries*. Cambridge: Polity.

Memmott, Carol. 2010. "Graphic Novel Offers a New Way to Look at 'Twilight'." *USA Today*, March 16. http://usatoday30.usatoday.com/printedition/life/20100316/twilightgraphic11_st.art.htm.

Middaugh, Dallas. 2012. "Manga Back on Top." *ICv2*, October 5. http://www.icv2.com/articles/news/24051.html.

Miller, Laura J. 2006. *Reluctant Capitalists: Bookselling and the Culture of Consumption*. Chicago: University of Chicago Press.

Miller, Laura J. 2009. "Selling the Product." In *The Enduring Book: Print Culture in Postwar America*, eds. David Paul Nord Joan Shelley Rubin, and Michael Schudson, 91–106. Chapel Hill: University of North Carolina Press.

Miller, Toby, Nitin Govil, John McMurria, Richard Maxwell, and Ting Wang. 2005. *Global Hollywood 2*. London: British Film Institute.

Munro, Craig, and Robyn Sheahan-Bright, eds. 2006. *Paper Empires: A History of the Book in Australia, 1946–2005*. Brisbane: University of Queensland Press.

Murray, Simone. 2004. *Mixed Media: Feminist Presses and Publishing Politics*. London: Pluto Press.

Murray, Simone. 2008. "Phantom Adaptations: Eucalyptus, the Adaptation Industry and the Film That Never Was." *Adaptation* 1 (1): 5–23.

Murray, Simone. 2012. *The Adaptation Industry: The Cultural Economy of Contemporary Literary Adaptation*. London: Routledge.

Napier, Susan J. 2007. *From Impressionism to Anime: Japan as Fantasy and Fan Cult in the Mind of the West*. New York: Palgrave Macmillan.

Negus, Keith. 2002. "The Work of Cultural Intermediaries and the Enduring Distance between Production and Consumption." *Cultural Studies* 16 (4): 501–515.

Nisbet, Robert A. 1966. *The Sociological Tradition*. New York: Basic Books.

Nixon, Sean, and Paul Du Gay. 2002. "Who Needs Cultural Intermediaries?" *Cultural Studies* 16(4): 495–500.

Nord, David Paul, Joan Shelley Rubin, and Michael Schudson, eds. 2009. *The Enduring Book: Print Culture in Postwar America*. Chapel Hill: University of North Carolina Press.

Nye, Joseph S. 1990. *Bound to Lead: The Changing Nature of American Power*. New York: Basic Books.

Nye, Joseph S. 2004. *Soft Power: The Means to Success in World Politics*. New York: Public Affairs.

Nye, Joseph S. 2008. "Forward." In *Soft Power Superpowers: Cultural and National Assets of Japan and the United States*, eds. Yasushi Watanabe, David L. McConnell, and Joseph S. Nye, ix–xiv. Armonk, NY: M.E. Sharpe.

Ono, Kent A., and Vincent N. Pham. 2009. *Asian Americans and the Media*. Cambridge: Polity.

Pagliassotti, Dru. 2008. "Reading Boys' Love in the West." *Particip@tions* 5 (2). http://www.participations.org/Volume%205/Issue%202/5_02_pagliassotti.htm.

Pagliassotti, Dru. 2009. "GloBLisation and Hybridisation: Publishers' Strategies for Bringing Boys' Love to the United States." *Intersections: Gender and Sexuality in Asia and the Pacific* 20. http://intersections.anu.edu.au/issue20/pagliassotti.htm.

Peters, John Durham. 1999. *Speaking into the Air: A History of the Idea of Communication*. Chicago: University of Chicago Press.

Peterson, Richard A. 1997. *Creating Country Music: Fabricating Authenticity*. Chicago: University of Chicago Press.

Pink, Daniel H. 2007. "Japan, Ink: Inside the Manga Industrial Complex." *Wired*, November. http://www.wired.com/techbiz/media/magazine/15-11/ff_manga?currentPage=all.

Prough, Jennifer S. 2011. *Straight from the Heart: Gender, Intimacy, and the Cultural Production of Shōjo Manga*. Honolulu: University of Hawai'i Press.

Radway, Janice A. 1984. *Reading the Romance: Women, Patriarchy, and Popular Literature*. Chapel Hill: University of North Carolina Press.

Radway, Janice A. 1999. *A Feeling for Books: The Book-of-the-Month Club, Literary Taste, and Middle-Class Desire*. Chapel Hill: University of North Carolina Press.

Reid, Calvin. 2009. 2008 "Graphic Novel Sales Up 5%; Manga Off 17%." *Publishers Weekly*, February 6. http://www.publishersweekly.com/article/ca6635333.html.

Rifas, Leonard. 2004. "Globalizing Comic Books from Below: How Manga Came to America." *International Journal of Comic Art* 6 (2): 138–171.

Sabin, Roger. 1993. *Adult Comics: An Introduction*. London: Routledge.

Sabin, Roger. 2006. "Barefoot Gen in the US and UK: Activist Comic, Graphic Novel, Manga." In *Reading Manga: Local and Global Perceptions of Japanese Comics*, eds. Jaqueline Berndt, and Steffi Richter, 39–57. Leipzig: Leipziger Universitätsverlag.

Sapiro, Gisèle. 2008. "Translation and the Field of Publishing." *Translation Studies* 1 (2): 154–166.

Sapiro, Gisèle. 2010. "Globalization and Cultural Diversity in the Book Market: The Case of Literary Translations in the US and in France." *Poetics* 38 (4): 419–439.

Sapiro, Gisèle. 2014. *The French Writers' War, 1940–1953*. Durham, NC: Duke University Press.

Sapiro, Gisèle, and Mauricio Bustamante. 2009. "Translation as a Measure of International Consecration: Mapping the World Distribution of Bourdieu's Books in Translation." *Sociologica* 2–3/2009.

Sassen, Saskia. 2001. *The Global City: New York, London, Tokyo*. Princeton: Princeton University Press.

Schiffrin, André. 2001. *The Business of Books: How International Conglomerates Took over Publishing and Changed the Way We Read*. London: Verso.

Schodt, Frederik L. 1983. *Manga! Manga!: The World of Japanese Comics*. Tokyo: Kodansha International.

Schodt, Frederik L. 1996. *Dreamland Japan: Writings on Modern Manga*. Berkeley, CA: Stone Bridge Press.

Schodt, Frederik L. 2007. *The Astro Boy Essays: Osamu Tezuka, Mighty Atom, and the Manga/Anime Revolution*. Berkeley, CA: Stone Bridge Press.

Sennett, Richard. 1998. *The Corrosion of Character: The Personal Consequences of Work in the New Capitalism*. New York: W. W. Norton.

Sennett, Richard. 2006. *The Culture of the New Capitalism*. New Haven: Yale University Press.

Sennett, Richard. 2008. *The Craftsman*. New Haven: Yale University Press.

Shimizu, Isao. 1991. *Manga No Rekishi* [History of Manga]. Tokyo: Iwanami Shoten.

Silverstone, Roger, and Leslie Haddon. 1996. "Design and the Domestication of Information and Communication Technologies." In *Communication by Design: The Politics of Information and Communication Technologies*, eds. Robin Mansell, and Roger Silverstone, 44–74. Oxford: Oxford University Press.

Silverstone, Roger, and Eric Hirsch, eds. 1992. *Consuming Technologies: Media and Information in Domestic Spaces*. London: Routledge.

Simmel, Georg. 1997. "The Philosophy of Fashion." In *Simmel on Culture: Selected Writings*, eds. David Frisby, and Mike Featherstone, 187–205. London: Sage.

Smith, Felipe. 2010. *Peepo Choo 2*. New York: Vertical.

Squires, Claire. 2009. *Marketing Literature: The Making of Contemporary Writing in Britain*. New York: Palgrave Macmillan.

Stallard, Karin, Barbara Ehrenreich, and Holly Sklar. 1983. *Poverty in the American Dream: Women & Children First*. Brooklyn, NY: South End Press.

Striphas, Ted. 2009. *The Late Age of Print: Everyday Book Culture from Consumerism to Control*. New York: Columbia University Press.

Suarez, Michael Felix, and H. R. Woudhuysen, eds. 2010. *The Oxford Companion to the Book*. Oxford: Oxford University Press.

Sugiura, Tsutomu. 2008. "Japan's Creative Industries: Culture as a Source of Soft Power in the Industrial Sector." In *Soft Power Superpowers: Cultural and National Assets of Japan and the United States*, eds. Yasushi Watanabe, David L. McConnell, and Joseph S. Nye, 128–153. Armonk, NY: M.E. Sharpe.

Taylor, Stephanie, and Karen Littleton. 2012. *Contemporary Identities of Creativity and Creative Work*. Farnham: Ashgate.

Terranova, Tiziana. 2000. "Free Labor: Producing Culture for the Digital Economy." *Social Text* 18 (2): 33–58.

Thompson, Jason. 2007a. *Manga: The Complete Guide*. New York: Ballantine.

Thompson, Jason. 2007b. "How Manga Conquered America." *Wired*, November.

Thompson, John B. 2005. *Books in the Digital Age: The Transformation of Academic and Higher Education Publishing in Britain and the United States*. Cambridge: Polity.

Thompson, John B. 2010. *Merchants of Culture: The Publishing Business in the Twenty-First Century*. Cambridge: Polity.

Thompson, Luke Y. 2009. "Dragonball Evolution: A Surreal Mess." *E! Online*, April 9. http://uk.eonline.com/news/_lt_i_gt_Dragonball_Evolution_lt__i_gt___A_Surreal_Mess/118209.

Thornton, Patricia H. 2004. *Markets from Culture: Institutional Logics and Organizational Decisions in Higher Education Publishing*. Stanford: Stanford University Press.

Tobin, Joseph J. 1992. "Introduction: Domesticating the West." In *Re-made in Japan: Everyday Life and Consumer Taste in a Changing Society*, ed. Joseph J. Tobin, 1–41. New Haven: Yale University Press.

Tobin, Joseph, ed. 2004. *Pikachu's Global Adventure: The Rise and Fall of Pokémon*. Durham, NC: Duke University Press.

Ursell, Gillian. 2000. "Television Production: Issues of Exploitation, Commodification and Subjectivity in UK Television Labour Markets." *Media, Culture & Society* 22 (6): 805–825.

Valaskivi, Katja. 2013. "A Brand New Future? Cool Japan and the Social Imaginary of the Branded Nation." *Japan Forum* 25 (4): 485–504.

Venuti, Lawrence. 1995. *The Translator's Invisibility: A History of Translation*. London: Routledge.

Venuti, Lawrence, ed. 2000. *The Translation Studies Reader*. London: Routledge.

Wacquant, Loïc. 2004. *Body & Soul: Notebooks of an Apprentice Boxer*. Oxford: Oxford University Press.

Watanabe, Yasushi, David L. McConnell, and Joseph S. Nye, eds. 2008. *Soft Power Superpowers: Cultural and National Assets of Japan and the United States*. Armonk, NY: M.E. Sharpe.

Whiteside, Thomas. 1980. *The Blockbuster Complex: Conglomerates, Show Business, and Book Publishing*. Middletown, CT: Wesleyan University Press.

Wolk, Douglas. 2007. *Reading Comics: How Graphic Novels Work and What They Mean*. New York: Da Capo Press.

Wright, Bradford W. 2001. *Comic Book Nation: The Transformation of Youth Culture in America*. Baltimore: John Hopkins University Press.

Yadao, Jason S. 2009. *The Rough Guide to Manga*. London: Rough Guides.

Yamanaka, Chie. 2006. "Domesticating Manga? National Identity in Korean Comics Culture." In *Reading Manga: Local and Global Perceptions of Japanese Comics*, eds. Jaqueline Berndt and Steffi Richter, 193–204. Leipzig: Leipziger Universitätsverlag.

Index